Subject
INDIA

BY HENRY NOEL BRAILSFORD

The John Day Company

NEW YORK

26373

Contents

vi

APPENDIX: THINGS SEEN

Preface

M<small>Y EXCUSE</small> for this book is that I have certain things to say about India which no one else is saying. That may be its condemnation.

To the American reader I must apologize for placing this book before him without the customary modifications. I have not even altered the words "we" and "our," which mean my own countrymen. This I have done deliberately, since the purpose of the book is first of all to prepare British readers for a new departure in policy. But I believe that India is the concern not merely of Britain but of all the United Nations, and that America with China may have a part to play in shaping its future. For that reason after correcting a few slips I am placing its pages, in their uncensored frankness, before Americans exactly as I wrote them.

India in these days is inaccessible to the unofficial traveller. I could have wished to include in this book some descriptive chapters giving a visual picture of the present activities of Congress and the actual condition of the masses. As an inadequate substitute I have included in the appendix "Things Seen" several chapters from an earlier book of mine, *Rebel India*, which give my impressions of the civil disobedience campaign as I saw it in 1930, and of village life. There have been changes, needless to say, in twelve years, but in its broad outline and design I think the picture may still be near the facts. Part of Chapter V is taken from the same book but has been recast. I am greatly indebted to *The New Republic* for its permission to reprint these chapters.

It is a pleasure to acknowledge my debt to other writers whose books I have freely used. I would name first *The Rise and Fulfilment of British Rule in India*, the work of two of my friends, Edward Thompson and G. T. Garratt, whose death

vii

was a loss as much to the India he loved as to his own country. I have drawn freely on Professor Buchanan's *The Development of Capitalist Enterprise in India* and on Dr. Vera Anstey's *Economic Development of India*. I found three recent books by Indian writers particularly suggestive, above all, (1) *India Today* by R. Palme Dutt; (2) *The Problem of India* by K. S. Shelvankar (a Penguin publication) and (3) M. Masani's stimulating and optimistic *Our India*, addressed to boys and girls in senior schools. I have, of course, used the standard official publications, especially the "Linlithgow" Report of the Royal Commission on Agriculture. In giving references I have used the authors' names only, omitting titles, *e.g.*, Thompson and Garratt, Anstey, Dutt, Linlithgow.

I would ask the reader to remember charitably that in wartime the processes of printing are necessarily slow. There is apt to be a long interval between the passing of the proofs and publication, during which much may happen.

My warm thanks go to two Indian friends who helped me with criticisms and suggestions—Miss Anima Sen Gupta, who took great pains over some very troublesome statistics, and Mr. Suresh Vaidya, who was kind enough to read the proofs. My debt is the greater, since there are passages in the book with which they do not agree.

H. N. Brailsford.

London, 1943.

SUBJECT INDIA

I. Rulers and Leaders

ON A summer day during this war I saw on the edge of Sherwood Forest one of the most inspiring sights a lover of our English land could wish to see. It was a great field of several scores of acres on which was ripening a splendid crop of wheat. A year ago this ground had been waste, which fed a few sheep, and that had been its condition since Anglo-Saxon times. But the County authorities had taken it over, set their tractors to work upon it, ploughed in the accumulated fertility of its turf and assisted Nature to produce this noble harvest that awaited the reapers. I walked on past other great fields, in which men were busy, some ploughing, some cutting, into the village of Laxton. A comely young woman was driving a tractor down the road past its beautiful old church, which followed Gothic styles of several successive centuries. Laxton — or, as its American duplicate spells the name, Lexington—is one of the most venerable survivals of our primitive English way of life. It still has its three great open fields, which its peasants cultivate in long strips without a hedge between them, as the Lassings or Lessings used to do, when first they arrived from the Teutonic fatherland and built their "town" on a clearing in the forest. Yet with all its conservative charm this village thrives: it learns: it innovates. It will use tractors today where once its teams of eight oxen used to plough for co-operating groups of neighbours. And today it is proud that its ancient common land has served to feed the nation in the extremity of its need.

It happened that on the day of my visit to Laxton I was thinking, none too happily, about India. The sight of that waste land which the mechanical plough had ripped up and made fertile, recalled to me a vision of the impossible future that used to cross my mind amid the stagnant poverty of the

Indian countryside, when I saw it some years ago. There too are waste common lands. From their sparse yellow grasses, herds of emaciated and nearly useless cattle draw a pitiful subsistence. The village retains, as Laxton does, its ancient way of life. But it does not learn: it does not innovate: nor does it thrive. I could more easily conjure up a picture of an elephant in Laxton, than I could imagine a comely Indian brunette, with a saffron *sari* round her shoulders, driving a tractor past its temple. I had wanted to plough up that waste land and sow it with vetches or *berseem*, so that those starved cows might yield milk for its equally emaciated children. If that could be done, I thought, there was a chance they might grow up alert, combative, ambitious men, who would fling off the loads of debt, inertia and ignorance that keep them poor. Nothing in India had stirred me so painfully as the sight of the children of its villages. Their famished bodies revealed the ravages of malaria, and I discovered that after they were weaned they rarely tasted milk. At the best there was buttermilk for them, but all the butter went to the usurer. That is one of the many discoveries which shatter complacency in India. But I dared not hope that in my lifetime I shall ever see a tractor performing in India the miracle wrought at Laxton.

Why not? Why is it difficult to entertain that hope? This question vexed me, as I left Laxton behind me and tried in my memory to juxtapose my fresh impressions of its adaptability and prosperity with my recollections of Indian villages. If I could answer this question, I thought, I should learn much about India; perhaps I might even be able to cast her horoscope. The answer at first sight is not obvious. Laxpore—if I may invent a name for a typical Indian village—follows in its temple and its fields a very ancient way of life. Its religion, like its land system, has been inherited from the immemorial past. But that is equally true of Laxton, where religion has survived two millennia, while its open fields are still what Tacitus described, before our ancestors crossed the water. As for the men who in the last resort govern Laxpore, who are they?

The cousins and sons of the men who govern Laxton, selected by competitive examination to fill the Indian Civil Service.

As I summoned some of these men before me from the shelf of memory, I grasped the first difficulty. They are what we all know them to be, hard-working, able, conscientious and incorruptible officials, but they cling to *laissez faire* and lack the driving power and creative imagination to carry through a startling experiment in innovation. The authority which ploughed up Laxton common had compulsory powers in reserve. But there was no need to use them: the village was eager to make its contribution. But if the alien British Raj had overcome its traditional disinclination to undertake such a task as this, and tried to help Laxpore to a better way of life without its consent, it would have encountered a total lack of comprehension, and the village might have resented the attack on its immemorial rights with furious rioting. Then how might its consent have been won? Laxton listens to wireless talks, and every villager reads, if not a daily at least a Sunday newspaper. But Laxpore is so indigent that not a single wireless set is to be found in it. Not more than one or two men in it can read, and the one weekly paper in Hindustani that reaches it is not disposed to help the Government in any of its undertakings. Finally, if all these difficulties were overcome, where would the authorities find a tractor to plough up the waste? When at the outbreak of this war we urgently needed some thousands of tractors for the ploughing up of our waste lands and pastures, we made them. But in all India there is not a single concern capable of manufacturing a tractor. That is an understatement. So backward still is Indian industry that no plant exists capable of making an internal-combustion engine of any kind.

By this line of thought we have stumbled across some of the basic facts of Indian life. Dwarfed by our imposing imperial structure, we have caught a glimpse of the Indian villager as he stands beside it, a puny figure, under-nourished, illiterate, impoverished, short-lived. If we should wish to help him, by using modern machinery to improve his diet—the first step in any advance to a higher standard of life—we had to realise that we could not do in his villages what we can do as a matter of course in our own. With all its virtues, our bureaucracy lacks the creative imagination for a social experiment of this kind. It is so little trusted by the people that it could not carry them with it if it were to try. Worst of all, this vast subcontinent lacks the means to construct machines essential for the technique of our modern existence. These are discoveries which we should find disquieting, if the world were tranquil and we were at peace.

But in fact we are at war, and uncertain, from one month to another, when the test may come to India. In this hour of danger a great part of her population is in revolt—a word which its leaders themselves have used, although it entered the struggle against us unarmed. We know little of what is going on, but a terse record in *The New Statesman* (December 5, 1942) of the happenings in a single week in September last conveys a sharp impression. It was a relatively quiet week : the casualties were on a small scale and there is no mention of the employment of planes to mow down crowds or of the use of troops:

We have before us a batch of Indian daily papers for the early part of September. Column after column is packed with the news of the revolt and the repression, in dry, brief paragraphs, for nothing but the matter supplied by the semi-official agencies may be printed. On this evidence the activities of Congress are, or in this period were, by an overwhelming proportion non-violent. The offences punished by *lathi* charges, imprisonment and fines were chiefly the holding of meetings, processions, peaceful picketing, the shouting of slogans and hoisting flags. For writing slogans in the sand three girls were sentenced to two months' imprisonment and a fine of Rs. 100 or another month. Some of the sentences for nominal offences of this kind were even more severe. Given the poverty of Indians, the fines were often crippling. As in 1930, women, including students, play a great part in these demonstrations. In one instance the police charged a procession of schoolgirls with canes. Two sentences of flogging were reported. Ten men were sentenced to flogging at Cawnpore for "assault," which may have meant that they had defended themselves against the police. Two students of Loyola College, Madras, were sentenced to flogging for having stones in their hands which they may have intended to throw at a passing train. Three editors were arrested for publishing news other than that furnished by the semi-official agencies. The outstanding news was the infliction of collective fines, Nazi-fashion, on villages and towns for Congress activities. In every case Muslims were exempted. On one day in villages round Madras these fines totalled Rs. 235,000. One little town, East Khandesh, was fined Rs. 30,000. The cases of serious violence were not numerous—two or three instances of arson and one of destroying sleepers on the railway. We have reported the punishments for disloyalty. It remains to report the reward of loyalty. The Raja of Kallicote, who wished to travel from Cuttack to Delhi to attend the National Defence Council, had reserved a first-class carriage. Three "European gentlemen" appropriated it and physically prevented him from entering it. The station master was powerless to deal with them. If "European gentlemen" treat a reigning prince in this way, how do they treat their coolies?

Of the many reflections which this record provokes, the most disturbing is the impression it conveys that we have here in gestures and demonstrations the verdict of the masses on our rule in India. There is no reason to suppose that any but a small proportion of this nation would welcome the Japanese, if they should attempt an invasion. On the other hand, we have lost the chance of rallying them as our comrades in arms. The probability is that the great majority of them would behave as the people of Burma and Malaya did: that is to say, they would be neutral and indifferent, because to their thinking, one foreign conqueror is much like another—not so decidedly better or worse that they would risk their skins for the difference between the two. This state of mind is not as recent or as superficial as we might like to think. During my stay in India in 1930, a period of civil disobedience, on the whole of a mild and non-violent type, I was surrounded in an out-of-the-way place by a crowd which manifested without restraint their dislike for the white skin of an unknown European. They did not touch me, but their slogans and verbal insults betrayed their hostility. I had other experiences which conveyed the same lesson in more subtle ways. At the end of my stay, by an absurd series of accidents, I missed a train at a wayside station in the Punjab which should have carried me to the junction on the main line, where I had to catch the express for Karachi. Thence with only a few hours to spare I was to fly to London. I had then, after an interval of only two days, to cross the Atlantic by a boat which would bring me to New York just in time to give a series of lectures at Columbia University. On this local train at Harappa depended my journey round half the globe. I asked the station master if he knew of any conveyance, car or lorry in the neighbourhood which I could hire. Without being positively offensive, he was as unhelpful and unsympathetic as any man could be. There was, he told me, no car of any kind within fifty miles. I sat down to study the map. I should have to walk twenty miles through the night over an unknown road. Happily there was a moon, but I did not like the prospect. As it chanced, my pocket-book, which I had laid on the table, had my name on it. Presently the station master from behind me was peering at it. His whole manner suddenly changed. "Are you," he exclaimed, "that good man, that just man, that true friend of India whose articles I have read in the papers?" I confessed that I had been writing articles which Indian papers had copied. He went straight to the telephone, and in ten minutes a car was waiting for me at the station gate. I reached New York on time.

It should not surprise us that our racial arrogance can evoke an answering resentment even in this gentle and courteous nation. Englishmen commonly assume that, while educated Indians may be critical of us, the dumb, illiterate millions are our firm friends. In this crisis of destiny I believe this is an inversion of the truth. Educated Indians may criticise us and even revolt against us, but they, or at least the more sensitive among them, have absorbed what is best in Western civilisation and share with us a respect for its values. With them we have much in common. The tragedy of our relationship with them has been that we refused to recognise these men as friends, when they pleaded with us to be worthy of ourselves. As for the millions sunk in unlettered poverty, what glimpse have they had of our treasures?

THE PROLONGED CONQUEST

How DID we get into this relationship of estrangement with this gifted but often puzzling nation? I will attempt in the following pages a rapid survey of the record, standing at some little distance from the crowded canvas of memory, so that I may see it with the eyes of a stranger.

The early pages of the story are for most of us as dim as they are uncongenial. We do not like to be reminded of the fact that this relationship began under a chartered company whose sole motive in all it did in India was to acquire riches for its shareholders and its servants. Nor do the more sensitive among us like to remember that this company conquered India with the sword, though the cruder of us occasionally boast of it. Kindly men, who would prefer a title of another sort, persuade themselves that we have gradually won our sovereign rights by disinterested benevolence. A former Viceroy once rebuked me rather sharply for speaking of the conquest. His case was Seeley's, that in fact our ancestors won all their victories with Indian troops and Indian allies: in short, that Indians conquered themselves. The answer is simple. If in such a case there is any difficulty in identifying the conqueror, the surest test is to ask who got the loot. It was Clive and not his sepoys, after the easy victory at Plassey, who swept £234,000 into his own pocket and then stood "astonished at his own moderation." But it is not the conquest which happened in the eighteenth century that weighs most heavily on my social conscience. By far the graver fact is that we had to go on conquering India. The process had to be repeated at the Mutiny over a great part of Northern and Central India. Thrice in recent years, in 1921, in 1930 and again today, against Gandhi's movements of civil disobedience, we have had to do it again. For long periods in this reign of nearly two centuries Indians have seemed tranquil and acquiescent, because they were divided and disarmed. But we have never won their consent, and least of all can we claim it now. Our rule over India is a daily conquest.

But over these early years we need not linger. Clive was a brigand of genius, whose crimes were matched only by the splendour of his courage. Worse than anything he did was the feat performed in 1770, when, during a famine which wiped out one third of the population of Bengal, the revenue was collected in full with perfect punctuality, as Warren Hastings afterwards certified. At a later and more civilised period than this, the Duke of Wellington * could justify the right of the conqueror to levy a tribute on the people he subdued:

In return for the protection which that country [Bengal] undoubtedly receives, Great Britain has some right to expect remuneration. In fact, all conquered countries give the conquerors an advantage in some point of view, and Bengal gives none to Great Britain, excepting in tribute, which therefore the latter ought to take.

Warren Hastings was an incomparably abler and bigger man than Clive, but his methods were hardly more scrupulous, though when he robbed it was never for his private gain: but he liked Indians, took an interest in Oriental scholarship and felt from time to time some concern for the welfare of the people of Bengal. The predatory and disreputable phase ended with the reforms of Cornwallis. He left on record his first impressions of the land he came to rule (1789): "I may safely assert that one third of the Company's territory in Hindustan is now a jungle inhabited only by wild beasts." His chief boon

* Quoted in full by Thompson and Garratt, p. 657.

to India was the creation of a civil service, well trained and highly paid. He understood that rich men do not pilfer. As Sir Thomas Monro, the greatest administrator of the next generation, put it,* Cornwallis "purchased the integrity of the Company's servants" by "raising their allowances."

This early period of loot and bloodshed need not have ruined our relationship with Indians for all time. India has suffered many conquests, and in the end, after the long anarchy and the degeneration of a great civilisation which had followed the collapse of the Mogul power, this conquest brought peace and the reign of order. But unlike earlier conquerors the English in India never made their home in this country and never blended with its people. The reward they drew for their work, much of it of lasting benefit to India, went home to enrich their families and a *rentier* class in England. India would have suffered less from much more rapacious conquerors who had spent the proceeds of their robberies in the country. In India the British lived apart in their spacious and isolated cantonments, frowned on intermarriage and confined their dealings with their subjects to business, administration and the frigid intercourse of ceremonial occasions. Their arrogance was such that the clerks of the Company required every Indian they met in the streets of Calcutta to salute them, while its collectors in the interior of Bengal would allow only the most exalted of the local gentry to be seated in their presence. The French had been less aloof and more human: Dupleix, their ablest leader, married an Indian lady. The climate was only part of the reason that forbade the British to make a home in India. The Dutch in their tropical islands frequently settle, intermarry, and bring up children. In our case the responsibility must be divided. During the earlier generations of our rule, the rigid caste system of the Hindus made social intercourse difficult. The Mohammedan conquerors got over this difficulty by converting a quarter of the population to their own creed. For that solution the Christian faith of our traders and administra-

* Thompson and Garratt, p. 657.

tors was insufficiently robust, though it is probable that multitudes from the lower castes would have welcomed this way of escape from their degradation. For long the Company actually forbade the entry into its territories of missionaries. Its wishes for India's good found a vent, we must assume, through other channels.

The Company, as time went on, was served by some men of high character and unusual ability, Metcalfe, Sir John Malcolm, Sir Thomas Monro and Sir Henry Lawrence, but all of these have left on record biting criticisms of the principles that underlay its administration. Monro, who was Governor of Madras, wrote in his famous Minute * of 1817 that while other conquerors had been violent and cruel, "none has treated the natives with such scorn as we." They do, he went on,

"enjoy the fruits of their labour in tranquillity: but none of them can aspire to anything beyond this mere animal state of thriving in peace. . . . The consequence, therefore, of the conquest of India by the British arms would be, in place of raising, to debase the whole people. There is, perhaps, no example of any conquest in which the natives have been so completely excluded from all share of government of their country as in British India."

He adds that the same rule of exclusion prevails in the army. The result was not merely, as Monro put it, to make the native "abject," but in Malcolm's words to render our rule "repulsive." The system these great administrators condemned remained virtually unchanged for a century after the date of Monro's Minute.

As our system of administration became fixed towards the close of the eighteenth century, it began to modify the structure of Indian society profoundly. The Company created over part of its territory a new class of functionless landlords, entitled to levy tribute on the peasants, where none had existed before. This it did partly because it regarded a squirearchy as

* Reproduced in full with corroborative evidence, Thompson and Garratt, p. 657.

a blessing to any nation and partly because it reckoned on the support of this new class. Its law-courts and its revenue officers, hardly aware at first of what they were doing, gradually introduced into India conceptions of individual property, especially in land, alien to her traditions, and often with unhappy results. The economic relationship repeated that which had driven the American colonies into revolt. India was regarded as a great market for British goods, especially cotton cloth: her function was to serve as a plantation for the raising of such exotic crops as indigo and tea and as a source of raw materials. The exquisite native handicrafts were ruined, at first by deliberate fiscal devices, and then by the irresistible competition of the new age of power-industry. From first to last the British in India were primarily merchants, with the psychology of this class. The Company was, down to 1813, a monopolist, who forbade competition. No one, not even one of its own servants, could open a coal-mine without its licence. This atmosphere did not foster enterprise. It is surprising how few in India and how relatively unenterprising were the pioneers who "develop" a country by great engineering and industrial projects. The characteristic structure of British business in India revolved round certain long-established firms, who acted as agents for promoters and investors in England, ready to sink money in India, but not to "open up" the country by their personal work. Such a firm of agents might manage a hundred enterprises of the most diverse kinds—a tea-garden and indigo plantation, a gold mine and eventually a railway, with a dozen mills. The system is very costly and it does not favour creative daring.

Round about the year 1833 we are conscious of a new atmosphere among the British in India. We are on the eve of the Victorian Age. The typical Englishman of the new era is a Whig and often an Evangelical, who will abolish slavery in Jamaica, while he fights the first Factory Acts in Lancashire. He believes in progress and *laissez faire*, and will soon make free trade a religion. The belief was growing, both at home and on the spot, that we had a "civilising mission" to fulfil in India. The Company was deprived of its trading functions in the Act of 1833, an indispensable first step, if its rule was to become in any degree disinterested. Macaulay's speech when he introduced this bill in the Commons is a landmark in the history of our relationship. He foresaw the end of autocracy—

the day when our subjects ... having become instructed in European knowledge, may in some future age demand European institutions. Whether such a day will ever come I know not. But never will I attempt to avert or retard it. Whenever it comes it will be the proudest day in English history.

The first result of this new attitude was that the Company now dared for the first time under Lord William Bentinck to suppress some of the survivals from the immemorial past which Hindu society, lacking since the Mohammedan conquest any strong leadership of its own, had never itself managed to throw off. Up to this date the Company had officially countenanced *suttee* (the burning, voluntary in theory, of widows). It was now forbidden. We are apt to forget, when we shudder in retrospect at ugly Oriental practices, how recent is our own European code of humanity. When the Company first settled in India, our forefathers were still burning heretics—an exclusively Christian rite. Landor has left a moving record of the last Englishwoman we roasted alive in public, as late as 1685, after Monmouth's rebellion.* Indians, in their turn, shuddered at our inhumanity when we took to hanging men for petty theft in Bengal, as our fathers did well into the last century at home. The fruits of this new attitude were not wholly good: the rising generation of Whigs and Evangelicals, which knew little of history and less of anthropology, developed a censorious contempt for Indian civilisation, and took to dwelling chiefly on its defects. None the less, our official policy was then, as now, to interfere as little as possible with Indian institutions: it tolerated social customs injurious to health, notably child marriage, and accepted even untouchability as an immutable fact in an environment it dared not alter. Our

* See *Imaginary Conversations*, "Lady Lisle and Elizabeth Gaunt."

courts, as time went on, took to administering Hindu law with an almost antiquarian fidelity. The result of this attitude was unquestionably to stereotype the past in a land that never has discarded it with ease. The best thing that happened in this period was that the abler and bolder minds among Hindus, notably the brave Bengali reformer, Rammohan Roy, were now thinking out India's social and religious problems afresh, under the stimulus of their contact with the more or less rationalist West.

A new element of revolutionary importance began to modify this too static relationship when we decided to promote education on an English basis in accordance with Macaulay's famous Minute. The original motive was to train clerks and junior officials for our own service, which explains why we were content to leave the vast mass of the population illiterate to this day. Macaulay was a Philistine of genius, who regarded Oriental civilisation with withering disdain. It was a great gain that the Indian *intelligentsia* should learn a Western language thoroughly. But it was a disaster that our schools and colleges should despise the study of India's own languages, her culture and her history. Even more fatal in its social and economic effects was the decision to give Indians a purely literary education. The natural sciences were neglected, and any provision we have latterly made to remedy this oversight has been tardy and inadequate. This was peculiarly unfortunate because the Brahman tradition suffered from this same one-sideness. The Indian mind enjoys literary studies, revels in logic and metaphysics and is at its ease in the subtlest legal debates. But it had felt little interest in physical science and has only recently begun to display its talent for this field of intellectual activity. In short, the Brahman intellectual and the classical scholar of the I.C.S., bred in a Public School, were equally indifferent to science and technology. The result was that Indians rushed into the legal profession and neglected the studies and careers which might have ended Indian poverty by the development of scientific agriculture and modern industry. This land was cursed with an unemployed proletariat of intellectuals, who found their solace in angry political agitation. We might have trained them to teach the peasants, work as engineers and qualify themselves as experts in modern farming; but all this lay beyond Macaulay's horizon, nor did Indians move spontaneously in this direction.*

The Mutiny of 1857 ended the Company's rule. It was an ill-organised revolt, but it made Englishmen in India aware of the insecurity of their tenure. The repression was stained with as much cruelty as the outbreak, and it left behind it in our minute and isolated garrisons a fear which still persists—the atmosphere that E. M. Forster's delicate art has reproduced in *A Passage to India*. They closed the doors of their clubs and drawing-rooms more tightly than ever, even to Indians "instructed in European knowledge." The common intellectual outlook that should have united the two races served only to give Indians a new sense of injury and neglect. Many of them now possessed a Western culture far beyond the attainments of the average member of the white colony, but still they were excluded.

One lesson of the Mutiny the rulers of India did learn. The rising of the Sepoys grew in the North into something approaching a national rebellion because of the resentment felt by the princes and feudal nobles whom we had deposed, especially during Lord Dalhousie's restless and ambitious reign as Governor-General. It was now realised that we had gone too far in this policy of direct rule and annexation. The Queen, in the famous post-Mutiny proclamation, promised that "We shall respect the rights, dignity and honour of the native princes as our own." That was a far from ingenuous way of defining a very much subtler policy. Here is Canning's account of it, written in 1860:

It was long ago said by Sir John Malcolm that if we made all

* Writing in 1934 Dr. Buchanan states (p. 479) that the sparsely settled State of Iowa, with 1 per cent of its population, had more students of agriculture, commerce and engineering than the whole of British India.

India into *zillahs* (or British Districts) it was not in the nature of things that our Empire should last fifty years; but that if we could keep up a number of native states without political power but as royal instruments, we should exist in India as long as our naval supremacy was maintained. Of the substantial truth of this opinion I have no doubt; the recent events have made it more deserving of our attention than ever.

The English language has degenerated since Canning's day. "Royal instruments without political power" is a stately, if long-winded phrase. We call the princes "puppets."

The formal proclamation in 1858 of a new era of racial equality awakened some hope for a brighter future. There was a period in the latter decades of Queen Victoria's reign when we seemed to have entered a slightly happier climate. There were in this generation many men among our officials who took a warm and scholarly interest in Indian languages, culture and anthropology and some who helped the awakening of Indian nationalism. The National Congress, when it first met in 1885, was effusively, even fulsomely loyal. Sir Henry Maine, perhaps the most sympathetic of the scholarly liberals who devoted their great talents to India's service, has left a record of the enthusiasm with which Indian students rushed to our universities, repeating the fervour and excitement of the Renaissance, when the new learning flashed on the scholastic darkness of Medieval Europe*.

What was it that went wrong after this new start? Traditional England soon discovered that it preferred traditional India—the inert India which asks no questions and ventures no criticisms. Our governing class developed a sudden preference for "the real India," by which it meant the more conservative Muslims, the hereditary soldiers content to serve without commissioned rank, and the always submissive princes. Disappointment turned to bitterness as Indians noted how slight and tardy was the influence of our famous proclamations of

* *Village Communities*, p. 277.

equality, first * made in 1833 and again in 1858. We never break our promises to India, but do we always fulfil them? Certainly the higher posts in the services were now open to Indians. But it was not till 1864 that the first Indian was admitted to the I.C.S.: three more entered in 1871. As late as 1915, after 82 years of equality, the Indians in the I.C.S. amounted only to 5 per cent: after 90 years the proportion † had risen by 1923 to 10 per cent.‡ Lord Ripon, a genuine Liberal, whom Indians respected, made a brave effort in 1883 to establish equality before the law between the races in the courts: but the furious agitation of the white community compelled him to compromise and whittle down his bill (the so-called Ilbert Bill) into a timid half-measure. English planters and men of business came out to India in increasing numbers after the Mutiny. Did our manners deteriorate in this period, or was it that Indians became more sensitive? Certainly crass and even brutal behaviour by Englishmen towards Indians was in this generation frequent, and it has not ceased in ours. Within an hour of embarking on the P. & O. liner for Bombay, in 1930, a lady of considerable assurance, who told me that she had lived eighteen years in Poona, flung at me the question, "Why don't they shoot Gandhi?" She went on to explain that "the whole trouble in India has come about, because the Government won't let us beat our servants. It's the only thing they understand." Arrived in Bombay, I heard this story from an Indian lady, who bore a name deeply honoured in the last century, of which by her carriage and her intelligence she was worthy. She was about to get into a first-class carriage, in which there were two English ladies. One of them, Lady X,

* The Act prescribes (Clause 87) that no native of British India "shall by reason only of his religion, place of birth, descent, colour or any of them be disabled from holding any place, office or employment" in the administration.

† R. Coupland, *Britain and India,* pp. 38 and 73, and Thompson and Garratt, p. 538.

‡ The figures today for the all-India services (I.C.S. with police, etc.) are 1,544 Europeans to 1,241 Indians.

came to the door and said gruffly, "You can't come in here." "And why?" asked the Indian. "Because you're black and I'm white," said Lady X. "I prefer my colour to your manners," was the neat retort. Other stories of this kind were more brutal and less amusing. A few years ago an Indian intellectual, a highly educated and attractive young man of slight physique, entered a first-class railway carriage in which were an Englishman and his wife. The Englishman ordered him out. He replied with the usual Indian gentleness, and finally, since the train had started, offered to change carriages at the next station. The Englishman opened the door and flung him out on the line. He was badly bruised. The strangest part of this story is that he assured me that he felt no hatred. The culprits in such cases were rarely the civil servants, whose code was fixed by their education. The merchants and soldiers who sullied our good name in this way were men who felt an inordinate pride in their white skins, because they had nothing else to be proud of.

The result of all this and of sundry acts like Lord Curzon's clumsy partition of Bengal was the arrival after the turn of the century of a more violent and menacing phase in the political life of India, marked by the rise of militant leadership in Congress and by terrorism in Bengal. Congress was at first content to criticise the slips and omissions of the bureaucracy, to assail the military expenditure and the financial "drain," and to ask, very gently, for the gradual concession of representative institutions. It had in Mr. Gokhale a moderate leader of great intellectual power and singular nobility of character, a liberal and a rationalist, who none the less worked with religious devotion for the good of the masses. He founded the Servants of India, a quasi-monastic order, whose members still labour with selfless zeal and courage, some to organise the workers, some to help the backward aboriginal tribes and others to train young Hindu widows as teachers or midwives. Gokhale and his generation accepted the British conquest as an unalterable fact decreed, as I have heard him say with a melancholy smile, "by the mysterious providence of God." His utmost ambition was at some distant day to achieve "colonial self-government." But providence moved so slowly that leadership passed to less patient men, to Tilak, a scholarly Brahman who was also a fighting man and a Mahratta, and to Lajpat Rai, the first Indian socialist. In retrospect I wonder would anyone now justify the imprisonment, often for long terms and usually for rash speeches, of these and other nationalist leaders? We had conceded municipal self-government, the participation of Indians in consultative councils, and the beginnings of representation under the ill-conceived scheme of Lord Morley (see below, p. 91); but broadly the picture was still government by an autocratic bureaucracy which had to rely with increasing frequency on coercion. An honest commentator must add that the problem was not easy. If there were leaders like Gokhale who would have shone among the rulers of any country in the world, there were at the far end of the scale the primitive aboriginal tribes, and between these extremes the illiterate mass of peasants and workers. The urban workers were soon to form their trade unions, but the organisation of the far more numerous peasants had hardly yet begun, whereas the educated middle class was ripe and even over-ripe for responsibility. India lives on many levels and in several centuries, and in their advance her millions cannot always move in step.

In this generation, from the 80's of last century onwards, there began, very late in the day, the establishment of modern power industry. The great coalfield of Bengal and Bihar developed very slowly, and the use of hydro-electricity lay far ahead. The Bombay cotton-mills ran on coal imported from Natal or even from England. At this time, so slight was our acquaintance with India's natural resources that even the ablest Englishmen honestly believed that, save in a few seaports, she was destined to remain a purely agricultural country. These infant industries had a hard struggle for life, but learned to thrive by the ruthless exploitation of their workers. The rulers of India had an unshakable faith that free trade must benefit every nation as certainly as it had benefited Lancashire. Factory legislation was long delayed and was until the other day wholly inadequate. Protection for Indian industries even against British competition was finally adopted but only after the World War—much to the credit of her British rulers, for it struck hard at Lancashire's staple trade.

With the war in 1914 came yet another chance for a new start. India displayed a generous and unanimous loyalty and gave lavishly both in blood and treasure. She expected her reward, but before it could reach her, disappointment and economic distress drove the Punjab to the edge of revolt. Our first reply, in April 1919, was one of those deeds that poison history, the massacre in an enclosed garden at Amritsar of an unarmed crowd: of whom 379 were killed and 1,200 wounded. All India was roused, and Gandhi became the unchallenged leader of Congress and made his first essay in civil disobedience against our "Satanic Government." Indians were ready for a decisive struggle. Not since the Mutiny has the British Raj been in graver danger. Prices soared, and the value of the rupee was halved. A firm alliance united the Hindus with the Muslims, who were angry over our attitude to Turkey and its Sultan, the last Caliph of Islam. So close was the fraternisation that Hindus were invited to preach in the mosques. British cloth was boycotted. With startling unanimity city after city declared a *hartal*—something between a day of mourning and a general strike—when the Prince of Wales attempted a royal progress through India in 1921. The National Volunteers were drilling, though they were unarmed, and thirty thousand political prisoners lay in British gaols. Gandhi's tactics favoured a gradual *crescendo*, but the peasants were calling on him to give the signal for tax resistance. He hesitated and they began to act without him. Then the villagers of Chauri-Chaura in the United Provinces were led into a horrifying atrocity. In February 1922 they burned down their police-station with twenty-one policemen in it.* Blaming himself for what had happened,

* I do not know what provocation they had received. In a parallel case, at Chimur, in 1942, it is alleged that six women had been raped. So too, in 1942, though two British airmen who crashed were murdered, it must be remembered that crowds were machine-gunned from the air.

Gandhi then announced that India was morally unfit for the struggle and, to the amazement of his followers and the world, called off the campaign before it was well begun. Was this his real reason? Certainly it was only one and probably not the chief of his reasons. Tax resistance by peasants in the North would have involved a strike against rent. It is significant that Gandhi and his Working Committee went out of their way to assure the landlords (*zemindars*) that Congress would scrupulously respect their legal rights.* This singular man is a born conservative whom history has turned into a revolutionary. The British Government saved him by a public trial and a heavy sentence from the unpopularity that might have engulfed him —a mistake it never repeated.

Meanwhile the British Government by the Act of 1919 had bestowed on India a tardy reward for the loyalty she had already repented. It was, as usual, "too little and too late." Ten years earlier it would not have seemed negligible. The new All-India Legislative Assembly and Council, partly elected on excessively narrow franchises, partly nominated and diluted by officials, had severely limited powers, but they served to focus public opinion. In the provinces, however, certain of the less important ministries were entrusted to Indians responsible to mainly elected Councils, subject to the Governor's veto, while the more important were still directed by officials. "Dyarchy," Mr. Montagu's invention, was not an easy system to work, and it was received with much scorn and little gratitude. Congress refused to co-operate.

In two provinces, Madras and the Punjab, where a strong local party existed which chose to make the most of the reforms, they had some effect. In the Punjab the Muslim Minister of Education, a man of some originality, carried out some rather daring and salutary ideas of his own, which could never have found a lodging in the brain of a bureaucrat. But in Bombay (to take a more usual case) I found that the Ministry of Education was run, virtually without reference to successive

* For the documents see Dutt, p. 317.

Indian ministers, on commonplace lines by its senior British official. I did not blame him. The ministers were careerists as destitute of dignity as of ideas. They had no mass-party behind them and could not have imposed themselves, even if they had had the wish to do so. More significant than these reforms themselves was the pledge of August 20, 1917, which heralded them. Mr. Montagu spoke the language of Macaulay and saw, though still in the undated future, the approach of "the proudest day in English history." "By successive stages," at a pace to be determined by the British and Indian Governments, he promised, for Mr. Lloyd George's Cabinet, "the increasing association of Indians in every branch of the administration and the gradual development of self-governing institutions, with a view to the progressive realisation of responsible government in India as an integral part of the British Empire."

How came it that promises and declarations of this kind had an effect so slight upon the minds of Indians? In the first place, we had made too many of them. Worse than this, in occasional outbreaks of honesty, leading members of the ruling class would from time to time utter their real thoughts, oblivious of the fact that Indians were listening. Lord Birkenhead had been Secretary for India, had administered the Montagu-Chelmsford reforms from Whitehall and appointed the Simon Commission to report on further advances towards self-government. But in 1929 he was capable of addressing these words to the House of Lords:

What man in this House can say that he can see in a generation, in two generations, in a hundred years, any prospect that the people of India will be in a position to assume control of the Army, the Navy, the Civil Service, and to have a Governor-General who will be responsible to the Indian Government and not to any authority in this country?

An indiscretion of this kind is suitably rebuked in the English Liberal press, and a week later most of us have managed to forget it. Indians do not forget. They draw two conclusions.

Firstly, they assume that when we do abandon some of the outworks of our citadel, it is only that we may hold its inner keep the more securely. Secondly, they infer that Englishmen are no honester than the rest of mankind.

MAHATMA GANDHI

WITH THESE early post-war years began the reign over India of Mahatma Gandhi, who for good or ill has shaped her destiny to this day. It is not easy for us to understand his influence: the last saint who moulded our history was Thomas à Becket. Few can meet him without submitting to his charm. So vital is he, so lucidly intelligent that one hardly notices the emaciated little body or the irregular features: he talks with his quick, shapely hands and his remarkable eyes. His good manners put the stranger at his ease, and as one gets to know him one learns that he has the gift of humor and can even indulge in playful fun. In public he speaks as he talks, quietly and simply, without rhetoric or display, though he can on occasion coin a memorable phrase. I have watched him doing business with streams of callers: he was prompt and shrewd and knew how to dismiss careerists. He shines in the patient exposition of his opinions to a roomful of questioners. At first I thought him the most original, the most obviously self-moved human being I had ever met. Everything he thinks and utters seems to come from the deep well that is himself. Whether he writes or speaks, he seems always to be conducting a dialogue with himself, audible, rational and wholly his own. In times of perplexity he is like a chess player, playing against himself. He reads and has read surprisingly little. In history and science he takes little interest, and in the aesthetic side of things none at all. Life and, incidentally, politics are for him always and entirely an absorbing ethical problem. He pores over the Hindu scriptures, but he studies the Gospels and the Koran as well. In his early life Thoreau, Ruskin and Tolstoy influenced him, but thereafter his mind turned on its own axis. In short, it is a reflective, rather than a perceptive or an enquiring mind. But I soon came to modify this reading of him. Is it really Gandhi who solves every problem of conduct, public or private, in confident decisions in the clearest English? Something much older than Gandhi is speaking through him. He is the Hindu conscience. These are the responses of an oracle which had its spokesmen in past centuries in the hermits, ascetics and teachers of this ancient land. I can believe that the priest whose statue was dug up in Mohenjo-Daro spoke much as he does now, three thousand years before Christ. He likes to reason everything out. But I think he merely clothes in logic what instinct has already spoken within his subconscious mind, and it is the heir of the Indian tradition.

That is why this singular genius means more to the Indian masses than any man who figures in our records. What he says is startling because it is so homely and familiar. He may say it in English, but it is not an echo of Burke or Mill: it is Indian thinking. I dare not try to expound it, for I find it neither congenial nor wholly intelligible. To me it seems negative, reactionary, pessimistic and other-worldly, not merely a creed but a habit of renunciation. Rigidly ascetic in matters of sex, I am not sure what place it allows to any of the satisfactions of the intellect or the senses. It aims at an equal love for all mankind, at justice and unflinching truth—honesty, that is to say, in social intercourse rather than scientific truth. Western science, and more especially medicine, Gandhi rejects with angry contempt. He would reduce daily life to a naked simplicity and dreads the complexities of Western technology. His ideal social and political structure is a loose commonwealth of old-world Indian villages, each mainly self-sufficient, under its elected *panchayat* (council) of elders. Handicrafts and village industries, above all spinning, are to be promoted, and agriculture improved by such sound and simple devices as the use of night soil. With Socialism Gandhi has no sympathy, though he does favour a type of trade union inspired by his own moral teaching. The lot of the workers is to be bettered, not by coercive legislation, and still less by expropriation, but by persuading employers and landowners to behave ethically as trustees of the property they hold for the common good. But on occasion Gandhi will combat exploitation, stubbornly and as in all else without fear. He professes himself an orthodox Hindu, who will even defend caste, not as it exists today, but in what he believes to have been its ancient and simple form. But nothing in his long life has deserved the gratitude of mankind so certainly as his unflinching struggle against untouchability. In this he never rests and never compromises, and in an astonishingly short time he has already gone far to break an oppression as ancient as the Brahman ascendancy. Finally, the most characteristically Hindu of all his doctrines is his preaching of non-violence (*ahimsa*). It doubtless has its root in the Hindu taboo on the taking of life, which the Jains of his native Gujerat observed with literal fidelity. It is a way of life which enjoins love for one's enemies. What I have always failed to grasp is its use as a tactic of resistance which may strike at property and legitimate economic interests, though it will not wound or kill.

Was it this teaching that won the masses, or was it the unique personality of the teacher? The two are one. No saint has ever lived his creed more faithfully. Literally Gandhi stripped himself naked and led the life of the poor peasants he would serve. He has, indeed, renounced all the goods of life—save only power; and power, as the Hindu tradition believes, comes to the ascetic from his austerities. His fasts and his days of silence ranked him with the old hermits. The masses contrasted this man with the leaders they had hitherto known—most of them lawyers, busy over the details of getting and maintaining wealth, of which they commonly enjoyed a comfortable share. They understood him with ease, and noted that he spoke with authority and the assurance of absolute belief. He soon had his devoted disciples, who would toil for him and supply all the humdrum talents he lacked. The rich poured money at his feet, and the poor faced at his bidding the *lathis* and prisons of the police. All called him saint and some saw in him an incarnation of God.

Under Gandhi's leadership Congress became the national party of India. It was the first mass organisation to come into being and until the other day the only Indian party which could be so described. The Liberals were always a distinguished group of intellectuals, which included many able, wealthy and influential men, but they had no mass following, for they never knew how to touch the emotions of the multitude. It is only in recent years that the Muslim League and the Hindu Mahasabha have acquired a numerous membership. Congress, while it knew how to arouse swelling waves of emotion in the masses, also evolved a modern technique of organisation, an art which Indians had been slow to learn. It could be business-like, punctual and energetic, while it also loved colour, publicity and the picturesque. For the first time in Indian political life it interested the peasants in its doings and ideas and drew the women out of their seclusion. In later chapters I have tried to describe it more fully, as I saw it in action.* It has published no recent figures of its membership, which may not now exceed two millions. Its power was tested in the provincial elections of 1937, when, though severely handicapped in many ways, it was so successful that it formed the Ministry in eight provinces out of eleven. I am not sure whether the usual estimate that over all India it polled close on 70 per cent of the general electorates is strictly accurate, but it cannot be far out. Its strength is unevenly distributed. Its hold on Bengal is relatively weak, and in the Punjab its influence is negligible, while in Hindu India it is a great power. It is, none the less, a grave mistake to call it a Hindu party, as Mr Churchill has done. Its purpose is not to advance Hindu confessional interests, though in fact the great majority of its membership, as of the Indian population, are Hindus. (There is a rival organisation which frankly stands for these separate confessional interests, the Hindu Mahasabha, which is often sharply opposed to Con-

* See below, pp. 219-240.

gress.) Its Working Committee, as everyone knows, has for chairman a noted Muslim theologian, Dr. Azad, and on it there always sit other Muslims, Parsis, Sikhs and occasionally a Christian and an "untouchable." It does include every section of the Indian population, including some very active groups of Muslims, but the main body of its Muslim sympathisers are now grouped in separate local parties, which commonly act with it. It is easy to grasp its relation to Hinduism by a simple analogy. It would be absurd to call our Labour Party a Protestant party, although the vast majority of its members were baptised into some Protestant church. But Catholics, Freethinkers and Jews are at their ease and can rise to high offices within it. Above all, its purpose is not to serve Protestant confessional interests but to further those of the workers and the Socialist idea. Change the names and all this is equally true of Congress. The idea for which it stands is Indian nationalism.

The critics of Congress often accuse it of being a "totalitarian" party. There is some truth in this description, which it is important to grasp. Its spokesmen often exaggerate its influence, which is immense but not universal. At the Round Table Conference Gandhi claimed to be in his own person the representative of all the peasants of India. That he never was; but few Englishmen realised how near to the truth this boast came. The fact is that Congress is not conducting normal party politics as we have known them in England for a century or more. India has not yet won constitutional self-government. Congress cannot regard itself primarily as the rival of other Indian parties in an internal struggle for power and influence. It is engaged in a life-and-death struggle with the British Empire for India's independence. In such a struggle, with an external power, it is bound to demand unity and discipline among all the national forces. Stressing, as it must, this duty of national unity, it may be, on occasion, intolerant of other Indian groups which differ from it over tactics or in temperament and outlook. This is a familiar phenomenon in every national struggle in history. The old Nationalist Party under Parnell in Ireland offers a parallel which Sinn Fein repeated.

Each of them had to destroy its rival at home in order to present a united front to the Saxon. The Chinese Kuo-min-tang, which had to overthrow first the Manchu dynasty and then the warlords in league with foreign powers, presents another instructive case for comparison. In this sense, but in no other, the tactics but not the thinking of Congress have a totalitarian look.

This item in our diagnosis leads to another, which is more fundamental. Congress, as Gandhi has shaped it, differs from its older self and from the Liberals in its revolutionary conception of the struggle in which it is engaged. Though it has renounced violence, it relies on various forms of "disobedience" to the British rulers of India and preaches the duty of "revolt." The Liberals, who rely solely on politeness and persuasion to achieve their end by gradualism, stand at the opposite extreme. Given this starting-point, it is intelligible that Congressmen should hold that every patriotic Indian ought to be within their ranks. They have at times stressed this argument in ways that aroused the hostility of other Indians. But it is fair to add that in two provinces, Sind and Assam, they did form coalitions with other parties and had there their Muslim allies. During the negotiations with Sir Stafford Cripps at Delhi they made it clear that the national government they demanded would be a "mixed," that is to say a coalition, administration.

This national character of Congress is reflected in its social composition and the wide gamut of opinions it includes. It is a national front drawn up for a specific purpose, and its ambition is to include every man and woman with a dark skin. Impossible as that may be, it is astonishing that it can embrace in one family a variety so immense. Many of its leaders are Brahmans, yet it won at the provincial elections six times as many of the seats reserved for untouchables as did the Independent Labour Party formed for their protection by Dr. Ambedkar, himself an untouchable. It is true, as Mr. Churchill recently said, that financiers and industrialists wield a considerable influence within it, as such persons do in his own party. Their skins also are dark. But for many years there has been within it a strong Socialist group, with its own distinct organisation, whose leaders sit on its Working Committee. Recently it has also included a little Communist group, as the Kuo-min-tang once did. Some of its ablest leaders, like Mr. Rajagopalachari, who has now left it, are in outlook typical conservatives. But the differences within it are deeper than these party labels indicate. Few of the younger generation of intellectuals, whether they are nominally Hindus, Muslims or Parsis, accept Gandhi's philosophy of life. Most of them are rationalists and many of them incline to Socialism. The wealthy men who give lavishly to Congress are equally far from his old-world outlook: they aim at a vast expansion of power-industry in India, as from their own very different angle the Socialists and Communists also do. The peasants, who also have their own distinct organisations within Congress, are much nearer to Gandhi in outlook than the Socialist intellectuals or the industrial workers, but in the northern provinces they mean to sweep away the functionless landowners by political action, where he would be content to soften these men's hearts by moral suasion. Again, it is now manifest that only a minority of Congress, insignificant in its numbers, shares Gandhi's pacifism, the deepest of his convictions. Congress has managed to draw up from time to time by majority decisions an agreed constructive programme, which is a compromise between Gandhism and an advanced Liberal view of social reform, but this is secondary to its overmastering purpose. It is first of all and all the time a nationalist party bent on liberating India—the whole of India, as one vast unit—from foreign rule. For how long, after that end is achieved, will it hold together? Not, I think, for many years, nor for long after its leader quits this earthly scene, in which he lingers, a detached wayfarer. Very soon after India has made an end of the Conquest, she will have to face her acute social problems. The villages will insist on shaking off their parasitic landlords and usurers. When they attempt this in earnest, Congress will split. Its millionaire bankers and its Socialists will no longer collaborate as they do for a limited but all-important end to-day. Finally, it is only fair to repeat that Congress has never preached a totalitarian or Fascist philosophy. Its one rebel who did so, the dynamic but unstable Bengali leader, Subhas Chandra Bose, was driven out of its ranks. It does—too often but not always—obey Gandhi with a perilous fidelity, but it has never accepted the principle of dictatorship—what Germans call the *Führer-Prinzip*. On the contrary, at the cost of long delays, it requires the assent of an elected National Committee, of about 250 delegates, for any new departure, whether in policy or tactics.

Even a brief history would remind us, as this hasty sketch cannot, that in fact Gandhi has several times been defeated; over big issues and for long terms in his management of Congress. Some of his chief ideas he has never succeeded in imposing on it at all, notably his hostility to industrial development. His mystical view of non-violence appealed only to a minority: the majority were always content with the common-sense view that a disarmed nation would merely invite massacre, if it tried to fight. Always there has existed in Congress another and more positive type of leader, who had no sympathy with his peculiarly reactionary brand of nationalism. Personal rivalry there was none, for the outstanding fact in Indian life today is that the finest men among these progressive leaders still feel for him, when they steel themselves to resist him, a reverent affection. This was as true of that typical Liberal, Motilal Nehru, as it is of his Socialist son, Jawaharlal. I met the younger Nehru first as a prisoner in the cool crypt of an ancient Mogul keep beside the Ganges, and I have since enjoyed his company both alone and with others in London. Always the same impression persists—a personality stable and consistent in its dualism. He has everything Gandhi lacks —a trained sense for history which led him to spend his captivity, like Raleigh and Condorcet, in writing the story of mankind, an interest in natural science which won him distinction at Cambridge, an aesthetic endowment which he satisfies now with natural beauty, again by the close study of English poetry and when he pleases by writing a page of perfect English prose. His understanding of the mechanics of historical movement made him a decided socialist. Travel and his imaginative grasp of other cultures taught him his international outlook. Nature made him a fighting man and gave him an athletic frame and an instinctive dislike of passivity. But under his European culture and through his firm muscles flows Indian blood, and something answers when Gandhi rationalises his negations, his asceticism, his other-worldliness. Nehru will oppose him, will even defeat him, but in the end he falls back into the ranks again. During this war they have alternated turn and turn about as the two personal forces that dominated Congress. When it looked as if the British Government would compromise, Nehru prevailed; when it froze the wish of Indians to hope, then Gandhi led. They sometimes remind me of the primitive barometer, made of cat-gut, which farmers used in my boyhood. A smiling old woman and a frowning old man stood on the two ends of a revolving porch, and came into view alternately, as the atmosphere changed from dry to moist. So it was in India. Did the political weather seem promising? Then the friendly face of Nehru swung into view. Did the weather lower? Then the little old man of Wardha sprang out of his retreat. But both are glued to the same perch. Together, they are Hindustan.

After this rapid dissection, which has omitted all the varieties of race and language within the Congress party, we may be better able to estimate Gandhi's achievement as a leader. It is a nation rather than a party, and a continent rather than a nation he can lead, not merely to the ballot-box but when he wills it to prison. He appeals to its oldest traditions, and yet he can induce it to smash the most ancient, albeit the ugliest, of its institutions. No man in our day has done anything like it, for Lenin had to supplement his gift of leadership with military force and a machine of coercion. Indians, it may be, when once they accept a teacher, will bestow on him veneration more readily and with a more steadfast loyalty than Western peoples do. In the old days every youth of the higher castes would attach himself to his *guru*, at once teacher, saint and confessor, whose influence dwelt with him throughout his after-life. There are strong personalities among Gandhi's lieutenants, not merely Pandit Jawaharlal Nehru, but others whose names are unknown in the West. Among them are men and women whose outlook differs from his as the twentieth century differs from the twelfth. Yet when they disagree with him on an urgent issue of action, they are torn in sunder, like an adolescent when first he differs from a loved and respected father. In no other society have I met with anything near the intimate affection and the deep veneration this man inspires. It is possible to say this and yet to think, as I do, that Gandhi's political judgment is disastrously fallible. His, as I have suggested, is not a perceptive mind. Even England he does not know well, and with international affairs his acquaintance is slight. During some twenty years, as the leader and thinker who often spoke but seldom listened, he has built up a world of his own, in which the solid realities are moral principles and articles of faith. All men who hold a creed with intense belief do this in some degree: even Lenin, in some respects the most realistic of men, did this—on occasion with unfortunate results. This it is which gives such men the ability to make a leap in history. They refuse to see the obstacles they surmount.

In this personal world of faith Gandhi has deliberately entrenched himself, sometimes by retiring into the fastnesses of his *ashram* (monastery) and regularly on his days of silence and meditation. Gradually he has come to believe that men do in fact act as in his spiritual vision they ought to act. He has in his own technique of *ahimsa* (non-violence) a belief as absolute as Hitler may feel in the efficacy of *Blitzkrieg*. It may on occasion fail, but only because there was some impurity in his heart. Was he really certain that he could persuade the Japanese not to invade an unarmed India? Perhaps not, but it seemed to him likely enough to be worth trying. George Fox, who would talk pacifism hopefully to Oliver Cromwell, had this kind of faith, and so had his disciples who set out on foot across Europe to convert the Pope of Rome and the Grand Turk. Gandhi may be shrewder than these children of God, for, as he is fond of saying, he is by caste a *bania* (the trader's and money-lender's caste). But none the less, he is to an astonishing degree the architect of his own universe, and he listens to no rival interpreters, be they historians, economists or psychologists. The danger of this intellectual isolation is enhanced by the fact that he has been surrounded for twenty years by devoted disciples and an idolatrous multitude. His rule over Congress is none the less absolute because it is indirect. More than once he has withdrawn from it into the wilderness. At present he holds no office in it and is not even a member. It is directed by an elaborate democratic machinery. But in a crisis, if Gandhi is strongly moved, he can usually sway it. It is hardly just to call him an autocrat, but if he be one, he owes his power to the ascendancy of his own personality.

Other dictators can point to the overt successes they have won. No man can yet predict what tangible success history may one day place to Gandhi's credit. More in the past may be the fruit of his struggles than the India Office would like to admit. The future is for me obscure and overcast. And yet this man has triumphed. To all Indians who have come under the influence of his teaching he has given an inner sense of independence. They are free within. The yoke of the Conquest snaps when they stand erect and perform be it the most innocent act of rebellion. This subjective liberation was a mighty event in Indian history. For Indians were oppressed even more by their own fatalism and their own sense of racial inferiority than by the British Raj. These inner fetters Gandhi broke. The outer world does not yet reflect this inner light of freedom. But how high for this Mahatma does the outer world rank?

THE BUREAUCRATS

AFTER THIS brief survey of Gandhi's place in contemporary India, it may be easier to realise what went wrong in our relationship with its people. In this land the rulers were not leaders and the leaders never ruled. That is the ideal formula for the production of paralysis, frustration and unrest. This divorce between leading and ruling was inevitable when Englishmen decided to sojourn in India as foreigners, but it need not have been as complete as it eventually became. It was not necessary that British officials and residents should isolate themselves as a closed caste of "white Brahmans," which married, dined and clubbed within its own ranks. Nor was it inevitable that the civil service should be confined to the movements of its departmental treadmill. There was more play of personality, less isolation and much less bureaucracy in the early days. There were a few men in the Company's time, who were in some sense leaders. One of the Governors-General, Bentinck, may deserve the name. Lord Ripon, at the height of the Victorian Liberal era, had this gift and endeared himself to Indians. But these exceptions served only to emphasise the cold impersonality of the administrative machine. In the early days a district magistrate had to be a self-reliant man of action, who cultivated an adaptable and elastic habit of mind. But first he was tied to the end of a telegraph wire: then he was entangled in codes and regulations: finally, the man who had once toured his district at leisure on horseback, with eyes and ears open, now rushed through it, inaccessible, in his car. The isolation became in our day nearly absolute, and this was inevitable, because Indians who respected themselves had with few exceptions withdrawn behind their own entrenchments. The Indians whom officials did meet were first of all the criminals they tried, then the wrangling parties to a civil suit and finally the sycophants, the yes-men, the careerists who crawled after jobs and titles. A senior official in private talk once expressed to me a decidedly cynical view of Indian character. I was puzzled, for I had been spending a week in a big provincial town, during which I had met many of its leading men and women and seen what they were doing to raise its standards of life and culture. I had been impressed by their keen social conscience, their capacity for hard work that brought no tangible reward, and the blend of sensitive refinement with courage in the younger generation. Doubtless there were in this town prominent persons who were less admirable, but I sensed an atmosphere which gross egoists would not find congenial. When I gave my observations to this official in detail, I discovered that though he had spent more months than I had spent days in this place, he had met none of the leading citizens who had impressed me, nor visited any of their social experiments. For this separation, which in times of crisis comes near to boycott, Indians must share the responsibility. They sense the racial arrogance that underlies the superficial good manners of official Englishmen and they are not eager to encounter it. Every politically-conscious Indian knows by heart some of the frank utterances which this arrogance has found. Towards the end of the last century Mr. Seton Kerr, formerly Foreign Secretary to the Government of India, spoke of:

"the cherished conviction which was shared by every Englishman in India, from the highest to the lowest ... the conviction in every man that he belongs to a race whom God has destined to govern and subdue."

About the same time Field-Marshal Lord Roberts * said:

"It is this consciousness of the inherent superiority of the European which has won for us India. However well educated and clever a native may be and however brave he may have proved himself, I believe that no rank which we can bestow upon him would cause him to be considered as an equal by the British officer."

* Thompson and Garratt, p. 536.

In the end, this conviction of the *Herrenvolk* which won India will as certainly lose it.

These civil servants, let me hasten to add, have the virtues and the vices of their calling and their schooling. They are conscientious and hard-working, but they have evolved a routine as dilatory as it is exasperating in its lack of sympathy and imagination. I am not sure whether they are inspired in their work by a sense of duty chiefly towards their own country or towards India: the best of them would argue that there is no meaning in this distinction. In the higher courts of law, often with success, the best of the judges strove to be color-blind. The reign of law they established was much too complicated and too costly, while in the political field it was subject to recurring exceptions, but it ranks among our gifts. It would have meant more to the poor man and the villager if the police had been as admirable as the higher courts: how gravely it fell short I shall describe elsewhere.*

It is not easy to define the degree in which at various periods Indians under our direct rule have enjoyed civil rights. Everyone knows the too numerous exceptions. There is always, even in times of peace, a power to detain and imprison political suspects or offenders, for indefinite periods, without trial. Gandhi has been thrice imprisoned in this way. The so called *détenus*, kept in concentration camps, vary in numbers from a hundred or two to as many thousands, and are usually supposed terrorists. Newspapers were from time to time exposed to the vague charge of bringing the Government into "hatred and contempt," and required to deposit crippling sums as surety for good behaviour. It should be said, however, that the vernacular press is often excessively irresponsible. On one ground or another, power exists to suppress political organisations and to forbid meetings. Save when Congress launches a civil disobedience campaign, the sufferers are usually class organisations of the Left, the Communist party, for example, and the more radical peasant leagues. When this has been said, the fact, none the less, remains that Indians do enjoy a large measure

* See below, pp. 232-234.

of civil liberty. As a rule, subject to many exceptions, political offenders are tried. The press, in spite of irritating and arbitrary restrictions in periods of tension, is on the whole free, and its more responsible organs do in fact criticise the Government in fairly plain words, though they may have to write rather less strongly than they feel. In the towns, in normal times, the rights of meeting and association are on the whole respected. It should be added, however, that in the country, where few villages can find a man of education and independence to speak for them, these civil liberties may exist only in theory. The British Raj is a hybrid, half oriental, half Anglo-Saxon. It speaks English even when it acts Mogul.

To India these rulers gave what a competent bureaucracy and a disciplined army can give—order and peace. That is quickly said. To realise the value of these things, we of this century must read the wearisome chronicles of the eighteenth, with their monotonous tale of rapine, slaughter and starvation. Plague and famine, albeit tardily, these foreign rulers vanquished. To all this the historian has a final chapter to add, which tells how the engineers conquered distance, brought fertility to deserts and drew power from the Himalayan snows.

"What more," the reader may ask me, "would you have?" In the first place all these good things were imposed from above: they were not the fulfilment of this people's will. The people looked on, passive and unmoved. Those among them who had the right and capacity to lead felt themselves thwarted. A nation's will was lamed, while a sense of impotence and inferiority corroded its mind. The civilisation of India on the eve of the Conquest had fallen behind that of Europe in the sense that it was decadent and stagnant. But this disparity was relatively recent. In the golden age of the Moguls, under the Emperor Akbar, who was Queen Elizabeth's contemporary, there was no such inequality between the two civilisations. The arts in India were sensitive and alive: the handicrafts had evolved an astonishing virtuosity of technique. At this tolerant ruler's court bold thinking and eager speculative debate flourished: the administration was orderly and efficient and had a care for the public good. The two latent advantages which Europe then possessed bore their full fruit only in the next century—firstly, its capacity for movement, its readiness to criticise itself, its ability to adapt its social structure to the restless forces stirring within it and, secondly, its discovery of the experimental method in the natural sciences. These things gave Europeans the enterprise and the technique to conquer India. But under the conditions of the Conquest these two endowments, which made our superiority, were the last of the gifts we handed on. Indian culture remained, until the Bengali renaissance in this century, sterile and depressed. The natural sciences were until the other day neglected. It was only round about 1880 that the industrial development began, and then only on a small scale. The social structure remained rigid and inert, until the awakening of masses of men for movement and change began in our own day. To this a foreign bureaucracy could at the best contribute little, save the indirect stimulus of suppression. This it did supply.

Once in New Delhi a high official invited me to give him my impressions of what I had observed. Fresh from a stay in a group of poor villages, I tried to convey to him the scalding memory of poverty, ignorance, and misery they had left with me. They suffered not merely from neglect but from gross wrongs. His surprise was genuine. He did not seriously question my presentation of the facts, but he was astonished that I should hold the Government of India responsible. The business of government, as he put it in words that were an echo from an earlier century, was to maintain order with peace and to administer justice: this the Government of India did. As for health and education, to attend to them was no part of its strict duty, but a work of super-erogation: that might come in time. Another high official answered this charge of neglect by repeating at each count the same monotonous reply: "But India is a poor country, a very poor country." He meant, what is only too painfully true, that taxation cannot today be made to yield a revenue that could finance an adequate system of social services. What troubled me was the helpless fatalism of this answer. It had never struck this experienced and typical civil servant that poverty is not a fact to be accepted but a problem to be solved. It is not a congenial task to criticise the lifework of men who have observed their code. They went out to India with a faith in *laissez faire* as the most solid item in their equipment, and experience left it intact. India has sunshine, water and a climate that yields two and even three crops in the year. What more do her peasants need for wealth? Only science, freedom from debt and a rational system of land tenure. India has in abundance coal, minerals and the sources of hydro-electric power. What more does she need for a vast industrial development? Again, science with planning and a peasantry prosperous enough to buy its products. But this bureaucracy accepted the comfortable assumption that the function of India was to serve as a colonial estate for the raising of raw materials for export. It lacked the creative imagination that could have planned on a grand continental scale and the dynamic will that might have carried its plans against inertia and opposition. It could not have wrestled either with the resistance of the interests in England or with the obstruction of ancient customs and reactionary classes in Indian society. This work called for bold leadership. Perhaps no foreigners could have supplied it; certainly no foreign bureaucracy dare attempt it. These rulers can never lead: the time then has come when India's leaders must rule.

II. Round Table to Cripps Mission

SEVERAL TIMES, as we have seen, in our dealings with India, British statesmanship sought to make a fresh start. Of all these attempts the most nearly successful was the last, for which we have to thank Sir Stafford Cripps. None the less it failed, and failed disastrously. Our relations, since he returned from Delhi, have steadily worsened, and it is on us, in the eyes of our Chinese and American allies, that the responsibility falls. That may be a summary judgment, but there is this rough justice in it, that our ancestors did take on their shoulders the charge of this peninsula, and we must bear the weight until we can contrive to throw it off with honour. The most disturbing fact that confronts us is not merely that Congress, incomparably the biggest and most powerful of Indian parties, is in open revolt midway in what we conceive to be a war for human freedom; it is that other Indian parties, though they may regret and even censure its action, have come into line with its demands, and dare not lag behind it in their attitude of opposition. It may be said that Indians were excessively suspicious. That cannot absolve us from the duty of discovering the way out of this maze. The offer that Sir Stafford Cripps carried to Delhi was, in the light of the facts, defective: it did not achieve the end we had in view. One attitude only is possible for resolute and candid minds. We must ascertain why it failed. That Congress has never been an easy body to deal with is no adequate answer; nor shall we necessarily be any nearer to a solution if Congress can be crushed by physical coercion. The fact we have to explain is that every Indian party rejected this offer.

There is no need to demonstrate the nation's sincerity when it applauded this offer. Our military fortunes, when we made it, were at the lowest ebb. The least perceptive of us understood that the indifference of the peoples of Burma and Malaya was part of the explanation of our defeats in those dependencies. An early attack on India was expected. Who dare risk the same disaster there, if by any act of statesmanship we could win the wholehearted support of this nation? Opinions may differ as to how much more in man-power and industrial output India could contribute, if her heart were in the struggle; but only a very unimaginative man could fail to realise that Indian troops, if they ever have to defend India's soil, cannot fling all their ardour into the battle, if they must march and fight among a sullen and indifferent population, their own kith and kin. We knew, moreover, what our Allies expected of us, and the Government cannot have been insensible to the widespread anxiety which found expression as boldly in the *Times* as in the press of the Left. Sir Stafford Cripps, who should have known the mind of his colleagues, was willing to vouch for them. In so doing he assumed a heavy responsibility. India had in this Cabinet no friend but himself. Mr. Churchill had led the Die-hards against Sir Samuel Hoare's bill. On other questions, during his long political career, he has not been inflexible: only on this subject of India do his acts and speeches reveal the unbending consistency that comes from irresistible feeling. From first to last his powerful personality and his immense popularity have enabled him to dominate this Cabinet. Had he really changed his mind? But no one questions Sir Stafford's personal integrity. He had, moreover, by a previous visit to India proved his interest in this question, and ties of personal friendship bound him to some of her leaders. That many Indians wished for a settlement, who can doubt? The younger generation chafed at its inaction, and among the leaders there were virile personalities like Jawaharlal Nehru, by temperament a fighting man, who shared its feelings. It was becoming intolerable to them that they should stand idle much longer, while others with arms in their hands settled the destinies of their motherland and of Asia. Youth is always for action, but only we could give the signal that would release its energies.

Before we examine the Cripps offer, it is indispensable that we should see it in the context in which Indians had to judge it. Life had not stood still in this restless land during the years of war. Other and less satisfactory offers had preceded it. Congress had made in the early weeks of the war demands so reasonable that it is difficult to understand in retrospect why they should have been refused. Thereafter, its leaders had drifted in and out of prison. Even Mr. Rajagopalachari, ex-Premier of Madras, the most moderate of men, served a term in gaol. But the narrative must start a little earlier, with yet another of our efforts at settlement that failed—the Round Table Conference and the abortive plan of federation which emerged from it as Sir Samuel Hoare's Act of 1935. The defects in our earlier offers were so evident, and sprang so obviously from an attitude which Indians very naturally resent, that they were bound to colour our later approach. Every term and phrase we use today carries its memories for them, and these memories are loaded with suspicion.

I will start what is not a narrative but a reminder with the Round Table Conference which met in London in 1931. The idea of eliciting from a gathering of representative Indians a plan for the future government of their country sprang from a good intention. But in fact it was not Indians but the Viceroy and his officials who chose these representatives. What they did was to catalogue with scrupulous care every creed, every party, every racial minority, every interest in this peninsula. In St. James' Palace they did assemble princes and untouchables, Sikhs, Muslims, Hindus and Christians, spokesmen of landowners, trade unions and chambers of commerce, but Mother India was not there. From this nation of peasants not a single peasant nor any spokesman of the peasantry took his seat. The leaders of Congress were enjoying official hospitality elsewhere. A truce did, indeed, permit Gandhi to attend the second session of the conference, in an interval between two imprisonments; but he made a poor use of his opportunities. The delegates entered as Muslims, Sikhs or Hindus, and Muslims, Sikhs or Hindus they remained to the end. From such a conference no Indian idea, no decisive majority and no coherent plan could emerge. Indians talked: Whitehall drafted and Westminster legislated. The result, after a long parliamentary duel between Sir Samuel Hoare and Mr. Churchill—was it more than a sham fight?—was a constitution which every Indian party repudiated. Congress was pledged to resist it. The Muslim League rejected not merely this act but "the federal objective" altogether. Even the princes, who had begun by welcoming it, killed it in the end by pronouncing its terms for their adherence "unacceptable." It was an imposed constitution and it was better dead. It may have represented fairly enough what British opinion was at this period willing to concede. Mr. Churchill and his Die-hard group fought it with passion and perseverance, and there was no answering pressure from the Labour Party to enlarge it.

Part of this act came into operation and proved its value. The autonomy of the provinces came out of it: the rest was paper. Indians underrated this gain. It enabled them for the first time to set up in the eleven provinces governments responsible to elected legislatures, which had under their control the whole field of administration, including "law and order" with the police, as well as the social services. There was a partial transfer of power. But the criticisms of Indians were not unreasonable. In the first place, since the provinces depended for their revenues mainly on sources controlled by the still autocratic Centre, there was a severe limit to the expansion of the social services, pitiful though the provision made in the villages for health and education was. With great spirit and ingenuity, Congress gave its mind to the provision of cheap and partially self-supporting schools. Secondly, even in the provinces the Act of 1935 made only a halting advance towards democracy. The property qualification for the suffrage, low though it looks to us, in fact enfranchised only about 11 per cent of the population, which means, on a rough reckoning, one adult male in three, together with a negligible number of women. Industrial workers have special representation, but the landless rural

labourer and the poorer tenant and peasant are not represented. The special representation provided for landlords and
chambers of commerce was excessive and unnecessary. There
is also in some provinces an upper house. The caution and the
concern for property which inspire the entire act are well illustrated by the clause (Section 299, §3) forbidding the introduction, either at the Centre or in the provinces, of any bill or
amendment for the nationalisation of any private property or
enterprise without the previous consent of the Viceroy or Governor. Finally, the wide powers of veto vested in the Governor
gave deep offence to Indian self-respect. In fact, in some of the
provinces these powers have never been used at all, and only
five or six times over the whole of India. That is a remarkable
record, which bears witness both to the moderation of Indians
and the good sense of governors. But it would be a mistake to
conclude that the veto is inoperative. Ministers who know that
it is there in reserve must exercise a caution which may cause
their legislation to lag behind public opinion and the needs of
the situation, as they estimate it themselves. Gently though
governors have exerted their very extensive powers, they have
on occasion so used them as to remind Indians very sharply
that there are limits to the provincial autonomy they enjoy.
When Mr. Allah Bux, the Muslim Premier of Sind, resigned
his honours and titles by way of protest against Mr. Churchill's
deplorable statement of September 10, 1942, which most
Englishmen regretted, he was dismissed from office on the
ground that he had forfeited the Governor's confidence. In
practice, then, as well as in theory, British rule, even in the
provinces, is still a reality. Much has been surrendered and
much of the essence of autonomy has been won. But ministries are subject to a dual allegiance: they must retain the
confidence of the British Governor as well as that of the
electorate and its representatives. The Conquest goes on.

It was, however, in the part of the act which has never
come into force, creating an all-Indian federation, that
political interest mainly centred. The government of British

India under our direct rule has always been highly centralised. For Indians, struggling for the recognition of their nationhood, the key to their problem lay at the Centre and not in the provinces. Before the conference met, the astonishing response of a great part of India's population to Gandhi's call for civil disobedience had convinced all but the Die-hards among Conservatives that the time for mere concessions was past. It was necessary to produce a plan of ambitious and imposing proportions which might appeal to the imagination of Indians. The master-idea was accordingly to give to the whole of India, states and provinces together, a new organic unity within a federal constitution. After a period of transition, long or short, this federation would evolve into a fully self-governing Dominion. Had we displayed any clear intention of shortening the period of transition by hastening the Indianisation of the army, this idea might have had some success. But behind it there was at work a class strategy, which British progressives chose to ignore, though Indians grasped it at once. The introduction of the princes into the federation would make India a nation, but at the price of subjecting her to the ascendancy of property in its most reactionary form. The essence of the scheme was that the princes, with a few exceptions autocrats who rule with no respect for civil rights and popular liberties, would ordinarily nominate their delegates to the federal legislature, while the provinces would elect theirs. In short, the princes, as the gorgeous leaders of landed property, were brought in as the ideal makeweight against the Hindu *intelligentsia* and the peasantry. The franchise was, to begin with, conferred only on 10 per cent of the adult males and 0.06 of the adult females. So valuable for their purposes did the authors of this act feel the princes to be, that they gave them in both chambers of the federation a voting power far beyond any claim that could be based on the population of their states. It amounts to only 23 per cent of the population of the whole peninsula. But in the upper house, the Federal Council, the princes were to have

40 per cent of the votes.* In the Federal Assembly the nominees of the princes were to hold 125 out of 375 seats. Add to this third the fourteen British members, including those from chambers of commerce, the four Anglo-Indians and the seven large landowners' representatives, and a solid Conservative block of 150 votes was ready to dominate the Assembly. It need pick up only 38 votes, let us say from among the 82 representatives of the separate Muslim electorates, to secure a majority. In their turn the Muslims were over-represented in the ratio of two to one. As Sir Samuel Hoare himself told the Commons (March 27, 1933) after analysing these proposals: "it will be impossible, short of a landslide, for the extremists to get control of the federal centre." It is well understood in India that the princes are the disciplined vassals of the Viceroy and the British Crown. It has been characteristic of British rule during the past two generations that it has leaned for support on the more backward elements in the Indian social structure—the medieval princes, the functionless landowners rather than the industrialists, who are in the economic sense of the word progressives, and the Muslims, who were on the whole rather slower in accepting Western education and technology than the Hindus. This is the attitude of a power that has lost its self-confidence and its pioneering outlook.

Had the authors of this scheme trusted their ingenious invention, they might have won the support of conservative and propertied Indians. Here was a federal parliament, wielding immense powers over the provinces, which could by virtue of its composition do nothing dangerous or unseemly. But they

* This was one of several instances of flagrant partiality in the voting arrangements incorporated in this act. In the Federal Assembly 86 votes only were attributed to the caste Hindus and 19 to the depressed classes, making in all 105 seats for a Hindu population of 177.7 millions. The Muslims, with 67 millions, were awarded 82 seats. That is to say, each Hindu member represented 1,692,000 persons, while a Muslim sat with only 817,000 behind him, a ratio of one to two. Sir Samuel Hoare in his dealings with "extremists" left nothing to chance.

went on to load it with additional safeguards. On limbs incapable of movement they must needs fix fetters. It was the formidable apparatus of reservations and vetoes which offended Indian self-respect so deeply that the scheme failed to light even a momentary flicker of enthusiasm, and perished before it could be tested in action. India was offered, to be sure, a premier and some ministers, authentically Indian and responsible to houses elected in part by the upper strata of her population, nominated in part by her princes. But the army and foreign policy, under ministers responsible only to the Viceroy, were "reserved" subjects. It would lie with the Viceroy to make peace and war, and even to negotiate economic agreements with foreign countries: nor could India determine the size, cost or composition of her army. The conquest still went on. The Viceroy was charged with the duty of protecting the official services and the various minorities, with a general responsibility for order and a power of veto over all legislation. The most significant and the most deeply resented of his powers was his control over finance. An Indian finance minister there was to be, nominally responsible to the legislature. But the debt, the army and the salaries and pensions of the civil services were fixed charges which he could not touch. One mean little detail stung Indians sharply: the cost of the Anglican Establishment in India was also quartered on the Budget as an unvotable charge. The finance minister would in fact have control, as Indians reckoned, over about 20 per cent of the expenditure for which he would have to budget. It may be said that much the greater part of every national budget consists of charges which are at least morally "fixed" and can in fact be varied only within narrow limits—and usually upwards. But at home these charges were originally incurred with Parliament's consent: they were not imposed. Nor was this all. Currency and monetary policy were removed from Parliamentary control to be managed by the governor of a Reserve Bank appointed by the Viceroy. Finally, with an expert financial adviser at his elbow, the Viceroy was directed to veto any of the measures of the responsible finance minister, if in his

opinion they might have the effect, "whether directly or indirectly," of "prejudicing India's credit in the money-markets
of the world." The "world" in this connection meant the City
of London, since India borrows nowhere else. In the last resort
it seemed that India was not a nation, but a field for the placing of foreign capital. The final test to which the policy of her
government must submit was that it should merit the confidence of British bankers and investors. "You tell me," said
Gandhi, "that I am to be master in my own house, but you
keep the key of the safe and you station a sentry at the door."

From the passage of this act down to the outbreak of the
war, India lived through a relatively tranquil yet formative
period. The third essay in civil disobedience ended with a
confession of exhaustion after, as Congress reckoned, some
120,000 of its members had been imprisoned: fines, it is said,
were a more effective deterrent in this poor country than
prison. Nothing was changed in the outlook of this party. Some
hundreds of tons of human substance were transported to our
gaols, and that is all. The influence for a time within Congress
of that unstable and turbulent personality, Subhas Chandra
Bose, indicated, if anything, a swing of opinion to the Left.
Subhas Bose is a type difficult for Europeans to understand.
Emphatically he is not a mercenary or a quisling, but a highly
emotional man, capable of self-sacrifice. He threw up a promising career in the I.C.S. while a student at Cambridge and faced
in our prisons privations which ruined his health. He is vain
and quarrels with great facility. As Mayor of Calcutta he did
good constructive work for health and education. In several
talks with him, I judged his mind to be quick and active but
impatient and superficial. His ignorance of international politics was remarkable. In 1930 he seemed to be, in outlook, a
communist, passionately devoted to the Soviet Union. Official
Englishmen believed that he was in close touch with terrorists.
Later, as Indian observers assure me, he swung over to a
Leftish brand of Fascism. Finally, he persuaded himself that
he could trust the promises of the Axis to liberate India. The

clue to his evolution may lie in his quarrel with Gandhi, who eventually brought about his expulsion from Congress.

The remarkable victory of Congress in the provincial elections of 1937 enabled it, after a brief moment of hesitation, to form ministries in eight of the eleven provinces. It had a share, as a member of a coalition, in the ministry of a ninth province, Sind: with better tactics it could have played a big part in Bengal. Only in one province, the Punjab, is it a negligible force. The reality of power was a new and salutary experience. Indians felt an access of self-respect and hope. The record of these ministries was favourably judged even by Europeans, who seldom are indulgent critics. Some did good work for elementary education, and others were able to improve the lot of the over-taxed and indebted peasants. Even the decidedly conservative Government of the Punjab had to its credit some useful acts which benefited the tenants. Two Congress ministries at least, those of Madras and Bombay, were criticised from the Left for their conservative tendencies. Congress tried, by limiting the number of paid posts and the level of salaries, to preserve its old austerity and discourage careerists. India was absorbed in creative and constructive work, when the war crashed upon her.

INDIA IN THE WAR

As the shock approached, Mr. Chamberlain's Government handled India as the Empire always had handled her in the past. In August Indian troops were despatched to Egypt, Aden and Singapore. Secrecy was desirable, and the thing was done, as technically the authorities had a right to do it, without vote, debate or sanction from any representatives of the Indian people. A white hand moved these Indian soldiers like pawns across the chessboard of world politics, in a quarrel not their own. Thereafter, at Westminster, six hundred English gentlemen, with not a dark skin among them, passed an amending act, which in the event of war authorised the British rulers of India to restrict Indian liberties by the exercise of the most formidable emergency powers. We subjected ourselves, it is true, to similar though milder restrictions. There is this difference: with virtual unanimity our elected representatives had endorsed the policy which required these sacrifices: we ration our own liberties and have a sovereign Parliament to check any abuse of authority. That is not India's case. Finally, in response to a cablegram from Whitehall, a Scottish noble-man at Delhi proclaimed India a belligerent in this European struggle. Without their consent, asked or given, and without their representatives' sanction, India's millions found them-selves at war.

Mr. Chamberlain's Government acted in accordance with all the precedents. That was its error: it failed to realise that India is no longer the docile nation of limited ambitions which entered the last war, naïvely loyal. To these customary steps of routine Indians reacted as though they had been deliberate provocations. That they were not: they sprang merely from the defective imagination which is the curse of most of the dealings of Englishmen with Indians. The tragedy of this situation was that all that is best in India, including most of the leaders of Congress, favoured the Allied cause. They have even stronger reasons than we have ourselves for loathing the Nazi doctrine of racial ascendancy, for we rank as degenerate Nor-dics. But they have their self-respect. Unfree themselves, were they to fight at our bidding to free others?

Congress, accordingly, through its Working Committee, issued an impressive and dignified manifesto in which it must have come near to voicing the feelings of the whole nation. It insisted that "no outside authority" in this issue of war and peace can impose its decision on the Indian people. "Co-opera-tion must be between equals by mutual consent for a cause which both consider to be worthy." It went on to condemn "the ideology of Fascism," its "glorification of war," its "sup-pression of the human spirit" and "its violation of the recog-nised standards of civilised behaviour." But it recalled also the betrayals of freedom on our side that ran without a break from the Manchurian affair to the end of the Spanish Civil War. This led it to a request that the British Government should state its war aims. "If the war is to defend the *status quo* of imperialist . . . privilege, then India can have nothing to do with it. If, however, the issue is democracy and a world order based on democracy, then India is intensely interested in it." India is the crux of the problem, for she has been the "outstanding example of modern Imperialism." In particular, was Great Britain prepared "to establish full democracy in India"? There followed a precise definition of this claim: "the Indian people must have the right of self-determination to frame their own constitution through a Constituent Assembly without external interference and must guide their own policy." A free India would "gladly associate herself with other free nations for mutual defence against aggression and for economic co-operation." But the most important part of this manifesto was the urgency of its concluding sentences. Any declaration that the Government might make must take "immediate effect, to the largest possible extent," for "only this will convince the people that the declaration is meant to be honoured. The real test of any declaration is its application to the present."

This was a plain-spoken document, but it contained no threats. It was so drafted as to make a possible basis for negotiation. The Liberal Moderates, who declared themselves a little later, were much more precise in their demands, for they appealed to the Government "to hasten the replacement of the present form of Central Government by a government responsible to the public."

The sequel to this manifesto was that the Viceroy had several conversations with Gandhi and Pandit Nehru. Very properly he then invited the leaders of other parties to meet him. In all, as he stated, he saw fifty-two persons. This was, it may be, to display an excessive receptivity. The effect, if not the intention, was to underline the fact that many varieties of opinion exist in this Indian subcontinent, more particularly if one searches for them. These "marked differences of outlook" were stressed in Lord Linlithgow's lengthy reply. What was missing in his analysis was any reference to the fact that Congress had recently won a majority in the All-India electorate, while some of the discordant opinions came from groups which had scored only a negligible poll. The one grave fact in this unweighted census of opinions was that the Muslim League, henceforward the only spokesman of Muslim opinion that New Delhi recognised, now for the first time declared itself against federation in any form. These divergencies bulked even larger in Lord Zetland's speech for the Government in the House of Lords, and the *Times* played on them with a practised skill made perfect during many generations of British rule in India.

The Viceroy's reply came out of the ruts of routine. For a statement of our war aims Indians were referred to Mr. Chamberlain's speeches. If they were curious about the future, they should review the pledges of former viceroys and secretaries of state, to the effect that "the natural issue of India's progress is the attainment of Dominion status." He then reaffirmed his belief in the soundness of the federal scheme in the Act of 1935, but recognised that some amendment of its details may be necessary at the end of the war. For that purpose he promised "consultation with representatives of the several communities, parties and interests in India and with the Indian princes" —apparently yet another Round Table Conference. In short, at this tense moment in history, while we embarked with Indians on a war that must at the best be perilous and prolonged, we had nothing new to say to this nation about its relation with us, its comrades in arms. As for the present, Congress had asked for some immediate earnest of our loyalty to democracy. The Viceroy's offer was to form "a consultative group" with which he would from time to time discuss the conduct of the war. As a substitute for "responsible government at the Centre" this device failed to impress Indians.

The publication of this wooden statement of policy as a White Paper (October 17, 1939) drove Congress to action. It had already in August withdrawn its members from the All-

India Legislative Assembly as a protest against the dispatch of Indian troops abroad. This was not an irreparable step: the Assembly is at best a powerless body, and the dissenters could at any time resume their seats. Its next step was, to my thinking, a grave error. It called on the Congress ministries in the eight provinces it controlled to resign their offices. They obeyed, with the result that in seven of them the governors took over the administration and carried on without the elected legislature. In Assam, however, an alternative coalition was formed, and later the same thing happened in Orissa. Congress had proved that its executive could secure the obedience of all the Hindu provinces. In so doing, unhappily, it alarmed the Muslims. This gesture gave emphatic expression to Indian anger and disappointment, but, like all gestures, it rapidly lost such psychological effect as it may have had in the first days or weeks. For the sake of this fleeing impression on public opinion, Congress threw away a very real basis of power. Had these ministries existed two years later, they might have taken positive collective action in the constitutional crisis. Together the premiers of the eleven provinces might have spoken for India with more authority than its party leaders. This gesture illustrated Gandhi's characteristic tendency to negation. Always his first instinct is to renounce and withdraw.

A year passed, however, without any graver developments. But the communal tension was increasing, and in March 1940 the Muslim League for the first time formally adopted the Pakistan scheme as its official policy. Congress, however, took a generous step in the middle of the summer which unhappily passed almost unnoticed. This was, after Dunkirk and the collapse of France, our blackest hour. Pandit Nehru, who is a citizen of the world as decidedly as he is a patriotic Indian, was at this period the dominant personality in the party. He had won a double victory, first of all over the pacifism of Gandhi and then over the provincialism of colleagues who could think only of their country's narrower interests, which they interpreted, as two great powers still did at this time, in an isolationist sense. The result was an offer of unstinted co-operation in the war effort: the Congress Party, as its resolution of July 7th, 1940, ran, would "throw its full weight into the efforts for the effective organisation of the defence of the country." This was far in advance of the average attitude of Indian opinion and a generous offer from men who had all served long terms in our prisons. Conditions, however, were attached to it. Congress asked for an acknowledgment of India's right to independence, while "as an immediate step . . . a provisional National Government should be constituted at the centre, which, though formed as a transitory measure, should be such as to command the confidence of all elected members in the Central Legislature."

To this overture the Government's response was the unhappy "August Offer" (1940). It was proposed that the Viceroy's Council should be enlarged, and that representative Indians should serve on it. This was a well-intentioned effort to satisfy Indian self-respect, but it fell too painfully short of any real transfer of power. Judging from what was actually done a year later, the key positions would still have remained in British hands. In addition to the Viceroy himself and the Commander-in-Chief, British officials remained in charge of finance and (as the Home Member) of the whole apparatus of police and security. To the additional Indian members there could have fallen only duties secondary even in time of peace. The promise of Dominion status was renewed with two significant additions. For the first time it was dated. It was to be implemented after the war "with the least possible delay." Secondly, the framing of the new constitution "should be primarily the responsibility of Indians themselves." The method, however, was not precisely indicated, but the reference to the setting up of a body representative of the principal elements in India's national life was not reassuring. The phrase could hardly mean any sort of constituent assembly: did it mean another Round Table Conference? But these inadequacies, though they largely cancelled the gains registered in this August offer, were not the details that ruined it. Its salient feature, on which Indians concentrated, while English commentators in their innocence ignored it, was a resort to the customary tactic, which centres round our scrupulous concern for minorities. The main passage which turned an offer into a provocation ran thus:

It goes without saying that they [the British Government] could not contemplate transfer of their present responsibilities for the peace and welfare of India to any system of government whose authority is directly denied by large and powerful elements in India's national life. Nor could they be parties to the coercion of such elements into submission to such a government.

Every Indian reader could translate this passage into concrete terms. The Muslim League was now accepted by the Viceroy and the India Office as the sole spokesman of one "large and powerful element." It had announced that it was opposed to federation on any terms. It had also demanded separation by adopting the Pakistan scheme. If it were to change its mind, there were still the depressed classes, another large if not powerful element, and here again it was Dr. Ambedkar, the extremist leader of a minority among their representatives, whom alone New Delhi recognised as their spokesman. Knowing in advance that these two "elements" would dissent from any democratic scheme of federation, the British Government deliberately armed them with a veto. Was this the way to promote a compromise? Nor was this all. A further reservation laid it down that British consent to the future constitution was "subject to the due fulfilment of the obligations which Great Britain's long connexion with India has imposed on her." This rather pompous language opened up several unpleasant vistas, but it was generally read in India as an intimation to the princes that they too, like the Muslim League, would be sustained in their use of their veto. Certainly there are limits to the coercion of minorities which civilisation prescribes. But in the presence of exceptionally exacting minorities is it statesmanship to assure them in advance that they shall never be coerced? Short of coercion, there are ways of promoting reasonable conduct among minorities which we have never used. The paradoxical result in India of our too sensitive concern for minorities is not that we manage to avoid coercion. It is the majority we coerce.

This offer, which Indians felt to be dishonest—if the reader will forgive a plain word—as well as inadequate, was flatly rejected both by Congress and by the Muslim League. The Hindu Mahasabha, now, in the rising communal tension, a growing organisation, came into line with Congress by demanding complete independence. Congress reacted by inviting Gandhi—who had suffered a heavy defeat when it made its useless offer to co-operate in the war effort—once more to guide it in action. He did so in September 1940 by proclaiming civil disobedience, though on a limited scale. He explained that he did not wish to do anything which would help the Axis or prejudice the British in their struggle against it. He refrained therefore from mass action of any kind. Under his direction, one by one, the leaders, national and local, made slightly seditious speeches—an easy thing to do in India—or announced that they would do so, and so got themselves arrested. It was not an impressive procedure. Too decent to strike hard, while we were struggling for survival, Congress struck feebly. But in all about 12,000 men and women were imprisoned or interned, among them six ex-premiers of provinces, twenty nine former ministers and 290 members of provincial legislatures. Among our prisoners was Nehru. Midway in a war for freedom, could there have been a more painful spectacle?

The distress of progressive Englishmen and moderate Indians was not wholly ineffective. In July 1941 the Viceroy carried out the enlargement and Indianisation of his Council. It now had a majority of non-official Indians, though the key positions—defence, finance, the home department and transport—remained in British hands. The effect on Indian opinion was slight. A generation ago this would have seemed a startling concession. Today Indians are struggling no longer for the symbolic recognition of racial equality, but for the reality of power. So long as the Viceroy selects at his own discretion safe and moderate Indians who represent only them-.

selves, there has been no surrender of power. Only one of these men, Dr. Ambedkar, could be said to represent a party: assuredly he is not a "yes-man," but unfortunately he is at feud with all Hindus. An advisory War Council was also set up—a concession which interested nobody: it was promptly boycotted both by Congress and by the Muslim League. What little good might have been achieved by the partial Indianisation of the Council was undone by one of Mr. Churchill's characteristic indiscretions. He made a statement on the Atlantic Charter which seemed to confine its scope to Europe and to exclude Indians from its benefits. He did, indeed, qualify this disastrous discrimination by explaining (September 9, 1941) that the two problems were distinct: "We are pledged by the Declaration of 1940 to help India to obtain free and equal partnership in the British Commonwealth with ourselves, subject of course to the fulfilment of obligations arising from our long connection with India and our responsibilities to its many races and interests." This heavily qualified promise of Dominion status was very far from placing Indians in the same position as the peoples of Europe. India in the process of liberation would remain a British possession, whose affairs are our exclusive concern. In plain words, Mr. Churchill had announced that our allies, America, China and Russia, will have no such say in the settlement of India's future as they will have in deciding the destinies of the Balkan Peninsula. This affirmation of the rights of empire is still a corroding poison in Indian minds. But the Indian majority on the Viceroy's Council did do something, a few months later, to justify its existence. Early in December 1941 most of the Congress prisoners were released, on the ground that their offences had been merely "symbolic." The Working Committee of Congress at once reciprocated. Once again the tendency which Nehru and Dr. Azad personified was in the ascendant, and at his own request Gandhi was relieved of the burden of leadership. Civil disobedience ceased to be the policy of Congress: once more it was ready to brush the Mahatma's pacifist scruples aside and play its part in the defence of India—on terms. The path to yet another attempt at settlement was open. But the reader who has had the patience to read through these preliminary pages will realise how formidable was the task that confronted the activists who wished to lead India to a settlement. Himself blinking, as it were, in the sunlight after some months of imprisonment, Jawaharlal Nehru had against him not merely the powerful influence of Gandhi but all the cumulative distrust aroused by our previous offers. Worst of all, few Indians, under the influence of our poor military performance in Malaya and Burma, believed that we had the capacity to defend their country against a Japanese invasion. At this dark hour an Indian need not have been a pacifist by conviction to share the Mahatma's reckoning that passive resistance might be as effective as any military tactics based on the Singapore model. But a new influence came in at this critical moment and told powerfully for national resistance. In February 1942 Marshal Chiang Kai-shek visited Delhi, and boldly addressed an outspoken though tactful appeal to Britain and India. His presence gave life to a new idea that began to fire the young manhood of India. Why should not Indians do what the equally unwarlike Chinese had done—form a people's army which, however ill-armed it might be, would baffle the invader by guerrilla tactics and overwhelm him in the end with its irresistible numbers? Students in the Punjab began to drill, and in the Mahratta country an unofficial school was opened for the study of guerrilla warfare.

THE CRIPPS MISSION

THREE DAYS after the fall of Rangoon, the choice of Sir Stafford Cripps for a mission to India was announced to the Commons by Mr. Churchill (March 11, 1942) in a statement which avoided some of the old pitfalls and struck a new note of urgency. It read like the utterance of a man who wished for success, because he realised the gravity of the military peril. "The crisis in the affairs of India arising out of the Japanese advance has made us wish to rally all the forces of Indian life to guard their land from the menace of the invader." It ended with a happy reference to India's sense of comradeship with "the valiant Chinese people" and to the part their country may play as "one of the bases" for "counter-blows" against the common enemy. This was a happy opening, while on the score of his personality and record Sir Stafford was generally regarded as the ideal choice for a mission of goodwill. On that score, however, there is something more to be said. His is one of the most formidable minds of our generation, but, like Gandhi's, it is not primarily perceptive and lacks the gifts of intuition and instinct which enable men endowed with much less powerful intellects to read the thoughts of their fellows. His former comrades remember with gratitude his unrivalled capacity for hard work and his almost prodigal generosity, while they try to forget the lack of tactical skill and judgment which neutralised his great qualities.

A word must be said about the preparation of the offer. Two courses were open. Soundings might have been taken through some unofficial go-between to discover whether what the War Cabinet had in mind would satisfy the Indian leaders. Failing some such preliminary step as this, the offer might have been made in an elastic form, capable of modification as the talks proceeded. In fact neither of these courses was adopted. There were no preliminary soundings, nor was the offer capable of amendment, save in minor details. It was a rigid formula which Indians must accept or reject as a whole substantially as it stood. To deal with an inevitably suspicious people in this lofty manner was to incur a grave risk of failure at the start. It may be said that Sir Stafford Cripps was well informed, and so he was. But it is clear that until he arrived in Delhi he did not realise that the centre of gravity of India's attention had shifted from the future to the present. This was already evident in the first manifesto of Congress after the outbreak of war, which ended, as we have already noted, with the emphatic statement: "The real test of any declaration is its application to the present." The reason for this is obvious, though it may not be flattering to our pride. Indians lacked the instinctive conviction which sustained us in our darkest hour, that somehow we should defy reason and probability by winning this war. Accordingly the care and pains spent by the authors of this document over the long-term proposals were largely wasted, although this part of the offer marked an appreciable advance on anything that had preceded it. What Indians chiefly noticed was that the immediate part of the offer, conveyed in one brief sentence, was vague and not, as it stood, particularly attractive. As a whole the offer was dismissed by Gandhi as "a post-dated cheque on a tottering bank" which might come back with the endorsement "No effects." This attitude ought not to surprise us. Apart from the military uncertainty, Indians may have reflected, when they read over this plan for their self-determination, which should come into force a few years hence, that Irish home rule was embodied before the last war in an act which had passed one house and survived the veto of the other, yet it never came into force, and Ireland in the end got her freedom only after rebellion, civil war and partition. *Absit omen.* The result was that Indians gave all their attention to that part of the offer which was drafted in the present tense and took little interest in the future plan on which Sir Stafford had concentrated.

There were other respects in which the offer showed a defective psychological management. Mr. Churchill's statement to the House was good, but it was impersonal. It struck me at the time that if he could have brought himself, then or later, to address Indians directly over the air with that warmth and generosity of language of which he is a master, he might have turned the scales for acceptance. As the chief opponent in the past of India's liberation his words, if they had rung true, would have meant more than any other man's. But he kept silence. Again, in drafting the offer we avoided the two words which are the keys to India's emotions. The promise of Dominion status with the right of secession did mean in effect independence. That was understood. But for Indians the Dominion idea has no magic—neither the name nor the thing. It would have made some little difference if we had boldly offered independence, which India should enjoy at her free choice within the British Commonwealth or outside it. But Sir Stafford Cripps did himself supply virtually these words, when he faced Indian journalists at one of his conferences in New Delhi. Here is the exchange of question and answer:

Question: Will the Indian Union be entitled to disown its allegiance to the Crown?

Answer: Yes. In order that there should be no possibility of doubt, we have inserted in the last sentence of paragraph (cii) the statement: "but will not impose any restriction on the power of the Indian Union to decide in the future its relation to the other Member States of the British Commonwealth." The Dominion will be completely free either to remain within or to go without the Commonwealth of Nations.

Sir Stafford, it should be said, conducted his press conferences brilliantly. Mr. Amery has also said that India would have *de facto* power to secede from the Commonwealth.*

It was still more unfortunate that we could not bring ourselves to offer a national government today, and we shrank from using the words. At the bidding of a government they could have called their own millions of Indians would risked death, but for an enlarged Viceroy's Council would any man lay down his life? Finally, it was not tactful on Sir Stafford's part to announce, somewhat brusquely, that to settle the destinies of four hundred millions of his fellow-men, two weeks was as much of his time as he could spare. But the real criticism of this offer was that it was rigid, and subject only in minor details to negotiation.

Let us deal first with the less controversial and at the moment the less important part of the offer—the plan of self-determination. It avoided some of the pitfalls that had beset previous offers. It was precisely dated: it would come into

* Commons: April 28, 1942.

force "immediately upon the cessation of hostilities." The entire responsibility for shaping the future constitution fell upon Indians. Instead of the discredited device of some conference of all the communities and interests, an elected Constituent Assembly would perform this work. The method suggested for choosing it by proportional election from the newly elected provincial councils was workmanlike and fair—though it might be objected that property would still have, as it has today, an excessive representation. The constitution so framed would create an Indian union, which would at once become a Dominion with full rights. The old idea of a transitional period with vetoes and reserved subjects was swept away. Finally, this Indian Dominion would rest not on an act of the Westminster Parliament, but on a treaty. So far this was substantially all that India could ask.

What, then, had become of the old stumbling-blocks—the princes and the minorities? The answer to the first question is deeply disturbing. Here there was no advance. As before, the princes might nominate their delegates: there was no provision for election. This would mean that a solid block of one-third or more of the constituent body would shape the constitution in a reactionary sense. Worse still, the princes would not vote as native conservatives, but as tools of the paramount power. Worst of all, if they failed to get their way in defending their immunity from all control and interference, they would stay outside the federation. A glance at the map should show what that would mean. These states interlock with the British provinces like the pieces in a child's jig-saw puzzle. They cut across rivers, railways, telegraph wires and electric grids. In them the imperial power would still be able to station British troops. The princes, so long as they remained autocrats and British puppets, were in a position to serve the Empire by a formidable process of blackmail. If they came in, they would condemn the Indian Union to a long night of reaction: if they stayed out, it would lie at the mercy of their master. In either event independence was a vain hope.

The reader may reply that I am making too much of a detail. "Surely", he may object, "this little matter of arranging for the democratic representation of the princes' subjects would have been adjusted in due course. This was obviously an oversight." Nothing of the kind. Controversy had raged round this question since the Round Table Conference met. The grey eminences of the India Office in their own limited field of vision have clear sight. It knows that once the princes honestly concede responsible government with civil rights, they will become useless to the Empire. Their subjects will vote much as their cousins in the British provinces do: that is to say, most of their delegations will join the "extremists" in the Constituent Assembly. It is significant that, as far as the record goes, Sir Stafford Cripps made no attempt to meet this obvious objection to his offer. This is no mere detail. While it stands, it completely vitiates the plan of self-determination. The tactics of the Die-hards are obvious to any cool observer. They yield, very slowly, one point after another, until they produce an offer which looks to the ill-informed public plausible and even generous. They keep in reserve, however, a strategical key which suffices for their purpose. So long as they hold it, they command India. But why should I try to say in my own words what the leading official expert on this subject, Professor Rushbrook-Williams, had said so much better? About these princes he wrote:—

Many of them owe their very existence to British justice and arms. . . . Their affection and loyalty are important assets for Britain in the present troubles and in the re-adjustments which must come. . . . The situation of these feudatory States, checkerboarding all India as they do, are a great safeguard. It is like establishing a vast network of friendly fortresses in debatable territory. It would be difficult for a general rebellion against the British to sweep India because of this network of powerful, loyal Native States.*

* *Evening Standard*, May 28, 1930. A reference to *Who's Who* shows that this professor of Indian history has held several highly responsible positions both under the India Office and for the princes, whose shepherd he was at the Round Table Conference.

What Canning saw so clearly in 1860 the India Office does not forget today. While it holds these "friendly fortresses," India can never achieve her independence.

On the other hand, the provision for the minorities did show an advance, though the price of it might be the division of India and the creation of a Muslim Ulster. The gain lay in robbing the minority of the right it had hitherto enjoyed to veto any advance whatever. This defect in past offers was at last frankly recognised by Mr. Churchill when he pointed out that the new offer

would avoid the alternative dangers either that the resistance of a powerful minority might impose an indefinite veto upon the wishes of the majority, or that a majority decision might be taken which would be resisted to a point destructive of internal harmony and fatal to the setting up of a new Constitution.

Difficulties might, indeed, arise, whether over other minorities, or on financial questions or over the status of British traders in India, during the negotiation of the treaty between the nascent Indian Union and the British Government, but there is no need to anticipate such minor troubles as these. The grave new fact was that the offer did contemplate as a possibility the refusal of the predominantly Muslim provinces to enter the union and made provision for the separation from it of Pakistan.

The reactions of the various parties to these long-term proposals were interesting, but in no case were they decisive. The princes accepted, as they had originally done in the case of the 1935 constitution, but this meant little or nothing, since they stressed the inviolability of their sovereign rights. The working of their minds was revealed in the somewhat farcical suggestion that a third separate federation might be created, consisting of some of the princes' states under the name of Rajistan.

It was not the future proposals that led Congress to reject the offer. It recognised that future independence might be implicit in these proposals and that self-determination had been accepted in principle. But its demand had always been for "independence for the whole of India." The scheme completely ignored "the ninety millions of people in the Indian States" and treated them "as commodities at the disposal of their Rulers," a "negation both of democracy and self-determination." "Such States may... become barriers to the growth of Indian freedom, enclaves where foreign authority still prevails, and where the possibility of maintaining foreign armed forces had been stated to be a likely contingency."

On the subject of Pakistan, Congress, after declaring that it was wedded to Indian unity, deplored the encouragement which the offer gave to the idea of separation. "Nevertheless the Committee cannot think in terms of compelling the people of any territorial unit to remain in an Indian Union against their declared and established will."

The Hindu Mahasabha was, as usual, less liberal than Congress. Its ably-drafted resolution raised several issues, notably defence, but its chief reason for rejection may have been the one it placed first. It stood without compromise for the unity of India and disputed the right of any province to exclude itself from the Indian Union—a plan which might, it predicted, lead to civil war.

The more important of the minorities registered their flat rejection of the scheme. The Sikhs feared Pakistan and said in a bitter letter that they would "resist by all possible means separation of the Punjab from the All-India Union." Dr. Ambedkar and Mr. Rajah, who claim to speak for the depressed classes, complained of a "breach of faith," made no positive suggestions for amendment and rejected proposals which would, they said, "place them under an unmitigated system of Hindu rule."

It was believed in the official world that Mr. Jinnah, supposing at first that Congress would accept, had drafted a resolution of acceptance for the Muslim League—doubtless with reservations. This he is said to have torn up when Congress rejected the offer. In its place he substituted a resolution rejecting the scheme on the ground of its rigidity. Muslims refused to enter any constituent assembly which could take decisions by a bare majority. They claimed, moreover, that Muslims alone should vote in any plébiscite taken to determine whether a province should adhere to the Indian Union. On these grounds, since the scheme had to be accepted or rejected as a whole, they registered their rejection.

It may be well to leave this big issue of Pakistan and Hindu-Muslim relations to the next chapter. We have now to consider the grounds on which the Working Committee of Congress rejected the offer. Critical as it was of some vital aspects of the proposals for the future, it was on the arrangements for the period of the war that it based its decision. "In today's grave crisis it is the present that counts," as its resolution put it, and again: "Only the realisation of present freedom could light the flame which would illuminate millions of hearts and move them to action." In short, it held that only a real and immediate transfer of power would enable the leaders of Indian opinion to organise the people for the defence of a country which they could feel to be their own. The break came at the end because they felt that the Viceroy's Council which they were asked to enter would not be in any true sense a national government. But from first to last the real issue was defence; they asked for power in order that the people of India should play their part in its defence. Before we attempt a brief survey of these rather puzzling negotiations, it may be well to remind ourselves of the outstanding facts in this Indian problem of defence.

THE PROBLEM OF DEFENCE

THE FIRST fact, as Indians see this problem of defence, and the main fact which concerns us is that as Europeans understand these words India has never had a national army. The Indian army, as we know it, evolved from the mercenary troops, the sepoys, raised by the Company as it gradually overran and conquered the Peninsula. After the Mutiny, when its forces came under the Crown, changes occurred which reflected the fear and distrust of the minute minority of white men who ruled and garrisoned India. The artillery was up to 1935 exclusively British, and the rule was adopted of brigading one British with two Indian battalions for greater safety. The commissioned ranks were up to recent years exclusively British. But the chief change which took place in the composition of the Indian army was the new reliance on the so-called "martial races," and this also was a reflection of the modern attitude of distrust. A curious accretion of legend has grown up around these races, drawn chiefly but not exclusively from the Punjab and the North-West frontier. Soldiers, who are not always close students of military history, tell us that out of the vast population of India, only these few races make good fighting material. It is customary to exaggerate the share of the Muslims in the military records of the Peninsula and to underestimate that of the Hindus. In fact at the time of the Conquest the leading military powers in India were the Hindu Mahrattas and the Sikhs, whose religion is a reformed Hindu faith which has abandoned caste. More curious still, the troops with which the British defeated these two martial races were drawn chiefly from the supposedly unwarlike populations of Madras and Bengal, which at that time extended farther westward than it does today. Regiments composed of high-caste Hindus, including Brahmans, served the Company up to the Mutiny: at the other end of the social scale "untouchables" were enlisted until late in the last century and made good soldiers. I have heard from an able student of history, who had himself served both in the army and the Indian Civil Service, a curious explanation of the modern preference for the "martial races." British officers are much concerned with the appearance of their men. The northern stocks tend to be tall and handsome, while the southern Dravidians, though sturdy, are shorter and less imposing. However this may be, the real recommendation of the "martial races" was that they formed an hereditary military caste. In successive generations sons followed fathers as recruits, who entered the same historic regiment. They were proud of its tradition and of its past victories won in the King-Emperor's service. Armies, especially victorious armies, can absorb and win over alien elements to a degree few of us realise. Once a man puts on a uniform and marches in step he acquires the outlook even of a foreign army. In 1919, soon after the armistice, I sailed down the Vistula on a boat manned by a Polish crew. The men, only recently demobilised, were still wearing their old German uniforms. We got talking (in German). What they wanted to talk about were all the glorious victories "we" had won. They gossiped endlessly about the army in which they had served, and even about "our" officers and "our" generals—most of them Junkers. This kind of loyalty is not a political sentiment.

Some care was taken of these men's material interests. To poor men the pay and the pension were a sufficient inducement, and often they might hope to receive a grant of land when they left the army. Most of these martial races come from a part of India, the North-West, which has been less influenced than the rest of the country by the nationalist movement, and they have little interest in politics. Some of them, notably the Pathans and Baluchis, are decidedly primitive. "Mercenary troops" is in our modern vocabulary a somewhat derogatory term. It was not always so: the famous Swiss mercenaries, poor mountaineers like many of these Indians, regarded service under the French monarchy as a respectable profession, which had its own code of honour. The man who enlists in this way will be true to his salt. There is no need to emphasise the gallantry these Indian troops have shown in this as in previous wars. To retain the goodwill of these "martial races" came to be one of the fixed objects of British policy. The Punjab has always been a favoured province, since it breeds men and horses for the army. More was done here and earlier than elsewhere to help its peasantry and to foster its agriculture. Here, for example, the co-operative banks and experimental research in farming originated. Here too and in neighbouring Sind all our most spectacular engineering works are to be found—the irrigation colonies, the Sukkur Barrage and the hydro-electric scheme. In its most beneficent incarnation the British Raj means water. I saw it at its best in these irrigation colonies, where the engineer has turned desert into garden, and in the villages tall men and stately bullocks reap rich harvest beside the canals. But even there it was pitiable to hear Sikh giants, whose great hands made mine look like a boy's, complain of the petty oppressions of the police. Canal water, which authority may withhold or bestow, made from the earliest times, in Egypt and Sumeria, a sure foundation of autocracy. It does so still. When I asked these stalwart yeomen whether Congress had much hold in their district, they answered: "Our water would be cut off, if we joined it." Their fear may have been excessive: enough that they felt it. Even so, care had to be taken not to put too severe a strain on the loyalty of men who enjoyed these favours, by using them recklessly against their own countrymen. In 1930 a part of the Garhwali Regiment, Hindus, did in fact refuse to fire on Muslim rioters at Peshawar and flung down their arms. But such cases had been rare. It was Gurkhas from Nepal, who do not feel themselves to be Indians, though they are either Buddhists or Hindus by religion, who were used in the horrible affair at Amritsar. In short, these "martial races" are so far a military caste, distinct from the general population, that the British rulers of India can usually rely upon their loyalty even in times of political unrest. According to religion they were, following the latest figures available, 32 per cent Muslims, 49.5 per cent Hindus, 8.5 per cent Sikhs and 6 per cent Gurkhas. The reader will note that even when judged by these figures the popular impression that Hindus are in some special sense unwarlike is mistaken. Plainly, such a force as this, officered as it used to be entirely by Englishmen, was as far as possible from being a national army.

A new policy was adopted when the epoch of reform set in after the last war. The undertaking was given that the army should be gradually Indianised. Indians became eligible for the King's Commission: an Indian "Sandhurst" was opened to train cadets, and at first eight units and afterwards sixteen were selected which are to be officered entirely by Indians. The process of eliminating British regimental officers will however be slow, and the creation of an Indian higher command and staff is not yet in sight. A beginning had been made before this war in mechanising the Indian army. The old distrust has so far vanished that there is again an Indian artillery and that in the air force Indians are admitted to the rank of pilot, though in very small numbers. At the outbreak of the war the active formations of this Indian army numbered about 150,000 men.

Yet another phase was reached in this war. The policy of relying exclusively on the "martial races" was abandoned and in some degree, at least in principle, the army was thrown open to general recruitment.* Some of the old regiments, long ago disbanded, were revived, notably in the supposedly unwarlike province of Madras. Recently, as many as 70,000 recruits have been accepted in each month, and the total of our Indian troops is now nearing the second million. This is, needless to say, a surprisingly small number to draw from a population of nearly four hundred millions. So far as I can learn, political motives played a small part in the enlistment of these men. India is a poor country.

Could India, if arms were available, provide a much larger army than this, of good fighting quality? The question is difficult to answer, for many prejudices and traditional opinions stand in the way. There is some truth in the usual English belief that part at least of the Indian population is unwarlike. The physique of the poorer peasants and coolies is so wretched that they would be useless as soldiers. Seven stone is in many regions a quite usual weight for full-grown men. Under-nourished, undersized and riddled with malaria, they lack both

* The principle has, I think, been carried out subject to very severe limitations. In November 1942 the Legislative Council of Bengal passed a resolution calling for the recruitment in this province of an army of 100,000 men. The inference would seem to be that up to this date the recruitment of Bengalis cannot have been favoured on any considerable scale.

the spirit and the staying power that would be demanded of them. I have heard an experienced English regimental officer say that the first thing to do with new recruits is to teach them to eat; yet he was talking of Punjabis, who are usually big and sturdy men. Again, it is true that in the past Hindu society was specialised more absolutely than European society ever was, even in the Middle Ages. The life of active government and war was confined to the higher castes, and they were expected to cultivate the virtues of self-reliance and courage. The lower castes, craftsmen, merchants and tillers of the soil had in turn their own appropriate virtues, but not these. Courage was no more expected from them than the early Victorian Age expected it from Englishwomen. But this specialisation of function and virtue is rapidly becoming a thing of the past. An Indian acquaintance of mine, an able man, once said to me with the frankness Indians so often show and Englishmen so seldom: "My father was a coward: I am a half-coward: my son will be a brave man." During the past generation the old ascetic attitude towards the body has vanished and Indians are taking with enthusiasm to sports and games. At an advanced school in Calcutta I saw a very fine exhibition of lathi-play (fencing with the quarterstaff) by the girls. This is a sport that demands more than a quick eye and sure movements: it tests a girl's physical courage. Even more characteristic of the spirit of the times were the enthusiasm and organising ability which Congress showed in raising its so-called "militia" of elder boys and young men, on something like Boy Scout lines. It was, of course, unarmed, but it liked to drill in military formation. The motive for the new cult of gymnastics, sports and drill was manifestly military. The same current of thought explained the popularity of aviation among wealthy young men. Young India was getting ready to fight.

It is, then, highly probable, even after due allowance has been made for the poor physique of some of the lower strata of this vast population and for the traditional pacifism of another section of it, that many millions of young men would emerge from the scrutiny who would furnish fighting material as good as the "martial races," while much of it would be more intelligent and better educated. But these young men are nationalists and in their outlook rebels. Some have passed through our prisons. Others have shown their vitality and initiative by organising peasant leagues in the villages or trade unions in the towns. Activities of this kind, carried on in defiance of authority, demand a high order of courage. In short, the type of man who would make the best soldier in a war of freedom is the last who will enlist under the conditions we have made in India today. If Congress had been less scrupulous and more realistic, it might have urged all its spirited young men to enlist, reckoning that if they permeated the ranks, independence was as good as won. This it would not do. Instead, it appealed to us to make it possible for a nation of free men to defend their own liberties.

The defence of India, when Japan set the East ablaze at Pearl Harbour, had in any event to be improvised on a wholly new plan. For this emergency the Empire was unprepared. The first line of India's defence was the Fleet, and it had lost the command of the seas. On land our guns were pointed in the wrong direction. The army was grouped primarily for the defence of the North-West Frontier: if the plans of the staff took account of any enemy more formidable than its tribesmen and the Afghans, that enemy was the Soviet Union. Until the other day we and the Americans had been supplying the Japanese with motor spirit, copper and scrap iron. The little professional army, British and Indian, which we had in the Peninsula, imperfectly mechanised and with its stations far removed from the probable scenes of danger, was at this time and for many months manifestly unequal to the tasks it might have to face. What was to be done? The activists among Indians had their plans. Nehru worked out a scheme for raising an army of five million men. Obviously the gravest problem was how to arm it: this would have demanded the transformation at a rapid tempo of Indian industry. Nehru had studied at close quarters in Spain and China two people's armies, from whose experience much could be learned. The Chinese offered to send instructors. In Spain it was the workers' own organisations, parties and trade unions which furnished the leadership, and some of the best shock troops, which eventually learned to take the offensive with success, were led by men who started life as peasants or craftsmen. The Chinese guerrillas, highly trained for their own congenial tactics, furnished another model which might have been adapted to India's needs. These would have been the mobile forces. For static defence Indians pointed to the precedent of our own Home Guard. Rifles were lacking: but hand grenades and even knives are useful weapons easily manufactured. Above all, such Indian forces would have been able to count everywhere on the backing of the villagers, who would have scouted for them, fed them and hidden them at need. But manifestly forces of this kind would have a personality of their own, with a patriotic morale and an essentially civic discipline wholly unlike that of the professional Indian army, which its British officers had taught to fight, as an automaton, anywhere, for any cause, with its mind hermetically closed to any political idea.

It may be that Pandit Nehru, Mr. Savarkar, Dr. Moonje and other Indian activists asked too much of human nature, when they expected British generals to smile on such plans as these. They were, for a time, considered: I gather that some British soldiers did favor them, and it was even proposed that Major Tom Wintringham, who learned his military science chiefly in Spain, should go out to help. The decision in the end went the other way. There will be no Indian people's army and no home guard. India will be defended, should the Japanese attack, by a professional army fighting with a sullen population behind it, whose active help we have failed to enlist.

THE DELHI TALKS

THE STORY of the negotiations in Delhi has now to be told. The record is defective. We have heard the British version in ample detail, and it has been possible to supplement it by private enquiry. But the Congress version is known only from the documents included in the White Paper. Between the two there are some discrepancies. Of the talks between Sir Stafford Cripps and other Indian leaders no record has been published. One outstanding fact should be noted: at no stage of the negotiations did the Viceroy meet any of the Indian leaders. We have no record of the talk between General Wavell and the two spokesmen of Congress, Dr. Azad and Nehru, though it may well have been decisive. It had no fortunate effect. General Wavell, brilliantly articulate on paper, can observe a monumental silence in conversation. Finally, it is remarkable and perhaps regrettable that Sir Stafford met only these two and had no chance of addressing the Working Committee as a whole or of answering its questions. This body numbers fifteen persons, but if current statements are correct, only twelve of them voted in the final decision. Mr. Gandhi, who is believed to have been for rejection from the start, left Delhi at an early stage of the talks, on April 3, for his distant home at Wardha, and can have taken no part in the final debates, though, as rumor has it, he may have telephoned to one of his more intimate disciples.

What we have now to consider are the proposals for the immediate present, that is to say for India's share as a nation in the war. Nothing else counted. To realise the atmosphere of these talks, we must recollect that the Japanese were steadily advancing in Burma, that they had occupied the Andaman Islands and won control by air and sea of the Bay of Bengal, and that their bombers had raided both the eastern coast of the Peninsula and our bases in Ceylon. The general belief was that an invasion was imminent.

Here is the War Cabinet's offer:

During the critical period which now faces India and until the new Constitution can be framed, His Majesty's Government inevitably bear the responsibility for and retain control and direction of the defence of India as part of their world war effort, but the task of organising to the full the military, moral, and material resources of India must be the responsibility of the Government of India with the co-operation of the peoples of India.

His Majesty's Government desire and invite the immediate and effective participation of the leaders of the principal sections of the Indian people in the counsels of their country, of the Commonwealth, and of the United Nations. Thus will they be enabled to give their active and constructive help in the discharge of a task which is vital and essential for the future freedom of India.

This is as vague as it well could be. What does stand out in sharp definition is the negative aspect—the British Government meant to "retain control and direction of the defence of India." Her leaders were left to guess how much or how little might be meant by the phrase which left to the Government of India the task of organising to the full her "military, moral and material resources." And what, again, was meant by the second paragraph, which said nothing with precision? It was soon explained. The Viceroy's Executive Council was to be composed entirely of Indians representing the leading parties; that is to say, the Viceroy would appoint them. The sole but all-important exception was that the Commander-in-Chief, General Wavell, would retain his seat as Member for Defence.

This was manifestly impossible. The proposals offered everything save the one thing that mattered: no Indian might touch defence. But Sir Stafford perceived that he had failed before he had begun, and on March 30 he secured from the Viceroy a vague suggestion—it was at first no more—that he would "see whether it were possible to designate an Indian to some office connected with the Government of India's defence responsibilities." Time passed, however, before the sanction of Whitehall could be secured. A talk with General

Wavell was suggested, but he was in Calcutta and could not meet the Indian leaders until April 5.

The Mission, it will be seen, had opened ill, and already on April 1 Sir Stafford was anticipating the "tragedy" of a "breakdown." He was facing a situation he had not anticipated. What Indians cared about was not the kind of status that one Indian union or two or three would enjoy at the end of the war, but how they were to arm and fight as free men today. The Working Committee of Congress lost little time in making up its mind about the offer as it stood. It passed a resolution of rejection which was communicated to Sir Stafford Cripps on the evening of April 2. Gandhi may have been present, but the draft reads like Nehru's work. This resolution was conceived, however, rather as a record of the Committee's first impressions than as its last word. It was still prepared to negotiate, and it is clear that it did so for a day or two in a relatively optimistic mood, for Sir Stafford Cripps was in his conversations with its spokesmen using language which seemed to meet its demands half-way. The paragraphs of the resolution dealing with the long-term offer have already been summarised: here is the essential passage:

Any proposal concerning the future of India must demand attention and scrutiny, but in today's grave crisis it is the present that counts and even the proposals for the future in so far as they affect the present. The Committee necessarily attached the greatest importance to this aspect of the question and on this ultimately depends what advice they should give to those who look to them for guidance. For this the present British War Cabinet's proposals are vague and altogether incomplete, and there would appear to be no vital changes in the present structure contemplated. It has been made clear that the defence of India will in any event remain under British control. At any time Defence is a vital subject; during war-time it is all-important and covers almost every sphere of life and administration. To take away Defence from the sphere of responsibility at this stage is to reduce that responsibility to a farce and nullity, and to make it perfectly clear that India is not going to be free in any way and her Government is not going to function as a free and independent Government during the pendency of the war.

The Committee would repeat that the essential fundamental prerequisite for the assumption of responsibility by the Indian people in the present is their realisation as a fact that they are free and are in charge of maintaining and defending their freedom. What is most wanted is the enthusiastic response of the people, which cannot be evoked without the fullest trust in them and the devolution of responsibility on them in the matter of Defence. It is only thus that even in this grave eleventh hour it may be possible to galvanise the people of India to rise to the height of the occasion. It is manifest that the present Government of India, as well as its Provincial agencies, are lacking in competence and are incapable of shouldering the burden of India's defence. It is only the people of India, through their popular representatives, who may shoulder this burden worthily. But that can only be done by present freedom and full responsibility being cast upon them. The Committee are, therefore, unable to accept the proposals put forward on behalf of the British War Cabinet.

The next step on the British side was, if possible, even more unfortunate than the opening move. It was proposed that an Indian should fill the office and bear the title of Defence Member, while General Wavell in charge of operations and strategy should be known as the War Member. This looked like a well-meant concession, until the list of subjects was produced of which the Defence Member should have charge. Here it is:

I. (a) public relations, (b) demobilisation, (c) petroleum supplies, (d) representation on Eastern Group Supply Council, (e) amenities and welfare of troops, (f) canteens, (g) certain non-technical schools, (h) stationery, printing and forms for the Army, (i) reception of foreign missions.

II. Certain questions "difficult to locate"—e.g. denial policy, evacuation from threatened areas, signals, economic warfare.

What enemy of England and India drafted this list? Or is there at Headquarters in New Delhi a reckless satirist? But perhaps we should admire the patient industry which scraped up these odds and ends. Petroleum, canteens and stationery: but why not red tape and pipeclay? One tries to imagine Nehru in his first broadcast as Defence Minister rousing a liberated people to a delirium of warlike enthusiasm by reading it out—"stationery, printing and forms for the Army."

The comment of Nehru and Dr. Azad was admirable in its brevity. They remarked that the list was "a revealing one" and rejected it.

Sir Stafford then tried again. The second effort was rather better. This time the formula defined the scope of the War Department. It was to deal with all proposals emanating from General Headquarters, Naval Headquarters and Air Headquarters, to represent the Government in all that concerned these three and act as liaison between them and other departments. The Defence Member would deal with "all other matters." But what were these other matters? A list was asked for, promised but never produced: it was not clear that they would amount to much more than the original catalogue. So far both sides may have taken a rather narrow view of the meaning of defence. In his final review, after the rejection, Sir Stafford broadened the argument by pointing out that many of the other departments which Nehru would control would be concerned directly or indirectly with defence. Of these, three at least were of considerable importance. The Supply Department would have charge of supplies for all forces and munitions. The Civil Defence Department would control air-raid precautions and all forms of civilian defence. The Labour Department would deal with man-power. This strong argument, unfortunately, was produced only after the negotiations had failed, and so far as is known there were no discussions in which it might have been tested and amplified. The last letter from Nehru and Dr. Azad records their final impression:

As regards the division of functions between the Defence Minister and the War Minister, you did not give an illustrative list as requested by us, and referred us to the previous list of the Defence Minister's functions which as you know we had been wholly unable to accept. In your letter under reply you mention certain subjects directly or indirectly related to the war which will be administered by other departments. So far as the Defence Minister is concerned it is clear that his functions will be limited by the first list that you sent.

No one has suggested any restrictions on the normal powers of the Commander-in-Chief. Indeed we went beyond this and were prepared to agree to further powers being given to him as War Minister. But it is clear that the British Government's conception and ours in regard to Defence differs greatly. For us it means giving it a National character and calling upon every man and woman in India to participate in it. It means trusting our own people and seeking their full co-operation in this great effort. The British Government's view seems to be based on an utter lack of confidence in the Indian people and in withholding real power from them.

You refer to the paramount duty and responsibility of His Majesty's Government in regard to defence. That duty and responsibility cannot be discharged effectively unless the Indian people are made to have and feel their responsibility, and the recent past stands witness to this. The Government of India do not seem to realise that the war can only be fought on a popular basis.

The last sentence may give the clue to the real feelings of these Indian leaders. Even in this crisis the British Government did not trust the Indian people, did not mean to arm it and did not intend that it should defend its own country, as the Chinese had defended theirs. In the way stood that draconic Arms Act which measures the length even of the Indian housewife's kitchen knife.

In the last stage, though defence was still the real issue, the negotiations turned rather on the political meaning of the offer. What would be the position of Indian leaders if they entered the Viceroy's Council? Would it be, in effect, though not in legal form, a cabinet, a national government?

It may be well to remind ourselves, at this stage, of the traditional character of this Viceroy's Council. It had been, until the other day, a committee of civil servants, sitting as heads of departments, over which the Viceroy, usually an aristocrat, presided. Its members came to it after a working life spent in the atmosphere of bureaucracy. Often men of marked ability, they might on one question or another hold decided views, but they had been trained to silence: they had no party or public following behind them: their life-work had been to carry out policies prescribed to them by their official superiors. In short, they were expert administrators, not politicians: still less were they party leaders. The Viceroy dealt with them much as a minister in Whitehall may deal with his senior departmental officials, who commonly know more of the business under discussion than he does. The Viceroy may and on occasion does veto the majority opinion of his Council, but in that case any two of them may appeal against him to the Secretary of State in London, with whom the last word lies. Such a council has little in common with a British cabinet, It more nearly resembles the American cabinet, whose members are not responsible to Congress, with this deadly difference: that the Viceroy is not a president elected by the Indian people. He is the executive hand of the distant India Office, with which he is in daily contact by cablegram, and may be overruled or dismissed by the Secretary of State.

The plan which Congress, and indeed all the Indian parties favoured, was that this ancient bureaucratic institution should, without any legal changes, be transformed by an informal agreement—"by convention" as the Indians put it—into a *de facto* cabinet. There was no time during war to remodel it by act of Parliament. At the end the spokesmen of Congress got involved with Sir Stafford Cripps in a rather barren debate over the nature of this constitutional change. Certainly the Indians wanted something wholly new, a genuine national government: what was in law merely a council should become in fact a cabinet. But they were not asking for an act of Parliament.* What they wanted was an assurance from the Viceroy that he would treat them as a constitutional monarch treats a British ministry. What did this mean? I am not sure: we have not got the Indian case in any detail. I think some such assurance over the use of the veto might have sufficed as the Viceroy actually gave in 1937 to the provincial cabinets. What was essential was the recognition of the collective responsibility of ministers. At this point I must stress a matter that has been generally overlooked. Congress has been assailed by innumerable critics, from Mr. Churchill downwards, on the assumption that it was asking for absolute power for itself. That is a careless if it is an honest mistake. What Nehru and Dr. Azad proposed in these documents was a "mixed," by which they meant a coalition government. "We are not interested," they wrote (p. 15), "in the Congress as such gaining power, but we are interested in the Indian people as a whole having freedom and power." The Congress press wrote throughout on the assumption that the Muslim League must share in the *interim* government. It was even suggested that Mr. Jinnah should form it. The significance of collective ministerial responsibility would have been this —that the council or cabinet could have done nothing to which the Muslim minority took serious objection. If it had infringed the rights or injured the self-respect of the Muslims, their members would have broken it up by resigning. In other words, in such a cabinet the Muslims could have protected themselves: they would not have had to rely on the Viceroy or the India Office. In no other way than this can India attain independence or even self-government.

In the last stage of these talks, Sir Stafford, who had acquired the authentic accent of New Delhi rather rapidly, raised the familiar objection of the minorities. We could not, as he put it, allow the minorities to be subjected to "an autocratic majority in the Cabinet," nor could His Majesty's Gov-

* In any event a formal amending act would have been necessary to cancel the statutory requirement that at least three members of the Council should be officials with ten years' service.

ernment forget the pledges it had given "to protect the rights of those minorities." Listening to such language from a man of the Left, Indians asked in dismay whether we really had any intention of abandoning these sacred if self-imposed duties of guardianship, even in the post-war future. This tenderness for the minorities was superfluous. Inside the cabinet they would have had all the power they needed. Finally, though this matter was not explicitly raised, to me personally it seems essential that the Council, if it ever becomes a *de facto* cabinet, must have an Indian premier, capable of guiding it, speaking for it and holding it together. In other words, the Viceroy must cease to be premier and become a constitutional king.

Was this a feasible plan? Everything depended on the willingness of Lord Linlithgow to accept this delicate and important, if less authoritative position, in the last year of his long reign. Was he willing? Only he could say. When Nehru and Dr. Azad pressed Sir Stafford on this matter, they were told (p. 11) "that nothing could be said at this stage even vaguely and generally about the conventions that should govern the new government and the Viceroy. This was a matter in the Viceroy's sole discretion, and at a later stage it could be discussed directly with the Viceroy." In other words, Indians must first accept: they would then be told what powers they would enjoy. Was this a way to treat men who respected themselves and their country? Lord Linlithgow's share of responsibility for the wrecking of the Cripps mission has been generally overlooked.

Rejection was now inevitable. Two tactless actions may have contributed to it. Lord Halifax anticipated it in a broadcast from America. Sir Stafford may have precipitated it by an ultimatum in which he announced that the time had come when he must fly back to London. The view of the majority of the Working Committee can be put in a sentence. They felt that the offer fell seriously short of any real transfer of power. The British case, as stated first by Sir Stafford and afterwards by Mr. Amery, was that power could not be transferred to a cabinet which would be "responsible to no one but itself." In other words, there was no Indian parliament which could, if it abused its powers, remove it by a vote of no confidence.

Was this a sufficient reason for rejecting the idea of a national government? To me it has a ring of pedantry. The enemy was at the gate: at such times we may have to dispense with some of the safeguards of democracy. At home we suspended the Parliament Act. Indians may not have felt that either Mr. Amery in London or Lord Linlithgow in Delhi was a perfect substitute for a parliament of their own. These Indian ministers would not in fact have been "irresponsible": they would have been responsible to their own parties and could not have continued in office, if either Congress or the Muslim League had called on them to resign. Finally, it would have been easy, as Congress suggested, to make them by their own declaration responsible to the elected members of the All-India Legislative Assembly. It may not be a satisfactory body from the democratic viewpoint, but as always we had seen to it that the minorities should be adequately represented in it. Whatever its defects, it is a rather more sensitive mirror of Indian opinion than the India Office in Whitehall.

It only remains to put it on record that the rejection of the offer by the Working Committee of Congress was communicated to Sir Stafford Cripps on April 10. It is generally believed that the vote was close—five for acceptance and seven for rejection: three did not vote. The reasons that decided the majority, which included Nehru but not Dr. Azad, have already been analysed. They are leaders of a great mass movement. They knew the state of Indian opinion as we do not. They realised that it had to be "galvanised", to use their word, into a fighting temper, not because it trusted the Japanese, but because it distrusted the British Government. This offer, as it finally emerged from the talks at Delhi, would not, in their opinion, have worked the miracle. Gandhi's attitude was in this sense an important factor: without his active support a bare majority of the Committee would have found its task difficult. It is clear that Sir Stafford Cripps was mistaken in his belief that the Committee had ever at an earlier stage of the discussions voted for acceptance. On the other hand, Nehru and Dr. Azad were influenced by their belief that there had been "a progressive deterioration in the British Government's attitude as our negotiations proceeded." This is more doubtful. I have satisfied myself by enquiry that the War Cabinet never intended to concede anything that could fairly be called a "National Government." None the less, Sir Stafford did publicly use these words. Again, it was widely believed, in London, as in Delhi, that the India Office ("a symbol of evil to us," as Dr. Azad put it) was to be merged in the Dominions Office, a department with a lighter touch, accustomed to deal with free men. The spokesmen of Congress believed that Sir Stafford had held out this prospect, and he has not denied their statement. Was this at one time in his brief? Or did he go beyond his brief? My personal impression is that the margin between acceptance and rejection was not unbridgeable and that Lord Linlithgow and Mr. Amery could have bridged it. But the offer was rigid and fixed: the limits within which it could have been amended by free negotiation were excessively narrow. Imperfect as it was, the Indians had to take it or leave it. Without exception every Indian party refused to take it. The offer was then withdrawn.*

AFTER THE BREAKDOWN

THE REST of the story is painful, and I will not linger over it. Inevitably after this failure, our relations with India deteriorated. Official propaganda laboured hard to cast all the blame on Congress, and across the curtain of the censorship there could be no reply. Within the ranks of Congress the

* Mr. Amery did not succeed in explaining with his usual lucidity what the withdrawal of the Draft Declaration meant. Our main purpose, that India should obtain full freedom, still holds, but some other method will have to be adopted. Commons: April 28, 1942.

influence of Gandhi was once again all-powerful. Thinking aloud, debating with himself, his mind was moving towards overt revolt, a final effort as he conceived it. There is this to be said for him, that he did nothing secretly; he warned us of his intentions and he gave us ample time, if we had been willing to make another effort at reconciliation. The Cripps Mission registered failure on April 10, but it was not till August 8 that the carefully timed revolt overtook us. Of these four months we made no use. In such a situation the best hope commonly lies in the intervention of a friendly mediator. The failure to bring India wholeheartedly into the war concerned the Americans and Chinese hardly less than it concerned us, and influential voices in the press of both these nations suggested some common effort to reach a solution. The Indians had the same inspiration. There is reason to believe that Marshal Chiang Kai-shek did suggest to Mr. Roosevelt that they should jointly offer their mediation. The President, possibly because he feared a rebuff, declined. This was, to my thinking, a misfortune for all of us. Any offer which America and China underwrote would have been accepted without hesitation by Indians. The mere fact that we had welcomed the mediation of these allies would have demonstrated our sincerity, for it would have proved that we no longer looked on Indians as our imperial property, but regarded them as one of the United Nations. To accept the mediation of foreign powers in a dispute between us and our subjects would certainly have been an unprecedented innovation. That was precisely what made it advisable. It would have proved that we have ceased to think of Indians as our subjects. When once they are convinced that this change has in fact happened in our minds, the details of the settlement will be easily adjusted. As yet none of them believe that this transformation has occurred—neither Gandhi nor Mr. Jinnah nor the princes. But for this great gesture we lacked the necessary wisdom and grace.

The task of explaining what Gandhi did is beyond me, for I am not a pacifist and doubtless I am an incorrigible Westerner in my mental habits. The difficulty in understanding him is that he is at once a man of the loftiest spiritual vision and a tactician who moves on the plane of everyday reality. In short, he compromises, where, as it seems to most of us, no compromise is possible. His slogan "Quit India" was well calculated to win the masses who looked up to him, but it aroused the maximum of resistance in us. He did not mean that Englishmen resident in India must quit it, and he even said—a surprising concession—that our troops might stay to fight the Japanese in case of need, though the Indian army should be disbanded. What he meant was that we must declare Indian independence and withdraw our government. That done, he declared, Indians would promptly come together and form a government of their own, which would be obeyed. This did not square with some of his recent utterances, for he has spoken, rather lightly, of the risk of a civil war between Muslims and Hindus. In this shape his demand was so manifestly impossible that I need spend no time in discussing it. We cannot withdraw our government until there is a provisional administration, acceptable to most Indians, ready to take over the reins of power. To walk out in the way he suggested would have been to invite the Japanese to walk in. None the less, even I can guess what Gandhi meant. He meant that when we really are, beyond any shadow of doubt, ready to transfer power, Indians will adjust their differences. Until that moment comes, they will bicker, with their brown eyes fixed on the white arbiter. There Gandhi is right. But there are ways of demonstrating our will to transfer power, without first putting up the shutters of the Viceregal Lodge.

On August 8 at Bombay the National Committee of Congress, with a negligible number of dissenters, adopted a policy of uncompromising revolt. The long resolution by which it was justified included much well reasoned argument, and ended with a call for mass civil disobedience. Indians revolted, albeit without arms, much as Irishmen revolted, at Easter 1915, during the last war. I am not going to argue that in so doing they wronged us, though I am convinced that the vast majority of this nation was at the time of the Cripps mission ready to concede the substance of independence. The wrong they did was to the family of nations. On the assumption of a widespread response to their summons, it was clear that for a time at least the defences of India would be imperiled, as in fact they were. They risked a Japanese success, which would have endangered not merely India's prospect of freedom, but also China's. The resolution included this curious sentence:

The Committee is anxious not to embarrass in any way the defence of China or Russia, whose freedom is precious and must be preserved, or to jeopardise the defensive capacity of the United Nations.

In words Congress repudiated a consequence which its acts were calculated to produce. The explanation of this inconsistency is, I believe, that Gandhi's unflinching belief in the duty of civil disobedience led him, in spite of previous experience, to exaggerate its efficacy. In the same way he had promised Indians independence by the end of 1921. He reckoned on a success so prompt that no serious prejudice would be inflicted on the good cause of the United Nations. This great man moves in a world of thought of his own. I can make no defence of what Congress did: it miscalculated and it forgot its international duty. But this question I will venture to ask: Have we always remembered ours? Toward the Czechs, the Spaniards and these same Indians? If so, then let us with our impeccable hands cast our accusing stones.

The Government struck first and arrested all the leaders of Congress, before Gandhi had actually fixed a date for the outbreak of the revolt. It is said that he would first have sought an interview with the Viceroy, but on this basis no useful negotiations could have taken place. The revolt that followed was spontaneous, and it seems to me improbable that the methods used can have been prescribed by Gandhi. If so, "non-violent" would be a ridiculous description. Rails were torn up and cables cut; police stations and other government buildings were set on fire; strikes broke out in the chief centres of industry. Our planes mowed down the rioters with their machine guns, and up to the end of December 1942, the police or troops opened fire on 538 occasions. In the same period 60,000 Indians were arrested, 940 killed and 1,630 wounded. The number punished by the unforgivable humiliation of whipping has been given by Mr. Amery as 958. It is possible that the revolt can for a time be crushed by physical coercion. The important new fact that concerns us today is that the other Indian parties, critical of Congress though they still are, are all now in line with its demands. All of them call for a national government now, and all of them claim independence.

Our chronicle of the doings of the British Government since the close of the Cripps Mission may be brief. It had failed and was, it seems, content to fail. It relapsed into majestic inertia, and neither itself tried nor permitted others to try to restore peace. Its sole conception of a policy was apparently to crush Congress: this it did with a will. While it declared that any further initiative towards a settlement must come from Indians, it made it physically impossible for them to take it. Manifestly, if they had first to agree on some joint proposals which they might present to us, it was essential that the leaders of the other parties should be permitted to visit Gandhi in prison. We need not dispute over the exact proportion of the Indian nation which Congress represents: no one doubts that it is much the largest of the Indian parties. Without it there can be no settlement. Even to the veteran head of the Anglican Church in India, Bishop Westcott, this facility was denied. The man best qualified for the office of mediator was, indisputably, Mr. Rajagopalachari, the ex Premier of Madras. He had advocated a conciliatory policy towards the Muslim League. He was prepared to abandon all opposition to the idea of Pakistan, provided Mr. Jinnah would join Congress in forming a national government now. He believed that if Muslims and Hindus had fought shoulder to shoulder for Mother India, the Muslims would in the end wish to prolong the partnership with their comrades in arms. To advocate this far-sighted policy, he resigned his membership of Congress. After talks with Mr. Jinnah which had been, as he believed, fruitful, he sought permission in November to lay his plan for a settlement before Gandhi, his former colleague and relative by marriage. Lord Linlithgow refused. About the same time he asked for a passport to visit London in the interests of peace. Mr. Amery refused.

It remains only to mention two of the Prime Minister's contributions to the Indian question. None of us can forget what we owe to his great leadership during the dark year when we fought alone: it is not easy to criticise Mr Churchill. His statement of September 10, 1942, as unjust as it was intemperate and inaccurate, was, none the less, regretted by most of us. In India it gravely aggravated an already ruinous situation. As they read it, Indians lost the last shred of faith in our sincerity. This was not, they felt, the speech of a man who would ever consent to their independence. *Divide et impera* rang through it from beginning to end. It did, indeed, confirm, as curtly as possible, "the broad principles" of the Cripps offer. Mr. Churchill then assailed Congress in the inimitable style which amuses us in his polemics against the Nazis. He called it "the Hindu Congress," but denied that it represented even the Hindu masses, jested about the manufacturers and financiers in its ranks, attacked it where it is least vulnerable, in its relations with the untouchables, and suggested that its activities had been aided by the Japanese. He then drew up in battle array against the Hindus all the forces on which he relies to defeat the claim of Congress to independence—the Muslims, the depressed classes, the subjects of the princes, the Sikhs and the Christians. Incidentally he handed out yet another veto—to the "martial races," who are "divided by unbridgeable religious gulfs from the Hindu Congress and would never consent to be ruled by them." He assured them that they shall never be "subjugated" by Congress against their will. He ended with the announcement that the "white" army in India is now larger than at any time in the British connexion.

This was the speech of a man who has learned nothing

about India since he served there as a subaltern in the Hussars. He has the gift of remaining young. The key to his romantic attitude may lie in his references to the "martial races," who for him are India—the land of the "Barrack-room Ballads." Many Indians gave their verbal answer to this speech: one of them acted, and he was neither a Hindu nor a member of Congress. By way of protest, Mr. Allah Bux, the Muslim Premier of Sind, resigned his titles and decorations.

Somewhat later, in his Mansion House speech (November 11, 1942), Mr. Churchill answered Mr. Wendell Willkie's speeches on India as follows:

Let me, however, make this clear, in case there should be any mistake about it in any quarter: We mean to hold our own. I have not become the King's First Minister in order to preside over the liquidation of the British Empire. For that task, if ever it were prescribed, some one else would have to be found and, under democracy, I suppose the nation would have to be consulted.

With this speech before me, I am driven to ask the question: Had there ever been an offer of independence to India?

The answer may be that before our reinforcements could reach the Peninsula over the long passage round the Cape, a rigid formula was carried to Delhi by an honest but unlucky messenger, who mistook it for an offer of independence. It failed in the opinion of all the Indian parties to transfer to them the reality of power today. It offered no prospect of independence tomorrow, because the Empire retained its "friendly fortresses" in the princes' states. The military prospect has improved since Sir Stafford Cripps flew to Delhi. The Prime Minister's tone has also changed and he has dismissed the herald of reconciliation from the War Cabinet. There is nothing to add to the story of our efforts to liberate subject India.

III. Hindus and Muslims

THERE ARE in the contemporary world several recognised ways of classifying men for political purposes. By adopting one principle of division rather than another, the rulers of a state define its character and determine its life. Men may be classified, first of all, according to the colour of their skins or the shape of their heads. They may next be grouped according to their religious beliefs. Finally they may be arranged according to economic status or functions; that is to say on class lines. Some would add an ideological classification, according to political creeds, but this will usually coincide roughly with the division into classes. In India all these principles of classification are at work. There is a colour bar: there are organised parties, while classes are rapidly coming to a consciousness of their distinct economic interests. But it is the classification according to religious belief that dominates the political scene of today.

This is no new fact. It was customary throughout the East and was, indeed, inevitable wherever the government was a theocracy. To this day the Emperor of Japan is a god incarnate. In Turkey, so long as it had a Sultan, he claimed to be the Caliph, who led the faithful in prayer, protected the Holy Places, and wielded the sword of God on earth. It could not be otherwise, in India or elsewhere, so long as the law of daily life was based on sacred books interpreted by a priesthood. It followed, when two or more religions divided the allegiance of a population, that each retained for certain defined purposes its own sacred system of law. That was still the case in Turkey when I first knew it. The bishop of a Christian flock was its political head. To his duties as its leader and guardian he was usually much more alive than to his functions as its spiritual pastor. He was the captain, sometimes militant,

sometimes subtle, who represented it in the face of the Turkish
power, always alien and often hostile. He had the charge generally of its collective interests and specifically of its schools
and the charities which took the place of social services. Theocracy in India was less highly organised: there is no Hindu
Church nor any hierarchy of spiritual chiefs. But there is a
Hindu legal code and a Muslim canon law which the British
rulers had to take into account, more especially in all that
concerned inheritance and marriage. For such purposes, therefore, the classification by creeds was unavoidable, as it also
was in the army, where the tabus of each faith, especially in
matters of diet, had to be respected.

The decisive step in the political field—as it seems to me,
the fatal step—was taken in 1909 by Lord Morley, when he
introduced the system of separate communal electorates into
the Morley-Minto scheme of reforms, which made some halting advance towards representative institutions. Morley, who
ossified noticeably in later life, had little sympathy with Indians and no belief in self-government,* while he confessed in
private talk a frank preference for Muslims over Hindus. The
problem, as he saw it, was to ensure that minorities should
secure their fair share of representation. Though he was at
home an advocate of proportional representation, he rejected
it as unsuitable in this case, and adopted the plan which the
more conservative Muslims favoured. The adherents of each
creed are entered in separate registers and grouped in distinct
constituencies, which vote apart, each returning a number of
representatives fixed in a rough ratio to population. The man
who thus accepted religion as the key to politics in India was
himself a secularist.

This system the Muslims have come to regard as their most
valued privilege, and it has survived and is likely to survive
the opposition of Congress and the Liberals, who offer in its

* "If it could be said," he declared, "that this chapter of reforms led
directly or indirectly to the establishment of a parliamentary system in
India, I for one would have nothing at all to do with it." (*Indian
Speeches*, p. 91.)

place a very simple plan, which allows all electors to vote together for whom they please, while ensuring that a minimum number of seats, proportionate to its share of the population, shall go to the minority. It is obvious that separate electorates must intensify religious divisions. It is inevitable on this arrangement that parties must be organised on lines of creed. If they co-operate at all, it can be only by way of coalition, after the elections. When men are grouped together on a religious footing, the mass-mind which emerges is likely to be abnormally conscious of creed, and can be swung with ease towards fanaticism. Candidates are driven to rival one another in zeal for the faith, and things of secular concern are thrust into the background. In the Hindu camp a lawyer, who is in fact the landlords' or usurers' candidate, may win peasant votes by swearing to protect the sacred cow. The corresponding trick is played with equal success in the Muslim electorate by a green-turbaned *hadji* (pilgrim) just returned from Mecca. The result is that the peasants of the two creeds never come together and with difficulty perceive the overwhelming identity of their common interests. On this segregation of Indians at the foundations of the political structure the rival conservative parties, both of them communal, the League and the Mahasabha, have thriven. Congress can and does promote the candidature of its own Muslim members in the Muslim constituencies, but with a diminishing record of success. If, on the other hand, Muslims and Hindus voted together, the opposite consequences would follow. A Muslim candidate, eager to win Hindu votes, would stress as much as possible their common interests and mention as gently and as seldom as he could the angry memories and crude suspicions that divide the two faiths.

FAITH AND ECONOMICS

How far in fact is this classification by creeds relevant to the realities of Indian politics? The question may startle the reader whose ears are fatigued by the din of these clashing faiths. Eccentric though this may seem, I venture to suggest that this classification is an audacious irrelevance, foreign to the actual concerns of daily life. India is no longer a theocracy. It is a very poor country struggling to reach higher levels in its economic and cultural life. Let us enquire first what matters do in fact engage the attention of the provincial Councils. The chief and in most provinces the overwhelming concern is agriculture in all its aspects. The peasant leagues may be demanding sweeping reforms in the system of land tenure. Should tax-assessments be lowered; should arrears be cancelled? One day the elimination of the functionless landlord will have to be faced. After this come more technical questions of the first importance touching irrigation, forestry, co-operative marketing and credit, the provision of better seeds and breeding stock, the utilisation of waste land, research and educational propaganda. From this we may go on to the passionate subject of usury. Where in all this, by what chink or crevice can the question of creed creep in? The relevant divisions are those which separate landlord from tenant; usurer from debtor. Left to themselves Hindu and Muslim peasants will feel, think and vote in exactly the same way. The one difficulty so far is that usurers are nearly always Hindus. Muslims do, on the whole, obey the prohibition of the Koran, though the Pathans are notoriously lax in this matter. But the Hindu usurer is no more popular with victims of his own creed than with Muslims. When we pass to the social services, again it is hard to see how creed can intrude. The poor of both faiths clamour for hospitals and both suffer equally from the curse of malaria and hookworm. They will not differ over factory legislation, for the trade unions include both communities. As little will they diverge over the means of transport. Finally, does not education present a difficulty? It exists, but it is less acute than one might anticipate. The official system is from top to bottom secular. One of the best things to be said for the schools, colleges and universities provided by the Government is that in them all Hindus and Muslims study, debate and play together. The Muslims have, however, a university of their own at Aligarh, and Hindus have theirs at Benares. Old-world schools of modest pretensions still survive, attached to mosques and temples in the remoter villages. The demand is audible and may grow for the provision of separate confessional schools and colleges, but as yet there is no controversy grave enough to compel believers of the two faiths to range themselves in separate parties for the defence of their rights.

From the provinces let us turn to the Federal Centre. As things stood in the Constitution of 1935, which never came into life, the main concerns of an Indian federation were to be finance, the customs, communications, defence and foreign affairs. Nothing here seems to call directly for the separation of the creeds. Income tax may be a painful and contentious matter, but it falls on all alike. Railways and posts can stir no religious controversies. Is the army a difficulty? The Muslims might ask for some guarantee that their numbers within it should not fall below an agreed proportion and great care would be necessary to escape jealousy over promotions at the top. They may feel in foreign policy some special sympathy for their Muslim neighbours, the Afghans and Persians. That need not hurt either the sentiments or the interests of the Hindus. In the broad functions of economic planning and development there may also lurk a risk, but of a vague and indirect kind. It happens that industry is largely in Hindu hands, though some big manufacturing concerns owned by Muslims do exist. Financiers, from the millionaire banker of Bombay down to the shady village money-lender, are also chiefly Hindus or else Parsis. Might a cleavage occur between town and country, agriculture and industry? Conceivably this may happen. But in that case need it or can it assume a religious form, as a struggle between the Muslim farmer and the industrialist?

This seems unlikely, for the simple reason that the mass of peasants, like the mass of consumers and the mass of urban wage-earners, are Hindus. Struggle and cleavage there will be between opposed interests and classes, but manifestly it must follow economic lines. Whatever the original intention may have been, the effect of this classification by religion is to delay the recognition of these economic issues as the urgent and substantial realities of political life. To distract attention from these issues is in effect to maintain things as they are. Religion is prostituted, not for the first time in history, to preserve the ascendancy of the propertied classes.

This argument amounts to a suggestion that with a more modern political structure than we have given her, India might manage to surmount the division into rival creeds that is her curse. In the meantime we have to face the fact that it is a disastrous reality. It may be well, then, to attempt some analysis of its origins and effects.

This feud began in the Middle Ages and it feeds on memory. The Muslims can never forget that they are a race of conquerors, and in their more romantic moods some of them in my hearing have talked of restoring their former ascendancy by the sword. Their record was a patchwork of good and evil. If in the early days their armies destroyed all they could not enslave, there were periods when it was their glory to construct and even to reconcile. If Muslims were content to draw their inspiration from the tolerance and justice of the Emperor Akbar, their love of the past would be a blessing. But more often it is of their military exploits that they think. The worst consequence of this habit is that it arouses an answering chauvinism in the Hindus, who also have their martial races and their military pride. Early in the present century, Tilak, a man as able as he was unwise, set to work to revive the cult of the Mahratta hero, Shivaji, the brilliant but ruthless warrior who began the process of destroying the Mogul Empire. This folly of his helped to keep Muslims aloof from the Congress party, during a period of vitality and expansion. Under Gandhi's influence Congress does not now offend in this way. He has always stressed the need for unity and mutual understanding, yet his own peculiar ethical outlook is so distinctly Hindu that it repels the average Muslim. But the militant Hindu tradition is still alive in the Mahasabha, which blends the fighting spirit of the sturdy Mahrattas with the pietism of the more orthodox Hindus of other stocks. It has evolved an attitude akin to that of the missionary and revivalist, which had hitherto been absent from this conservative community.

Students of this difficult question often lay stress on the ideological contrast between Islam and Hinduism. Assuredly it would be difficult to name two creeds, two attitudes to life so violently opposed. Islam, in its stark Unitarian simplicity, is positive and realistic. For it, in the beginning, was fact. It dwells in this visible world, in which it sees the will of God made manifest by the sword and sceptre of prophets, soldiers and kings. It has nothing that can properly be called a priesthood. Its ritual, if its form of worship deserves that name at all, is as simple as it is impressive: in its spacious and dignified mosques, open to the skies, the faithful prostrate themselves in prayer and affirmation. It felt like our own Puritan iconoclasts when it saw the efforts of the Hindus to visualise God in art. It will enslave the heathen, but it proclaims the equality of all believers and often in its history it has come near to realising this difficult ideal. Its confidence that it possesses the truth which all men should acknowledge made it in its period of expansive energy a warlike and intolerant creed. Its sensuous and possessive attitude to women has raised up formidable obstacles to their freedom and self-respect.

What Hinduism is, it is harder to define. What is it not? A lofty speculative philosophy, mystical and pantheistic. A museum of primitive customs. An oppressive system of priestcraft. In its cult of Krishna, which is what it chiefly means to most Hindus today, it is a gentle and lovable belief, based on a noble poem with an idealistic doctrine, a happy ritual and an attractive mythology. But side by side is the darker cult of Kali under many names. The violence of this climate, its pests, floods and famines, taught the Indian villager to dread the

cruelty of God. As Mahatma Gandhi teaches it to his countrymen today, it is an ethic of love and renunciation. At its best,
Hinduism turns away from life in an ascetic attitude of rejection and sees in this earthly existence of ours only a transient
moment in the soul's long journey through time. At its worst,
it separates men and degrades them by its institution of caste.
Its weakness is that it never denies, never rejects, never dis-
cards what is obsolete and unworthy of the noble core of its
beliefs. Islam was a Reformation which shook off the primitive
beliefs and rites of Arabia. But Hinduism, as we know it today,
is a Counter-Reformation, which restored Brahman ascendancy, after the humanitarian Buddhist revolt; its function is
to conserve. But it is not an organised church: it has no formu-
lated creed: it has never persecuted and has only lately begun
to proselytise. Rather is it an elaborate code of daily behaviour binding only on men born in Hindustan within its
fold. Accordingly it is tolerant. It saw in woman rather the
mother than the mistress, and within its society she can win
her freedom.

But this stark opposition, as we have set it out here, is misleading. In the first place, the form in which Islam reached
India was not the ultra-simple Semitic faith. What came to
India was Persian culture, with its exquisite art and poetry,
careless of orthodoxy, often inclined to mysticism and occasionally to free thought. In this form it was by no means uncongenial to the speculative Hindu temperament. Again, though
there are old Muslim families in India which trace their descent to the conquerors and even to the Prophet, the immense
mass of the Muslim population was originally Hindu by blood
and culture. In the villages it retains much of its traditional
outlook, its folklore and even traces of caste. This old-world,
rural population had long ago reached a fairly happy *modus
vivendi* between the two creeds. It is still customary in the
villages that they should, out of courtesy, attend each other's
religious festivals. Relations are much happier in the princes'
states than in British India. Finally, we must not forget that
a large part of the younger educated generation of both creeds

is, in one degree or another, rationalist in its outlook. Among Indian students in England the difference between Hindus and Muslims is hardly perceptible. It is fortunate that Indians, save in the South, have in Hindustani and Urdu a *lingua franca* which is widely understood even by men of little or no education. The two languages are basically identical, though literary Urdu uses many words of Persian origin. Unluckily each clings to its own peculiar script. If Muslims and Hindus are ever wise enough to adopt a common script for this beautiful language that unites them, the two cultures might intermarry to the gain of both.

If ideology is not the absolute barrier which some take it to be, what does so fatally divide these two? Broadly the origin of the trouble is in our day economic, and it results in a struggle for power. The Hindus were much prompter than the Muslims in adopting Western education and took more readily to commerce and industry. They are the more enterprising and consequently the wealthier of the two communities, though at both ends of the social scale in rural India there is little to choose between the well-to-do landlords at the top and the peasantry and labourers at the bottom who have nothing to lose but their debts. This disparity soon became a political issue, since Hindus tended to monopolise the jobs for which there is an educational test or a competitive examination. In a country where industry is seriously under-developed, official employment offers the most promising career open to the numerous intellectual proletariat. It was soon demanded that official posts should be distributed in accordance with the ratio between the two creeds in the population of a province. The Government, seeking to be impartial, in some cases reserved a fixed number of places for Muslim students in professional colleges. This was done, for example, in some veterinary schools: I cannot say whether the health of Indian horses gains by this arrangement. Hot controversies would rage between the two creeds before a professor of mathematics could be appointed in a leading university. Always the confessional calculus had to be observed, even in the academic world.

THE MUSLIM LEAGUE

W HEN the provinces attained full self-government an even acuter phase of this rivalry opened. Government means patronage, and patronage is in the gift of ministers. On the eve of the election of 1937 in the United Provinces a leading Muslim politician who had hitherto belonged to the Congress party deserted it, because he thought it would be defeated, and went over to the Muslim League with his following. He was mistaken: Congress was victorious and formed the ministry. This man then asked to be taken back to the fold and rewarded with a Cabinet post. Very naturally, but perhaps unwisely, Congress refused—as any British party in a like case would have done. The consequences were unfortunate and to the English mind rather astonishing. The Muslim League redoubled its attacks on Congress, and on the strength of this and similar cases accused it of being a totalitarian party which sought to monopolise power. It does claim to govern a province when it wins a majority, but it has been fair and even generous in giving posts to its own Muslim adherents. This is party government, as commonly understood. In absurdly violent language the Muslim League began to talk of persecution in the Congress provinces, and even of "atrocities." *
There was nothing in this charge; if there had been, the Governors would have interfered—which they never did. British

* The real charges, as Mr Guy Wint summarises them (*India and Democracy*, p. 179), were that Congress discriminated against Muslims in the public services, aided popular movements in the states of Muslim princes, used its tricolour as the national flag, taught children in its schools to salute portraits of Gandhi and to sing a national anthem containing "objectionable sentiments": finally, that it favoured Hindustani as against Urdu (see p. 98 above). All this, even if true, is pretty trivial and could surely be set right without splitting India in two. As to the last accusation, it is true that Gandhi takes a stiff Hindu attitude in the question of the script to be used for these two forms of the *lingua franca*. That is regrettable, but two scripts for the same language can hardly be taught in one school.

propaganda since the failure of the Cripps Mission has done its utmost to discredit Congress, but it has refrained from repeating this charge of "persecution," which would have been the most effective weapon it could have used.

For an objective judgment of the Indian crisis it is essential to have some idea of the extent to which the Muslim League may fairly claim to speak for the Mohammedan community. Mr. Jinnah frequently asserts that he represents 81 millions out of the 100 millions of Muslims in British India. This is an extreme claim. Even if we add the princes' states there are only 94 millions in the whole peninsula. There is only one numerical test to which we can appeal, but it is now out-of-date—the general election in the provinces in 1937. On that occasion less than one in four of the successful Muslim candidates (110 out of 482) stood under the League's auspices. Since 1937 it has undoubtedly gained ground. It had then no following in the Punjab, where it now has a hold. Elsewhere it has done well in by-elections, though I can discover no record of these sufficiently detailed to be trustworthy. Undoubtedly large numbers of the wealthy, conservative Muslim landowners have rallied to it. Conspicuous among them are the great landlords of Oudh, the *taluqdars,* who have often played a turbulent part in Indian history. This process may have been assisted by the official practice adopted during Lord Linlithgow's long tenure of the vice-regal office of treating it not merely as the chief but as the sole exponent of Mohammedan opinion. No other Muslim organisation was mentioned even in the White Paper dealing with the Cripps Mission. The semi-official news agency shows the same tendency. This preference has raised its prestige and may have increased its membership. it is the oldest of the political bodies drawn from this community, for it was founded in 1906 with the object of "promoting loyalty to the British Government" and placing before it "in temperate language" the aspirations of the Muslim community.

Some estimate of Muslim opinion outside the League we must try to form, though I know of no reliable figures. To

begin with, there are the Muslims within Congress, an unknown but considerable number, which includes some able and
influential personalities. Secondly, the Shiah sect, about 20 per
cent of the Muslim population, has in the past held aloof from
the League. Then there is an organisation which represents the
orthodox Sunni theologians and preachers, the *Jamiat-ul-Ulema*
(Hind), which claims 200,000 members, a large number, since
it has a high educational test. It has always been friendly to
Congress and has made several political pronouncements in
its sense. This is a highly significant fact, since it suggests that
religious differences are not the real root of the quarrel between Congress and the League. If Congress were an intolerant
Hindu body, these orthodox Muslim divines would not march
on parallel lines with it. We may discover a useful clue to the
quarrel, when we note that the Conference representing the
big Momin community has also, and quite recently, adopted
resolutions which repeated the demands of Congress and opposed the policy of the League. The Momins are diffused over
most of northern India. Some are Shiahs, and they are said to
be somewhat lax in their beliefs, but the significant fact about
them is that they include a large part of the Mohammedan
working-class, for they are by trade either cultivators or
weavers. Their ancestors were once Hindus of the lower
castes. They are poor men who cannot organise easily, and it
would be misleading to suggest that their Conference has
them all consciously behind it. Most of them are illiterate and
many are voteless. Here we are obviously in the presence of
a class antagonism between these proletarian Muslims and
the landowners of Mr. Jinnah's League. The same cleavage
confronts us in the great province of Bengal, where the biggest
Muslim party, as tested by the election of 1937, was the Kris-
hak Praja Party, a moderate peasants' organisation. Its somewhat opportunist leader, Mr. Fazlul Haq, was until recently
premier of Bengal. In the Punjab there are the Ahrars, an
organisation of tenant-farmers. Again, in the province of Sind,
the leading Muslim organisation was in 1937 the Azad Independent Party, which formed under Mr. Allah Bux a coalition

ministry with Congress support. As everyone knows, the North-West Frontier province, almost solidly Muslim, had a Congress ministry. It is said that its Pathan leader, Abdul Gaffur Khan, who used to be called "the Frontier Gandhi," has recently resigned his membership of Congress. That may be so, but whatever change his opinions may have undergone he is not congenial to the authorities, for like Gandhi himself he is in prison. This survey is summary and incomplete*, but I will not weary the reader with further details. The broad fact is that the workers and peasants of Mohammedan India are not represented by the Muslim League, and wherever they have managed to organise, they are opposed to it. But over the vast spaces of India it is not easy for poor men to organise on a nation-wide scale, especially if the official world in Delhi looks askance at them. Under all the political ferment in India, which seems on the surface to turn on constitutional issues and differences of religious belief, the underlying reality is this class cleavage. It is overshadowed today by the struggle against the Empire for independence. Tomorrow it will have to be faced. Already from their palaces the great landlords can see their peasants, Muslims and Hindus together, in the more advanced regions, marching in procession behind banners which display the hammer and sickle. That portent has caused them to rally to the League. Its appeal to religion offers the best hope of keeping their tenants divided. Like every privileged class, they must divide to rule. How far in this tactic they are succeeding, only a skilled observer on the spot could confidently say. For my own part, while I concede that the League has on its side wealth, social prestige and most of the press, which in India as elsewhere is necessarily in the service of property, I am content to point out that it is far from representing the whole of this community. It may be inevitable that the tension

* I have not included the Khaksars, a growing party with a Nazi ideology. It is equally opposed to Congress and the Muslim League, which it denounces as the party of the rich.

between the two communities should increase as the decisive hour approaches which will fix the shape of India's future. For my part, after a long experience of similar feuds between Muslims and Christians in Turkey, I doubt whether even in India the root of the quarrel really is the difference of religious belief. None the less, where the usurer is a Hindu and the debtors Muslim peasants, or where Muslims are imported, as sometimes happens, to break a strike of Hindu workers, a tinge of fanaticism will colour the quarrel. When that happens the result may be, in the slums of some of the larger towns, an outbreak of communal rioting. The tragic consequence of this struggle is that it divides, by an unreal partition, the mass of India's workers and peasants, whose interests are identical.

PAKISTAN

UNDER Mr. Jinnah's leadership, the Muslim League has now driven this feud to an extremity at which no compromise seems possible. This formidable man is as able as he is unbending, and he has brought the League under his own personal sway. A wealthy and successful lawyer, he was popular in Bombay and was during a great part of his political life a prominent figure in the Congress party, until a sharp dispute separated him from Gandhi. He is the last man who would naturally gravitate towards a party based on religion. He belongs to a sect commonly classed as heretical, and is linked by ties of marriage with the Parsi community. Though he wields immense power, he is not widely known to the masses, even of his own faith.

Mr. Jinnah's case is so simple and trenchant that it can be stated in a few lines. He denies the existence of an Indian nation and maintains that two distinct nations inhabit this peninsula, one Muslim, the other Hindu. Accordingly he proclaims the refusal of the Muslim minority to bow to the will of this alien Hindu majority. The only possible solution is separation. He therefore demands the creation of "independent sovereign states" in the north-western and eastern parts of the peninsula. To this Muslim state or states he gives the name of Pakistan.

If we grant Mr. Jinnah's premises his conclusion is irresistible. If Muslims and Hindus have in fact so little in common that they cannot work together as a nation, then they had better separate peacefully. To coerce even one unwilling province into an Indian federation would be criminal folly. But is the cleavage as deep as Mr. Jinnah now declares it to be? If so, it is strange that this able man should have discovered this basic fact of Indian life only in the last phase of a long public career. But, as we have seen, over the greater part of the field of political action, whether in the provinces or at the Centre, religion does not naturally intrude, and with a modicum of good sense need never intrude. The tendency in the two bigger Muslim provinces, the Punjab and Bengal, which have worked the present Constitution smoothly, is towards an alignment of parties on the basis of economic interests and functions. In the former, the Unionist Party, which represents mainly the landlords, is composed of Hindus and Sikhs as well as Muslims, and it enjoys a secure majority. In Bengal, a coalition held office for a time composed of the Muslim Peasant Party with a mainly Hindu group which has a similar agrarian policy and formerly belonged to the Congress Party. In both these provinces Muslims and Hindus have made the discovery that religious differences need be no obstacle to co-operation for common economic ends.

In effect Mr. Jinnah's position is that democracy is unworkable in India. Assuredly democracy can work smoothly only within a relatively homogeneous society, conscious of a unity that dwarfs the differences within it. Whenever two races, two religions or two classes flatly deny this unity, a revolutionary situation has arisen, which must end either in civil war or partition. Mr. Jinnah's logic seems flawless, until one notices that he applies it to any future Indian federation but not to the existing provinces. In all of these there is a religious minority, sometimes Muslim, sometimes Hindu. But in fact, in their legislatures, it does not happen—I think one may say it never happens—that a solid majority of one creed votes down a solid minority of the other. It is not apparent why an oppression which does not occur in the provinces must happen fatally and all the time at the Centre. This picture which Mr. Jinnah has conjured up of three Hindus invariably voting down one helpless Muslim is a creation of his fancy. This is a fallacy which democracy has often had to surmount. When the Levellers proposed manhood suffrage, Cromwell resisted on the ground that the landless majority would use their votes to abolish property. That fear delayed the coming of democracy to England for more than two centuries. The same ancient fallacy delayed the enfranchisement of women, for they too had a slight majority and might all have combined to vote down men. In fact the three Hindus are divided among themselves on lines of class and caste and will promptly bid against each other for the Muslim's support. In the last resort he is a tough fellow, capable of self-defence, and there are ninety millions of him. This nightmare of Mr. Jinnah's seems plausible only because we choose to classify Indians on theocratic lines.

Let us now examine Mr. Jinnah's practical solution, which has some manifest flaws. In the first place it would leave nearly a third of the Muslim population of British India still exposed to the mercy of the Hindu majority outside Pakistan, while within it there would be a big Hindu and a small Sikh minority. An exchange of populations has been suggested—a proposal as difficult to realise as it is repugnant. The uprooted Dravidian millions would find themselves in a strange land speaking an Aryan tongue. Again, it is hardly conceivable that Bengal as a whole should be included in Pakistan, for it has a Hindu minority numbering 25 millions. If its western portion were detached, the Sikhs of the Punjab would also ask to be excluded, while the Muslims of Assam might wish to be included. Again, it is not clear whether Bengal, separated from the Muslim North-West by a vast intervening territory, would form part of Pakistan or stand alone. Some have proposed to carve out a connecting corridor. So do the complications multiply: Indian geography is not as simple as Mr. Jinnah's logic.

The plausible aspect of the scheme is that the North-West of India, predominantly Muslim, does form a compact territory. To its three provinces (Punjab, Sind and N.W. Frontier) the state of Kashmir and tribal Baluchistan could be added. Some exponents of the scheme hope for a union with Afghanistan. In this way a big and overwhelmingly Muslim territory could be pieced together, speaking languages or dialects which are closely akin. But would this new birth be capable of life? Some of its territory is desert, or barren mountain, and much of it sparsely peopled. If the Punjab is relatively prosperous, the rest of it is poor. Two of these provinces, Sind and the North-West Frontier, have a standing deficit in their budgets, which compelled them to draw on the Centre. In Pakistan they would have to sponge on the Punjab. Worse still, the cost of defending the Frontier would fall on Pakistan. This is a formidable charge which accounted for a large part of India's military expenditure. It might be reduced by constructive aid to the wild tribes of the mountains, in the shape of roads, schools and assistance for the very little they can hope to develop in the way of industry and agriculture. Something has been done on these lines: more might be attempted, but, like blockhouses and barracks, it would cost money.

Some resources and advantages Pakistan can boast. It has a good port in Karachi. It is rich in rivers, as important for irrigation as for hydro-electricity. The coal it is said to possess in Baluchistan and Kashmir is of doubtful value and is still unworked. There is oil near Lahore, which for one reason or another has been worked only on a small scale. With these resources Pakistan could develop a number of light industries: a cotton industry already exists. But this country possesses neither iron ore nor coking coal. It follows that it could not create a heavy industry. It would remain a chiefly agricultural country, whose fertile regions would bear the cost of defending and policing its deserts and mountains.

This is not from the economic standpoint an alluring prospect, nor would it seem promising to a modern soldier. Man-power Pakistan would have of the first quality—though its Mohammedan soldiers are no better than the Sikhs and Rajputs. But it could never manufacture its own tanks, guns and aircraft, nor has it an exportable surplus of primary products of a volume that would enable it to import in sufficient quantities these indispensable aids to a just cause. In other words, until we can look forward to a disarmed world, the independence of Pakistan would be somewhat nominal. This conclusion may be at variance with the day-dreams of the more chauvinistic Muslims. I have heard them boasting of the ease with which they could reconquer Hindu India. They forget its steel mills, no less than its millions and its Mahrattas. If they imagine that Pakistan, standing on its own feet, could become a first-rate military power, they are living in the past.

We have still to consider the relationship of Bengal to Pakistan. Bengal is a relatively wealthy province, densely peopled, well-watered and in its western districts it has a growing heavy industry. It could meet the deficits of the poorer provinces: it might be able to pay for the defence of the North-West Frontier. But why should it take these burdens on its shoulders? With its participation, if it came in as a single whole, Pakistan might be capable of life: without it, the flimsy project loses much of its attraction. But it would be monstrous to force all Bengal into Pakistan. Its Muslim population is fairly compact and inhabits the region most distant from the rest of Pakistan—the East. The rest of Bengal, with its 25 million Hindus, cannot with any show of equity be included. It, however, is the industrial region. On the other hand, would the Bengalis consent to the division of their province? They took to terrorism when Lord Curzon did it and forced Lord Crewe to undo his partition, though there was much to be said for it on the score of administrative convenience. The unity of their province is dear to them and they are proud of their language. It is unlikely that a majority of the Bengali Muslims will ever vote for Pakistan, and certain that in any plébiscite of the whole population it would be overwhelmingly defeated. It is hardly necessary to probe further into the absurdities of this proposal. How, for example, will the army of western Pakistan ensure the defence of this remote and isolated eastern province? The Bengali Muslims, it may be noted, do not rank as a "martial race"; though that is no proof that they lack the military virtues. With Bengal, Pakistan would become at once a financial possibility and a geographical absurdity. Without Bengal, it is difficult to believe that the shrewd Punjabis will ever shoulder the economic burdens Mr. Jinnah's scheme would entail.

The reader may wish to know what support the demand for Pakistan can claim. The question cannot be answered with confidence. Outside the ranks of the Muslim League, whose total membership is not known, it can have little or no support, nor should it be assumed that all its members take the idea seriously. Mr. Jinnah's position seems to be that the demand of the League is enough, and he requires that the British Government and other Indian parties shall assent to it unconditionally. It is significant that he rejected Sir Stafford Cripps' suggestion of a plébiscite of the whole electorate in the provinces he claims. At that time it was doubtful whether any of them would have yielded even a bare majority and certain that some of them would have rejected it. Mr. Jinnah subsequently suggested a plébiscite of the Muslim electorate alone in these provinces—a test which no impartial authority could regard as appropriate. It may be that the idea is gaining in acceptance as men despair of a communal settlement. There is, however, a rather widespread doubt as to whether Mr. Jinnah himself is in earnest over this scheme. Is he soberly bent on realising it, or is it merely a bargaining counter, or a device for postponing indefinitely a federation of India on lines to which he is opposed? I do not know the answer to this question, but it is possible that though the plan may have been adopted originally as a tactical expedient, it has now become a political ideal which must be taken in earnest. My reason for supposing that Mr. Jinnah may have an eventual compromise in mind is that he has several times said that he would be prepared to co-operate with Hindus on terms of parity. That would be his condition for joining a national government as an *interim* arrangement for the conduct of the war. This is from his standpoint a logical proposal. If Muslims and Hindus are two separate nations, then, like sovereign powers, they must be regarded as equals. He insists, therefore, that ministerial posts shall be equally divided between them. This is an extravagant claim from a community which includes slightly less than a quarter of India's population. Hindus might be wise to accept it as a temporary concession during the war, but as a perma-nent rule it would prove intolerable. If it were to be pressed to its logical extreme, this principle of parity would also re-quire equality of numbers in the representative assembly of the federation.

If this should prove to be the only way of escape from a de-plorable deadlock, it might be preferable to imitate the struc-ture of the Austro-Hungarian dual monarchy. Its two halves formed separate states, united by the link of the Habsburg Crown, but they enjoyed internal free trade, a common system of defence, a common foreign policy and a linked system of communications. Delegations from their two parliaments met to discuss their common affairs. It was not an easy system to work, and it threw a heavy responsibility on the Crown. On this analogy, Pakistan and Hindustan would form two distinct federations, which would conduct their common affairs on a footing of parity. These common affairs would necessarily be confined to a somewhat limited field, but at least in this way economic conflict and civil war would be avoided, and the two would present a single front to the external world. But the British Crown could not serve as the indispensable link. The Indian fear that it would "rule to divide" would render that expedient unacceptable. There is nothing to be said for this solution, save that it would be preferable to total separation.

Separation few Englishmen could contemplate without a sense of defeat. Of the benefits which British rule has con-ferred on this peninsula, one stands out conspicuous and indisputable. We have given it unity, and with unity both internal peace and a vast free market for the produce of all its factories and fields. It obeyed a single system of law and there is in its world of thought the prospect of a marriage of cultures which it would be wicked to divorce. To erect once again a cactus hedge across this peninsula would be a crime against civilisation.

THE UNTOUCHABLES

THERE IS yet another minority whose case we must consider, and it may be convenient to do it here. The "depressed" or as they are now called the "scheduled" classes constitute the most painful and difficult social problem with which history has ever cursed a civilised people. The reader in considering it must summon his charity to his aid, as well as his pity. Europe never had any institution quite so degrading to human nature as this, but it may be well to recall the fact that serfdom was once universal throughout Christendom, that even in this island the Church itself owned serfs and that this mitigated species of slavery survived in Prussia down to 1808 and in Russia till 1861. The Negroes of the southern States are even now hardly "touchable" for the whites. The "untouchables" are and always were free men, but religion has laid on them the stains of degradation and uncleanness. They were aboriginals belonging to very backward races whom the Dravidians had conquered before the Aryans arrived. They remained outside the social systems of both these higher races, and to them fell the tasks which Hindus regard as unclean—sweeping, scavenging, working in leather and tanning. A group of them is to be found living at a little distance from most villages in abject poverty and squalor. They might not use the village well, nor might they, until very recently, enter its temple. They accepted their degradation meekly, as in the West Lazarus during the Age of Belief accepted his pre-ordained poverty. They believed that they were expiating in this life sins committed in a past existence. Our Western class divisions by no means coincide with the caste divisions of India.* Brahmans are often poor men: many of them earn their living as cooks. The untouchables are usually poor, landless proletariats but not always: some of them, as traders in hides, have become well-to-do. It must not be supposed that Indian society has always acquiesced in the institution of caste. For several centuries, the happiest period in the life of this peninsula, Buddhism, an essentially humane movement, swept it away. The Sikhs abolished it in their community. So did the Brahmo Somaj, the reformed Hindu Church, comparable to Unitarianism among Christians, which flourished among the intellectuals of Bengal during the last century and made a splendid contribution to the mental and moral growth of this nation. Above all, Congress under Gandhi's leadership has struggled in every possible way to rescue the untouchables from their degradation. Thanks mainly to it, the temples have now been thrown open to them pretty widely in many regions of India. I saw them serving as equals beside Brahmans in the volunteer "militia" of Congress. High-caste Hindus have opened schools and orphanages for their children. Gandhi made an untouchable girl his adopted daughter and took her

* The nearest parallel to caste in Europe is the rule of endogamy observed by its royal families and until recently by its prouder aristocracies, notably that of the old Dual Monarchy. Even in these cases, however, the rule was based on family traditions and not on religion. My own guess is that caste may have originated (if one accepts Mr. Hocart's theory of *Kingship* as he states it in his book with that title) with the royal Children of the Sun, who married their "sisters." Such rules tend to spread downwards in early societies, as on Mr. Hocart's showing the coronation rite did in the ceremonies of initiation and marriage. If "sister" be interpreted in a classificatory sense, we may have the origin of endogamy, which would appear first in the higher strata of society and then, as the Brahmans reduced life to a rigid system, in the lower also: *i.e.* this peculiar royal practice, when imitated, turned class into caste. Anthropologists will understand this too brief note, which I hope to develop in a later essay.

into his *ashram* (monastery). It was unworthy of Mr. Church-ill, usually a chivalrous opponent, to reproach Congress, of all parties, on this subject. All this, however, is only a begin-ning, an earnest of goodwill. An institution rooted in ancient habits of thought dies hard. Most of these unhappy men are still segregated, in their poverty, dirt and ignorance, as are the dwellers in our own slums, but with less hope of escape.

The easiest way of escape for these outcasts was to abandon the Hindu faith. Many in the past became Mohammedans. Islam, to its honour, knows nothing of caste or colour bar. In Turkey I have seen a Negro regimental officer commanding white troops. Some turned to Christianity, only to encounter our racial barrier. Dr. Ambedkar, the foremost of the leaders risen from the ranks of the depressed classes, adopted the Sikh religion. But it is only a small minority that is likely to avail itself of these paths to a happier status. Then can nothing be done by political means? It cannot be said that the British Government of India has done much for these unfortunates. Until very recently it used its police to exclude them from the temples, if ever they dared to force their way in. Little can be cited to testify to any constructive effort on its part to help them. Towards the end of last century it even excluded them from the army. So much Dr. Ambedkar has himself said in the plainest words.* But during the Round Table Conference they were raised to the dignity of a minority, which we are now pledged to protect. Mr. MacDonald proposed to give them, like Muslims, Sikhs and Christians, a separate communal elec-

* Speaking at the Round Table Conference, he said:—

"So far as we are concerned the British Government has accepted the social arrangements as it found them. . . . Our wrongs have remained as open sores and have not been righted, although 150 years of British rule have rolled away. We do not accuse the British of indifference or lack of sympathy but we do find they are quite incompetent to tackle our problem. . . . It [the Government] has not dared to touch any of these evils because . . . it is afraid its intervention . . . would give rise to resistance. Of what good is such a government to anybody?" (*Parl. Papers* 1931, Cmd. 3778, p. 133.)

torate of their own. Gandhi fasted by way of protest, and Dr. Ambedkar accepted a compromise which leaves them in the general Hindu electorate, while reserving for them a number of seats proportionate to their population. The results of this arrangement have been very interesting. Of these 151 reserved seats a majority, 78, were won in the provincial elections of 1937 by "untouchables" who stood as Congress candidates. Dr. Ambedkar's Labour Party won only 13 of these seats. Self-help is a sound principle and it is right and necessary that these proletarians should organise for their own protection. But need they do so separately? As landless labourers their economic interests do not differ from those of Hindu workers who stand above them on the ladder of caste, nor from those of Muslims. It would seem that in fact most of them are content to accept Congress as their champion. Dr. Ambedkar is a brave man who has fought a gallant battle against crushing odds. He would be a saint, if he could banish from his mind all hatred towards caste Hindus. But is he wise to use, as he seems to be doing, the veto which the Empire has thrust into his hands, to stave off the coming of Indian independence? However that may be, it is a mistake to assume that he has a right to speak for this vast "minority" of fifty millions. His following, devoted though it is in his own province of Bombay, is a mere fraction of that figure. The fact is, of course, that the vast majority of these unfortunates can hardly be said to have a political opinion. But they have all heard of Mahatma Gandhi and of what he has done for them. It goes without saying that the rights of this class as human beings and as citizens should be expressly recognised in India's future constitution, nor need it be emphasised that every Indian group and party which draws its inspiration from socialism or communism will in the future, as such groups do today, acknowledge its duty to these peculiarly helpless workers.

THE BRITISH ARBITER

IT WOULD be an evasion to conclude this chapter on Muslims and Hindus without some reference to our own conduct as arbiters. Have we sought to divide and rule? Indians with hardly an exception would answer with an emphatic affirmative: they assume it as a settled fact in all their discussions of our policy and history. Many, perhaps most Americans hold the same belief. Up to the Mutiny leading officials under the Company occasionally recommended it as a maxim of policy. English men of business in India will on occasion blurt it out today as an obvious truth which everyone takes for granted. This is not evidence. The situation lends itself inevitably to this suspicion and this interpretation. British rule could not have endured till today, if ever under good leadership the great mass of the two communities had for any length of time combined to end it, as under poor leadership during the Mutiny a part of them did. Can this risk fail to influence the calculations and policies of British statesmen and officials? But where on a crude view of the facts we do seem to be keeping the two apart, an innocent explanation is always possible. Even the most fatal instance, Lord Morley's separate communal electorates, can be excused by reference to a worthy motive. I have heard him defend it in private conversation, though his manner made on me the impression that he was not happy about what he had just done. Would not the two be less likely to quarrel, he argued, if they voted apart: would not contested elections, fought it may be on a low level of courtesy, aggravate their dissensions? If we classify them carefully and tabulate their rights with precision, it is because we mean to hold the scales even between them. Our tradition is that we arbitrate with as near an approch to impartiality as is humanly possible. This is, I do not doubt, a true account of what normally passes in the conscious mind of statesmen and officials. To discover any calculation or any aim more sinister than this, a psychologist would have to peer into the darkness of their sub-conscious processes. That is what Indians habitually do, and like all subject races they have sensitive antennae.

To speculate about motives is an unprofitable exercise. The sober student of this question will prefer to consider results. Two are obvious. In the first place, by classifying Indians according to creed in every conceivable relationship of public life we helped to make them abnormally conscious of their differences. They were haunted by religion—if this be religion—obsessed by it, until every other consideration that can unite men or divide them faded into the background. We labelled them Hindus and Muslims till they forgot they were men. In the second place, by dwelling on these differences and exalting our own function as arbiters, we persuaded ourselves and for a time we even persuaded some Indians that our rule was indispensable. Even now, when events have driven us to promise its early end, this theme of our sacred duty to the minorities constantly recurs in our official statements.

The historian, baffled in the attempt to read our motives, may turn to something less elusive, our political arithmetic. He may be startled, as perhaps the reader of the previous chapter was, when he discovers that Sir Samuel Hoare proposed to give the princes—but not their subjects—a voting power of 40 and 33 per cent in the two chambers of his federal legislature, though these subjects amount to only 23 per cent of the population of the Peninsula. He will marvel at the discovery that Sir Samuel over-estimated Muslims for voting purposes in comparison with Hindus in the proportion of two to one. On further research, he will discover that as usual in India this practice had tradition behind it. Lord Morley in the Morley-Minto reforms did the same thing in a still more staggering disproportion. To acquire a vote a Hindu must pay income tax on an income of Rs. 300,000, while a Muslim could achieve it with an income of Rs. 3,000: a Hindu graduate must have held his degree for thirty years, a Muslim for only three. To this principle the bureaucracy gives the name of "weightage." Chivalry and equity require that something should be done to weight the scales in favour of the minority. The historian, pondering on weightage, may next discover in the British Museum some persuasive arguments by Lord Morley in favour of the meticulously accurate system of proportional representation advocated by his friend Lord Courtney. Accuracy is for England, chivalry for India. Pursuing his enquiries, he may find that Mr. Ramsay MacDonald gave his name to some of these Indian communal awards. Now Mr. MacDonald was a somewhat violent opponent of proportional representation. But as I can testify at first hand, his view, which he would express with some heat, was that majorities rather than minorities should be accorded extra representation, in the interests of "strong government." But again, he too was thinking of Great Britain. In his bewilderment, the historian may then go on to scrutinise the minorities thus favoured by Lord Morley, Sir Samuel Hoare and Mr. MacDonald.* He will discover them without much trouble, in any of Mr. Churchill's speeches, arrayed on our side against Congress and "the extremists." He may sum up by applauding our "chivalry"—but I am hardly authorised to anticipate his conclusions.

The same historian, when he frames his questions, will have to consider not merely what we said but what we omitted to say. For half-a-century or more, every Secretary of State and every Viceroy has kept in his dispatch-case the notes of a stereotyped statement, which he has repeated with variations on every public occasion. The Simon Report made the case with ponderous detail and at inordinate length. Mr. Churchill will do it with a touch of passion and more than a trace of malice. We all know the pattern of this statement about India. It may mention the many languages and races. It mobilises all the interests opposed to Congress. It parades the statistics, not always impeccably accurate, of the minorities. And invariably

* Chivalry is a subjective principle, and we must be prepared for some caprice. In Mr. MacDonald's award the Hindus profit by it, as well as the Muslims, notably in Sind, where they are a small minority. But in Bengal, where they are a big minority, they are seriously underrepresented. But, as everyone knows, Bengali Hindus incline to disloyalty.

it dwells on the opposed religions and the depressed classes. Sometimes it is done in a tone of fatalistic regret, sometimes with an air of polemical triumph, but always the stress is on the divisions of India. And this India's rulers have been doing for fifty years and for much more than fifty years.

Was this the way to unite the jarring creeds? I can imagine an official speech on wholly different lines. Sometimes with Churchillian eloquence, sometimes with a touch of humour, but always with courtesy and persuasion it would have sought to induce Indians to forget their religious divisions. It might have reminded them that we once had our suspect Catholic minority and our dissenting untouchables. It might have communicated to Muslims and Hindus the discovery our fathers made long ago that creed is an irrelevance in modern politics. It might have asked them whether the Koran and the Vedic Hymns really differ irreconcilably over income tax, the rupee exchange and the best way of combating malaria and hookworm. If every day and in every way, each according to his temperament and opportunities, using the press and the wireless, schoolbooks and white papers, the officials and spokesmen of this mighty government had sought to minimise religious differences and promote an outlook of secular commonsense, and done this steadily for fifty years, is it certain that this feud would rage as it does today? They chose to make the other speech.

IV. Unity and Independence

Do INDIANS constitute a nation? For two generations the abler and more public-spirited of them have affirmed it. Mr. Jinnah is not the only man who has denied it: few of their English critics would concede it. The question has little practical importance. No one suggests that India should be a unitary state like France or the United Kingdom. The urgent political issue is whether an all-Indian federation can be created with a sense of unity strong enough to hold its many states and provinces together. The precedents of Switzerland, Canada and South Africa have taught us that two or more peoples, who differ in culture, language, history and religion, can work a federal machinery with success. Czechs and Poles, Greeks and South Slavs have now agreed to unite on a quasi-federal footing. Some of us believe that Europe must contrive to create preferably a true continental federation, but at least a closely-knit confederacy. In this species of union, it is not a necessity, though it may be an advantage, that its members, like the Australians or the Germans in the Weimar federal republic, should be conscious of a common nationality.

It is important, none the less, that we should decide this question in our own minds. We shall not understand Indians until we do. Round this theme of nationality the public life of the Peninsula has revolved for more than half a century. In English Liberals, from Byron to Lloyd-George, the idea of nationality has often stirred a deep and romantic emotion. Our own generation is more skeptical. We know what crimes and follies have been perpetrated in its name. We are aware of the sordid commercial motives and the pretensions to class ascendancy that may shelter behind it. We have come to doubt whether we shall ever be rid of war while it dominates men's minds. Can it unite men for good without dividing them for evil? Most of us incline to back a nation, and especially a little nationality, while it is fighting for its life against suppression; but when in the enjoyment of peace and freedom it stresses and organises the peculiarities that divide it from the rest of mankind, our sympathy turns to criticism. Yet, as Burke put it, in "the divine tactic of history" the "little platoons" in which we are ranged must contrive to march in step, and to them we owe both love and allegiance. Our national divisions may bring splendour to the life of humanity, if through them we can realise our unity amid diversity. Of all social experiences the most stimulating is the perception we enjoy in intercourse with Indian and Chinese friends that while we may differ in our beliefs as in our customs, our values in all that constitutes civilisation are the same.

The case for rejecting the Indian claim to nationality is so familiar that the briefest reminder should suffice to recall it. The anthropologist can distinguish several distinct racial stocks in this peninsula, as in our own island, intermingled in varying proportions. The diversity of languages is a real impediment to unity, though it is much less serious than most of us suppose. Only twelve languages need be reckoned. There are many more in Europe. Those of northern and central India, all of them derived from Sanskrit, are so closely akin that a quick-witted man who speaks one of them can with very little practice understand most if not all of the others with ease: the more individual Bengali is an exception. The Dravidian languages of the South are similarly akin. Hindustani, with its variant Urdu, and for the middle and upper classes English serve as common languages. The question of religion in relation to nationality we have discussed already.

By far the most serious obstacle to social unity comes from caste and its rule of endogamy, while the same prohibition of intermarriage and eating together separates strict Hindus from Muslims. But even of caste it must be said that while it divides, it also unites. A Brahman from the torrid tip of the Peninsula, whose mother-tongue is Dravidian, always felt himself the blood-brother of a Brahman reared among the Himalayan snows whose mother-tongue is Aryan. They would always dine together and intermarry. Muslims of South and North had the same sense of fraternity. But caste, as history describes it, is already a thing of the past. The promiscuity of factories and railway trains did much to break it down. The spread of rationalism and nationalism did more. Today it is only the older and stricter Hindus who observe the rules about eating and drinking apart. Marriages between Brahman women and men of lower caste are now fairly frequent, since some of the leaders of Congress set the example: indeed, my Indian friends tell me that they can now happen without an inner struggle or a painful division within the closely-knit Hindu family. Even in the South, under the influence of Congress, Brahmans are now making a practice of dining publicly with "untouchables." Liberal Hindus and Muslims will now eat together as a matter of course, but intermarriage between Muslim women and Hindu men is still difficult, if not impossible. Even this barrier will yield to time: it can endure only as long as the tabu on social intercourse. There are now young Muslim women, though as yet only the daring pioneers, who go about unveiled and enter general society.

As a consciously-held idea nationality is in India a recent growth. It is, even in Europe, a relatively modern development. Wellington said that among the Indians of his day the Mahrattas alone possessed it. During the period of the British conquest not adventurers only but princes of old families would side with the intruding power, as they had done during earlier invasions, without any sense of treachery to their native land. There are parallels in English history, up to Marlborough's day. Was the Mutiny a nationalist movement? Certainly it sprang from a sense that the differences between British and Indian ways were in kind and degree in a new class and of another order from those that separate the peoples of this peninsula. The unity achieved at this time may have been racial rather than national. Our own determination to remain foreigners in India, together with our arrogance, began it and fostered it to this day. The Mutiny was in part a reactionary

movement, a recoil from our disturbing and alarming innova-
tions—even from our railway trains which suggested black
magic. This reaction, one of the inevitable effects of conquest
on men of spirit, made itself felt long after the Mutiny and is
not wholly spent. Gandhi reflects it. Indians turned back with
an uncritical veneration to the Hindu past, idealised it, exaggerated its achievements in revels of fantasy and closed their
minds to any criticism of its defects. Some turned their backs
on science and revived its empirical system of medicine. Others
defended its ancient superstitions and its patent social evils.
Even the best we had to give, our science and the relative
humanity of our social structure, came to Indians linked with
our racial insolence and our economic self-seeking. But this
attitude is typical no longer of Indian nationalism. Today it
is the pride of India that her sons, several Nobel prize-winners
among them, contribute to the common culture of mankind.

Nationalism, as Mazzini understood it, may be a new force
in India, but long before the conquest this peninsula had its
common heritage of culture. Nor was the love of a beautiful
Motherland absent. The sacred duty of pilgrimage, often to
the remotest rivers and shrines, began it and came to express
it. Once in his life every Hindu aspired to see the Ganges.
Travelling afoot, he was everywhere received as a brother.
When the obstacle of Babel may have been more baffling than
it is today, there was evolved in prehistoric times that subtle
and elaborate sign-language, which is still legible in the gestures of Indian dances. Underneath the variety which history
and many invasions have brought to India, there survives
everywhere, in the tools men use, in the habits and customs of
daily life, in folklore and even in religion an underlying unity,
which is doubtless Dravidian in origin. The toy carts of clay,
dug up after five thousand years in the Indus Valley, are exact
models of those which its peasants use today. The exquisitely
engraved seals of the same period have themes whose meaning
scholars can decipher, because they are drawn from rituals
and myths that still survive. Shiva was God Almighty then as
he is still. But this unity is much more than an antiquarian

curiosity. It is something embedded in the Indian mind and even in the Indian body, something latent in the genes of this race, a physiological as well as a psychological fact. The foreigner detects it in the movements, gestures and tones of Indians, above all when they sing and dance. A habit in expression must reflect a way of feeling. These movements and gestures, especially of the hands and arms, have a grace and delicacy unknown in the West. The scale of expression is slighter, more economical and incomparably subtler than ours, though the sense for structure may be less developed. When our ears and eyes grow accustomed to the unfamiliar range and scale of movements and song the aesthetic effect can be intensely moving and even dramatic. Derive this habit of expression, as you please, from heredity or education, it bespeaks a common racial tendency. Assemble a group of Indian musicians. Their only common language may be English. Yet without a score, on their instruments, they will together improvise, as gypsies do, an elaborate composition, following a traditional pattern, upon a rhythm which the drummer indicates. What do we mean by a common culture? Is it a system of beliefs and opinions, a series of categories, a set of ethical values? Doubtless it is all this, enshrined in literature and art. But more important than all this is our way of reacting and responding to life, in lines, movements and tones, our habits of utterance which betray character. This cultural unity Indians possess, and the Muslims share it with the Hindus.

CENTRE AND PROVINCES

THE KIND of unity which federation requires is something more prosaic and less unusual. On the material plane it exists already. This peninsula is geographically a natural unit more solid and compact than Europe, and we have given it a good system of communications by sea, air, and rail. British India has had for several generations a system of law and administration and an economic structure which erred, if it did err, on the side of uniformity. The same civil and criminal codes are everywhere applied according to the same legal procedure. The vast administrative machine, whether it deals with the revenue, the police, forestry and what not, moves according to a uniform routine with few provincial variations. Of all the unifying forces the most patent has been education, though rightly and properly, as self-government developed, provinces and even cities have begun to give it some regional or local individuality. In the economic field the currency and customs were unified at an early date, under the Company. In spite of its formidable distances, India is in actual fact as well as by law a single market open to all its producers. Legislation in such fundamental matters as the Factory Acts has made the conditions of work uniform in modern concerns throughout its provinces. The only obstacles to the growth of internal trade on a gigantic scale is the poverty of the village and the self-sufficiency that belong to its oldest traditions. It usually buys salt and paraffin from the outer world and often cotton cloths and some tools; but there is still many a village in which the hereditary craftsmen, who serve it for an allowance of grain, or some acres of free land, will weave all the cloth it needs, hammer its hoes for it and turn its pots.

On this basic foundation of uniformity, a political structure has been erected which can readily be adapted to a true federal pattern. British India is divided into eleven provinces, comparable to the States of the American Union, which up to the early months of this war were functioning happily as self-governing units. Their boundaries might in several cases be redrawn with advantage, for they seldom correspond accurately to linguistic areas. But they will serve well enough to make a start. A demarcation exists between the functions and powers of the central government and those of the provinces. To adapt it to the eventual form of the future federation will be a thorny and difficult undertaking, likely to arouse prolonged controversy: but, again, for a start and during the *interim* period, the present arrangement will serve. There is already an

All-India Legislative Assembly, which serves as some index of opinion, though it rests on a painfully restricted franchise and is constantly over-ruled by the Viceroy. But even this impotent body might possibly be turned to use in the *interim* period. In this matter of the relative powers and importance of Centre and provinces, Congress and the Hindus generally tend to exalt the Centre, while the Muslims, if they are prepared to accept federation at all, would enlarge the powers of the provinces. For this ominous division of opinion there is a crude and simple explanation. In four of the eleven provinces the Muslims have a majority. The Hindus, on the other hand, if we must continue to think in these fallacious religious terms, will have a majority at the Centre—unless, indeed, Mr. Jinnah's too exacting demand of parity were accepted. There is, perhaps, another and subtler reason, why Congress lays what it seems to me is an excessive stress on the unification of India. Indian nationalists have had to struggle for this idea of nationhood against their British opponents, against all the baffling obstacles of history, almost one might say against the facts. In the deep places of their minds they know very well how precarious this unity is, and that is precisely why they must affirm it with passion.

I realised this during some frank talks with Gandhi in 1931, while the Round Table Conference was sitting. I shared his fears that any plan of federation likely to emerge from it would be unworkable, unacceptable and even dangerous. I thought he might do well to delay it and might have to reject it—which was in the end what the chief Indian parties did. But I differed from him in his estimate of the plan of provincial autonomy. Faulty though it was, I thought it both workable and valuable—as in the event it proved to be. I ventured to suggest to him that nine-tenths of what was needed to raise the level of the peasant's existence—questions of health, land-tenure, schools, debt, and the improvement of farming—could be dealt with in the provinces and depended only indirectly on the Centre. Further, I suggested to him that if strong and popular governments, loyal to the Indian idea, had for a few years won a firm base for action in the provinces, they might boldly seize the initiative, call a National Congress jointly, form a federation themselves, and present the accomplished fact to Whitehall. I conceded that this would be a bold and quasi-revolutionary course, but I predicted that reasonable men in England would view it with comprehension and even with respect as a constructive act. Meanwhile, I begged him to improve the provincial plan if he could, but in any event to accept it and work it. He dismissed the whole of this reasoning with a degree of irritation that astonished me. In the long run he did so far change his mind that in 1937 he consented to work the provincial scheme and Congress formed the administrations of eight of the eleven provinces. But in 1939 he threw this immense advantage away by calling on these governments to resign. From first to last the achievement of national unity has engaged the passionate interest of Congress: provincial self-government was for it a secondary matter. For this there was, round about 1930, an intelligible explanation. The Simon Report had conceded the autonomy of the provinces, but it had argued that Indians were unfit for any advance at the Centre. It was only natural that they should react as they did. At the Centre they located the citadel of our empire over them: all their strategy was directed to its conquest. It may be that they still underrate the importance of the provinces. From a realistic standpoint the justification for their view is that at present the provinces are largely dependent on the Centre for their revenues, a fact which sets a severe limit to the expansion of the social services.

The problems of the future federal constitution are too intricate for more than a mention here: they fall, moreover, to Indians and not to us for decision. There is much to be said for the idea of embodying in it, what was lacking in the abortive Act of 1935, a charter of civil and political rights, with a supreme court as its guardian. This would help to reassure the minorities: there is, however, a risk that, as in the United States, the court might become the watchdog of property. Again, the Muslims or the more conservative of them, can be placated by a division of powers and functions which allots the minimum to the Centre and the maximum to the provinces. This sacrifice may have to be faced, but it will mean that any hope of economic planning on a large scale will have to be abandoned. That would be suicidal. Social legislation, also, would be endangered. A progressive province will hesitate to make its Factory Act more stringent or to raise the cost of its social services, if industries which compete with its own enjoy easier conditions and lighter taxation in neighbouring provinces. This difficulty is a notorious impediment to social reform in the United States. The franchise presents several thorny problems. Congress, in spite of the general illiteracy, boldly and rightly demands universal suffrage.

The illiteracy of the village is a less serious obstacle than might be supposed. Its social structure is usually so homogeneous that the evils from which it suffers press on all alike. It tends, therefore, to think as a unit, and consequently when it has made up its mind, it votes solidly. At the worst it is split into two factions, each of which may vote as a block. There is usually at least one man who can read. I have watched the peasants sitting under a shady tree at evening to listen with close attention to the leading articles of the popular newspaper of the district. On one occasion, the clever man of the village read aloud first the Hindu and then the Muslim newspaper: some discussion followed. If the radio is developed as it should be, a loudspeaker should be installed free in every village, as in Russia, for instruction and entertainment. In the Punjab the Government subsidised touring companies of actors, whose plays sometimes conveyed a rather bold and salutary social moral. Some, to lessen this difficulty of illiteracy as well as that of the vast numbers involved, have suggested indirect election at one or two removes. Villagers might be grouped, say, in twenties: each of these groups would send a man to an electoral college which would choose the member for the constituency. Given well-organised peasants' leagues in a free community this plan might work well, but in the conditions that prevail today a landlord would find it even easier to intimidate one man or to bribe him than to deal with twenty. It would, however, be preferable that each village should elect a small council, a soviet or *panchayat*, to manage its affairs, and that this should send a representative to the electoral college or district council. The existing provisions for the representation of special interests—landlords, chambers of commerce, Europeans, among others—raise another set of difficulties. But the chief trouble centres in the communal electorates. Much as Congress dislikes them, it may have to appease the Muslims by prolonging their existence for a period of years. Without Muslim consent it will not be possible to get rid of them. In India a determined minority can usually get its way. The least controversial reform might be to adopt the plan of reserved seats accepted for the depressed classes. This ensures to the minority an allowance of seats in proportion to its numbers. But any elector may vote for any candidate—a plan which tends to discourage fanatics. To my thinking the best way of escape from this classification of men by religion would be to group them by occupation. Hindus and Muslims would vote together as peasants, industrial workers, miners, teachers, doctors and so forth. The choice of candidates should not be restricted to the occupational group. Peasants, for example, might wish to elect Gandhi and teachers Nehru, both of them lawyers. This is, of course, the Soviet system in its earlier form. It is interesting that Mr. Amery,* as well as Pandit Nehru, has advocated this radical solution. An experiment with it is being made in Hyderabad State. I will not dwell upon it, since it is for Indians to solve their own problems. I mention it in order that the pessimistic reader may realise that ways of escape from the religious tangle can be discovered. There were moments during my stay in India when I felt tempted to do what Shelley did in Ireland—to scatter broadcast a tract on *The Necessity of Atheism*. The publication for use in higher schools of an easy abbreviation of *The Golden Bough* might be even more useful. But without any frontal attack on religion as a force that divides mankind, its political entrench-

* *India and Freedom*, p. 31.

ments can be turned by methods that need not offend a good man's faith. On the essentials of conduct, a man's duty to his neighbours, Hindus and Muslims are not divided.

THE PRINCES' STATES

WE HAVE still to face the gravest of the difficulties that confront federation. Hitherto we have dealt only with the provinces under direct British rule and ignored the princes' states, which cover a third of the area of the peninsula and include a quarter of its population. Federation might, indeed, begin with the provinces, leaving the states as they are, under the suzerainty of the Crown. This dualism could only be provisional. In a very short time it would become intolerable. The territories of the states are scattered in a baffling patchwork in and around the provinces. Questions of defence, customs and communications are common to both. In race, language and religion the states repeat the pattern of British India. But the difficulties in the way of union are formidable in spite of this identical heritage from history. To begin with, the states number no less than 562 units, which range in area from the acreage of Hyde Park to that of the kingdom of Italy. Most of them are so small and so poor, that even if they were well-governed, they could not support the cost of a civilised administration. A group of these dwarf states might be able to finance the hospitals and higher schools their peoples need, but not one alone. Congress has proposed to group them in units with a minimum population of two million inhabitants. In other cases the territories of a prince are widely scattered, or else they cut across linguistic boundaries, as those of some provinces also do—a defect which makes needless difficulties for the administration and especially for the schools. A dictator with a good map in front of him and the statistics of the latest census would make short work of this confusion. But the least of these petty rulers can claim his rights as a sovereign, secured to him and his heirs for ever, through grant or treaty by the King-Emperor.

The next difficulty is that these states show an equal diversity in the level of their civilisation and the quality of their administration. Some of them, especially Mysore, Travancore and Baroda, are progressive, well-governed, and in some important matters ahead of British India. Like other travellers before me, I felt in Baroda an atmosphere of contentment and happiness which I encountered nowhere under British rule. There are other states in this fortunate class, but they are the exceptions. In general the states are backward and reactionary. Some of them retain a feudal system reminiscent of medieval Europe, under which their subjects are bound to perform the most onerous servitudes to the prince, to supply him on demand with food and contributions for feasts and other solemn occasions, and even to perform forced *corvée* labour for his benefit. In few of them are the civil rights of citizens respected, and there is rarely any liberty of the press or of association. Until lately there was hardly even a pretence of distinguishing between the state budget and the prince's private purse: he taxed as he pleased and took what he pleased: even now such improvement as there is is largely nominal. The prince fairly often appropriates a third or a fifth of the total revenue of his state. In 1926 the Raja of Jamnagar took £700,000 out of £1,000,000. Custom expects only a lax standard of personal conduct from the prince or his favourites. In short, most of these princes are autocrats and few of them are remarkable for their benevolence. Indians, it may be, are less impatient of personal rule than Europeans, and are said to prefer it, if it reaches an average level of decency, to the cold efficiency of our bureaucracy. In only twenty-three of the 562 states is there a consultative council of sorts: in the best of them it is elected at least in part and exerts some influence: in only one enlightened little state, Aundh, is there responsible self-government. Some check upon oppression is exercised by the British Residents and Political Agents, but it must be gross and notorious before they intervene: when they do so, the prince may be exiled or even deposed. But the prevalent belief in India is that Residents are usually more exacting in requiring a loyal and submissive attitude towards the paramount power than in imposing even a moderate standard of good government. The princes are tenants at will and most of them are aware of blots on their record to which the Resident could point, if they should incur his displeasure. Some of them, moreover, are so unpopular with their subjects that they could not maintain themselves were it not that British troops are available to restore what is misnamed "order." On occasion they have in fact been used for this purpose. There is no pretence of equality in this feudal relationship. As Lord Reading wrote in 1926 to the Nizam of Hyderabad, the greatest of the princes, in rejecting a claim of his which was at least arguable:

The Sovereignty of the British Crown is supreme in India, and therefore no Ruler of an Indian State can justifiably claim to negotiate with the British Crown on an equal footing.

It is their perception of this relationship of dependence which dominates the attitude of Indian nationalists towards the princes as a body. They look like Indians, but are in fact the bodyguard of the British Viceroy. Any proposal to bring them into Indian politics is inevitably viewed with suspicion. They would be, in any federal assembly, what "the King's men" were in the House of Commons of the eighteenth century, a disciplined faction which in crucial divisions would vote under the eyes, if not under the direction of the Imperial power. To dream of independence, or even of self-government if the Indian Union started with this handicap, would be to cherish a very silly illusion. Even if this fear could be dismissed as excessive, the fact remains that the princes would form a nearly solid conservative and even reactionary block. Their interests and outlook are those of great landowners, like the rest of their class in India, passive receivers of tribute, who perform no useful social or economic function. If they wielded, as was proposed in the Act of 1935, a third or more of the votes in the federal legislature, the chance that a progressive government would ever hold office would be negligible. This reasoning assumes that the princes would nominate the delegations from their states and expect them to vote as required. The word used in the Draft Declaration which was the brief of the Cripps Mission was "appoint." With very few, if any, exceptions, as things stand today, that is a reasonable reckoning. British Conservatives are usually frank in their utterances on this subject. They would call in the Old World to redress the balance of the New. Medieval India is to act as a barrier against Hindu radicalism and the spectre of social revolution. These are reckless and provocative tactics. If anything in our own staid island could arouse a revolutionary temper, it would be a rash use of the Lords' veto. The habitual use of the princes' votes to serve the interests of property would have in the hotter climate of India an even more explosive effect.

On this question, the attitude of Congress and other Indian progressives is what any democrat would expect of them. They aspire to a union of all India, and realise that without the princes' states it would be not merely incomplete but in the long run unworkable. But they insist that any state which enters the federation must be represented by a delegation freely elected by its people. This condition, as Congress made clear in its comments on the Cripps offer, must apply to the constituent assembly which draws up the constitution of the federation. This should not surprise us. Legal experts were mobilised, when the Act of 1935 was drafted, to study every model and precedent for federation. In no recorded instance have autocratic states federated with democratic states. It may be said that in the fulness of time, under the pressure of Indian public opinion, the princes would, one by one, give way, if they were within the federation, and would emancipate their subjects. That may be a correct forecast. But it would be a slow, anxious and turbulent process, which would put the statesmanship of the young commonwealth to an excessively severe test, for it might be complicated by issues both of class and religion. In the two biggest states, Hyderabad and Kashmir, the princes and the majority of their subjects are not of the same faith. The federation might have to send its troops to support an obstinate autocrat—an odious duty which might break it. But the chief objection to the easy-going solution of leaving this matter for time to settle is that the vote of the princes would at the constituent assembly and during the early formative years give to the federation an ultra-conservative structure, which might in after years prove difficult to amend. The princes, who cling to all the rights and trappings of sovereignty, would combine with the more conservative Muslims to reduce the powers and functions of the federation to the barest rudiments. This the Muslims, with scores of millions behind them, have every right to do, if they choose, but five hundred titled landlords ought not to weight the scales.

The straightforward way out of this tangle is that the provisional government of British India, when it invites the states to send their representatives to the constituent assembly, should stipulate that they shall be elected under conditions and by a franchise not less liberal than those which obtain in the provinces of British India. It is probable that in the atmosphere of hope and exultation which should prevail at this proud moment in Indian history, few of the princes would dare to refuse. If they did, the struggle between them and their subjects would be sharp but short—on one condition. It is that the paramount power should refrain from supporting the more reactionary princes. The proper course would be that the Viceroy should at the earliest possible moment issue a statement to the effect that the states must, like the rest of us, respect the ideals for which the United Nations fought, and that if they oppose the reasonable claims of their peoples, they can expect no support from the paramount power. That, in nine cases out of ten, would ensure a peaceful transformation. If in the tenth case it should be necessary to send troops, the prince should pay the suitable penalty for misgovernment —deposition. In our Indian record nothing has become us so ill as our maintenance of the gaudy and barbarous anachronism most of these states still are. In return for their submission, we have tolerated conditions that have kept scores of millions of Indians in a stagnant backwater, as unwholesome as it was outmoded. The relatively happy conditions of Mysore, Travancore, Baroda and two or three more of these states serves only to throw into relief the neglect and exploitation that prevail elsewhere. Into the legal intricacies of this question I have not thought it necessary to enter. Whatever be our obligations to these princes, we have always exacted some minimum standard of good government. Can we in the twentieth century reckon autocracy under that head?

WHAT IS INDEPENDENCE?

FOR THE first time, in 1929, Congress startled other Indians by a plain demand for "independence." Its use of the word was at that time tactical: in fact, Gandhi would have been satisfied with the status of a Dominion. If he could have got it then without equivocation and delay, he would have accepted the unavoidable transitional arrangements. Before this date, Mr. Gokhale had looked forward to "colonial self-government" in a somewhat distant future, while Mr. Tilak towards the end of his life flung himself into an agitation for immediate "home rule." Congress before 1930 had been content to use the vague but expressive term "swaraj" (self-rule). Today, when it says "independence" it means it, in the fullest juridical sense of the word. Not the least significant fact in the situation that now confronts us is that the other Indian parties, including the Muslim League, have had to come into line with it.

What, then, do Indians mean by "independence"? I put this question recently to a very able Indian friend. He paused for a moment and then replied: "I mean a state of things in which the British Government can no longer play off Muslims against Hindus and the princes against both." This is, I believe, what Indians chiefly mean by the word, though it may not be all they mean. If India were a Dominion, with the status laid down in the Statute of Westminster, and her right of secession expressly recognised, this definition would be satisfied. The tactics of division could no more be used against her than they can be used—where it would be equally easy to use them—against Canada or South Africa. That they can be used during her difficult passage to the status of a Dominion is, however, only too obvious. Thereafter the subtler risks that might infringe the reality of her independence would be of another order—the risks which lie in wait for every national state that has to depend on others for financial or military aid. If political conditions, expressed or implied, are attached to the grant of this assistance, to that extent its independence is infringed and may become a far from splendid illusion. But for the time being the attention of Indians is chiefly focussed on an objective more easily attainable. They want to shape their own future without our interference, be it interested or benevolent.

The Dominion pattern would satisfy this ambition. But neither the name nor the thing has any magic for Indians. We had talked about it through so many years of an always restless and unhappy relationship and relegated it so often to a distant and undated future, that few Indians could hear the word without irritation. The idea has for us associations that mean nothing to them. For us the Dominions are countries peopled by our kinsmen. There our own family names recur: the arrival of letters that link sundered brothers is an event to which we look forward, and so are the pilgrimages which cousins, born overseas, make to what is still for them "the home country." The political relationship, vaguely defined, with no organised institutional structure, befits the informal dealings of kinsmen. This tie, unlike anything else in history or the contemporary world, works best when the Dominion is solidly Anglo-Saxon, as New Zealand is, and very ill when it is alien in blood, as Eire is. What can this model mean to Indians—a people foreign to us in blood, speech and culture, whose memories are not of any cradle in this island, but of the great days when Asoka ruled with mercy and Akbar with tolerance? The mother and daughters analogy is ludicrously inappropriate here. Nor is there here the basis of casual, easygoing confidence that enables us to carry the Dominions with us in our external policy through the simple process of exchanging cablegrams and talking with their agents in London. All told, their white populations number little more than half our own. India, if she achieves her unity and prospers in liberty, will one day be conscious of a place in the family of mankind rather higher than we commonly assign to her. If ever these four hundred millions, literate, awakened, well-nourished and well-housed, attain self-respect with freedom, India will rank high among the great powers. Would the Dominion idea fit a member of that stature? Finally, let us realise that no tie of sentiment will ever link India with the other Dominions. Their empty spaces are not for her crowded millions. All of them have in one form or another erected against her emigrants the insult of a colour-bar.

It is, then, probable, if our future relationship with India is determined by any method resembling that of the Cripps offer, that she will avail herself, promptly or at an early date, of the right to secede from the British Commonwealth I am making throughout this chapter the speculative assumption that in spite of Mr. Churchill's Mansion House Speech, we would let her go. Sentiment will carry her powerfully in that direction. On the other hand, it is hard to see what Indians can have to gain by insisting, as Gandhi would now do, that their independence should be recognised in legal form at once. Would much or anything be gained in time, if the intermediate stage, during which India ranked as a Dominion, were omitted? Probably not. During the war, while British and Allied troops operate on Indian soil under a British Commander-in-Chief, the word "independent" might be used as a matter of courtesy, and changes might be rapidly made in ceremonial matters: but would this be "independence" as the word is commonly understood? Innumerable questions of detail, some of them of considerable importance, would have to be settled by negotiation before the separation could be completed—matters connected with the currency, the Reserve Bank, the debt, the rights of civil servants, the status of British residents and companies in India, and much else to which it would be folly to devote time and attention while the war had still to be won. Again, in the military sense, India, however frankly we might be willing to concede her political independence, could not stand alone, either during the war or for some time after it, and a treaty of alliance would have to be negotiated with the United Nations. In their councils India would possess the weight to which her realisable resources, human and industrial, entitled her. Provided that she had a national government which possessed the confidence of her people, it would make little difference whether it was in legal form the Viceroy's Executive Council, the responsible cabinet of a Dominion or the central authority of an independent Indian commonwealth. In any event, whatever her legal standing, India cannot consolidate her eventual federal structure until after the advent of peace, and even then, the process cannot be rapid. This is at all times a realistic world, but especially is it so amid total war. India will be as independent as the right hands of her armed men, her steel-mills and her engineering shops make her. Parchments and proclamations cannot confer independence, they can only describe what muscle and steel have won.

For the rest Indians would be wise to recognise that the method laid down in the Cripps offer, the road to independence through Dominion status and, if they choose it, secession is for them and for us the smoothest and not the longest. I cannot argue that our conduct towards them has in the past been so considerate that we have a right to ask from them some respect for our pride as a great empire. We must in any event face a surrender of power which is for the old-fashioned imperialist difficult and repugnant. Happily that old-world possessive attitude towards empire has grown steadily less confident and sure of itself since the early years of this century. But there are ways of surrendering power which fit our habits of thought and involve no sense of humiliation or defeat. The road through Dominion status has this merit.

Rightly or wrongly, the kind of surrender which Gandhi demanded, even if in details he consented to compromise, would affront all that is worst and much that is best in our instinctive and traditional attitude to life. If Indians reject the smooth and easy road, they will not win independence more quickly, and they may bring on themselves and on us a tragic and ruinous struggle, from which all that is sane and constructive in both our nations recoils in horror. Nothing in the logic of history requires it.

It would be wise and generous on our part, none the less, as an earlier page has argued, to use the word "independence" without hesitation. Let our solution be, when we revise the Cripps formula, an offer of independence, which Indians shall enjoy, at their free choice, within the British Commonwealth or outside it. But when this is said, Indians must join us in facing the fact that by two parallel lines of development the old-world concept of national sovereignty and independence has been profoundly modified in our generation, first by technical changes and then by the reaction to them of our social thinking. Never again will the gallantry of a little nationality find in its dykes, or mountains defensible ramparts for its independence. An industrially backward country, even if its man-power enables it to mobilise greater armies than the aggressor can put into the field, may have to abandon for a period of years, as China has had to do, immense and fertile territories, counting itself fortunate that vast distances and poor communications enable it to prolong its resistance in the far interior. Its hopes of recovering what it has lost depend on the precarious help it receives from wealthier powers which can manufacture the arguments of justice. In these days, when the Panzer divisions range at will over Europe, while a thousand bombers scatter ruin in a single night over her cities, how many nations are effectively independent? Mechanized warfare, but more especially air-power, have shattered the old-world concept of sovereignty. Independence has become what mathematicians would call a function of heavy industry.

In reaction against this brutal fact, how far and how fast

will social morality carry us towards an international organisation built on law, democracy, and mutual aid? That is a secret of the unknown future. The phrases of the Atlantic Charter are deliberately vague, and General Smuts, who doubtless reflects the main trend of Anglo-American policy, has warned us that such international organisation as may come into existence will be less ambitious than the Genevan League. Charters and covenants, councils and assemblies, formal definitions of right and obligations, are out of fashion. The prevalent conception of the future, if I grasp it correctly, is that the lesser states will accept the leadership of the two powers which possess an overwhelming superiority of military and industrial might, and these in turn will admit their smaller neighbours to informal and friendly consultation. The model for the world, as Mr. Herbert Morrison has told us, will be the British Commonwealth. Regional councils, a Pacific council, for instance, may continue to discuss the common affairs of the United Nations, but in the last resort the decision to set in motion the fleets, naval and aerial, of Britain and America, or to make available their manufacturing resources for the assistance of others will lie with the governments of Washington and London, and not with any international authority. In other words, the creation of an organically international police force subject to an international government lies in the distant future. In a degree difficult to foresee, the nature and amount of the assistance, military and economic, on which lesser powers can rely will depend on their willingness to conform to British and American policy. How much, for instance, will they receive if their economic tendencies are radical enough to incur the disfavour of Wall Street and the City? The picture is complicated by the existence of a mighty third focus of military power in Moscow, which enjoys less intimate relations with the other two. How long will it be possible to deny to Germany and Japan any place in this pattern of power? There is not in this dim vision of the post-war world much scope for independence as it has hitherto been conceived. As a social and ethical ideal many of us have outgrown it and will see it vanish without regret. This view of the future may for the moment flatter British and American patriotism. But to accept dependence without a federal structure and without representative institutions will not indefinitely satisfy the rest of mankind. It is already possible to foresee some of the ways in which nations of the second and third rank, facing the colossal bulk of the three surviving armed Great Powers, will endeavour to counter-balance their hegemony. They will try by regional groupings and costly armaments to alter the balance of power. Some will form a confederacy with their neighbours, as the Czechs and Poles and also the Greeks and South Slavs propose to do. Any group of states, like the first of these two pairs, that has the natural resources on which heavy industry and the manufacture of machine tools can be based, will endeavour at any cost to develop these sources of power. Not all of them are in this fortunate case—the second pair is not. It is a restless and unstable prospect and across it there may sweep revolutionary tides which as yet we cannot measure.

It is against this background that the problems of India's independence have to be envisaged. Her numbers promise her what her poverty denies—the stature of a great power. She has in abundance and high quality the iron which heavy industry requires, but she is still far from being able to supply herself unaided with the more elaborate weapons of mechanized warfare. It is to be expected that as soon as she governs herself, she will for economic as well as military reasons develop her heavy and machine-tool industries. She will also hasten to give her army its due complement of field and staff officers. Will she, for the sake of safety, during these early years content herself with the status of a Dominion, so that she may enjoy the protection of the British Commonwealth—a guarantee not quite as absolute as it looked before this war? Or will she gamble on the chance that no major war is likely to surprise the world for a decade at least? In that case, will she promptly exercise her right of secession?

It would be rash to venture on a confident prediction. The

ties formed by soldiers, lawyers, engineers and traders through two centuries may hold for a time, even if the sentimental bond is weak, and there are conservative Indians who may hesitate to break altogether with the past. But we may have to adjust ourselves to the prospect of a legal separation, which need not be an obstacle to friendly and helpful relations. There are tendencies which may carry India out of the British Commonwealth and into association with her Asiatic neighbours. They cannot be traced to her past history. This peninsula, until Europeans began to trade with it from armed ships and fortified "factories," had lived a life of relative isolation. From it Buddhist missionaries had carried its ideas over the Himalayas and across the seas. Muslim invaders had often penetrated it. But the rules of caste forbade Hindus to cross the dark ocean, nor did the Mogul Empire aspire to play a part beyond its natural boundaries. In our own day Muslims have been conscious of their links with other peoples of their own faith, more especially in the years immediately after the first World War. But even in the East religious sympathy is a diminishing force in international politics. The Turks have secularised their republic. Arabs, scattered over the immense belt of territory from the Atlantic to the Indian Ocean, may, over part of it at least, discover a principle that will unite them, but it will be rather their racial or nationalistic affinity than their common religion. Islam, in short, is today rather a powerful cultural link than a spring of political action. But in our generation there has grown up in the vast area that lies between Bombay and Tokio a new sense of the fraternity of the Asiatic peoples. The Japanese, with what success it is difficult to estimate, have sought to promote it and exploit it. Its negative meaning is readily grasped: it is a reaction of the self-respect and the instinct of self-preservation of the Asiatic peoples against Western imperialism and the white man's colour bar. Tagore made Chinese scholars welcome in his college at Santiniketan, and Gandhi would share his devotions with Japanese pilgrims in his monastery. Above all, during China's struggle for survival, the sympathy between the two great Asiatic peoples has grown into an active political force. Something wholly new in the history of Asia began to happen when Pandit Nehru shared the life of Chungking under a Japanese bombardment and Marshal Chiang Kai-shek visited Delhi. The paradox of this fraternisation is that it is our planes and our language which have made it easy. As yet it could supply a motive for action only to the more imaginative among the intellectuals of the two peoples, but such sentiments tend to spread downwards. Looking into the future Pandit Nehru has more than once made the forecast that a free India will find her closer ties rather with her Asiatic neighbours than with the peoples of the British Commonwealth. He has even suggested that an Asiatic league may one day be formed with India and China as its leading members.

This is an interesting and may be a prophetic suggestion. A sentiment of fraternity would not suffice to bring such a league into being. The realities of economics and "geopolitics" have also to be considered. In the economic sense India and China are not complementary. Both are chiefly backward primary producers. They do not need and cannot greatly help each other. All these Asiatic countries are still dependent on imported capital goods—that is to say on machinery, which they must draw in the future chiefly from Great Britain, the United States and possibly from Germany. The leading banks and shipping firms which dominate commerce are still mainly European, American or Japanese. If Japan fails by conquest to unify this vast region as her "Co-prosperity Sphere," is she capable of the political and moral evolution which would enable her to play a useful and acceptable part within it as the sea-faring and industrial power possessed of this most advanced technique and the greatest aptitude for organisation? Or have her militarists ruined her chances of peaceful leadership by their ruthlessness, as the Nazis may have ruined the prospects of Germany? Again, it is hard to foresee the economic changes that may follow the war. The Filipinos, for example, have been urged to grow for Japan the raw cotton which Indians used to export. Will natural rubber and oil be again the coveted materials they were in the past? Could Indian heavy industries, stimulated for the second time by war, expand so far in the first decade of peace that they might begin to supply the needs of other Asiatic peoples? The immediate foreground of the future is even more obscure than the European scene, for we do not even know how much longer Japan and the Soviet Union will remain at peace with one another.

The long-range tendencies may be easier to forecast. The old imperial *régimes* that were overthrown so easily in Malaya, Burma and the Dutch islands cannot be restored precisely as they were, though it may cost us some time and trouble to reach this conclusion. American interest in this part of the world has been greatly stimulated. America will not imitate any of the older forms of imperialism and will be impatient of such vestiges of it as we try to retain. She proposes, if Vice-President Wallace and his school have their way, to help the agricultural peoples, especially India and China, to enter the industrial age—or in plain words to supply them with machinery on long-term credit, or even on lend-lease terms. Like every relationship of dependence between unequal partners this plan of development may have its dangers, but it is incomparably less dangerous than the imperialist techniques of the past. So far from seeing in these Asiatic countries estates whose sole function was to furnish Western industry with raw materials and foods, it would emancipate them from this colonial status. Nor is it proposed that Western capital shall directly exploit Eastern labour by itself constructing and operating its own railways, steel-mills and factories under some form of privilege. The very grave risk that the borrowing Power may lose something of its political liberty in this way would be lessened, if the transaction were carried out or controlled by an international organisation. The alternative open to India and China is that they should imitate the heroic self-reliance of Russia, refrain from borrowing and build up their capital equipment rather more slowly by stinting their own consumption. The risk that India or China might run is not from the older and more brutal type of intervention. It is rather that Washington or London may make their aid dependent on the adoption or avoidance of some measure in social policy, or on the admission to power of some "safe" party or leader or the exclusion from it of another. It may be conveyed to the Asiatic client state by discreet channels that it need expect no economic help, if it should "liquidate" its landlords, or socialise its coal-mines, or if it should allow a Socialist leader to form a ministry, or again, if it hesitates to suppress its Communists; or else it may be required to cut down some item in its social services, of course for the sake of solvency. Pressure of this kind has been applied in the fairly recent past even to great European powers. A poor nation cannot escape it merely by proclaiming its sovereign independence. Assuredly if India and China stand shoulder to shoulder and manage to group some of their weaker neighbours round them, their liberties, political and economic, are the less likely to be infringed by the great capitalist powers of the West. How far they could manage without external help to ensure their own military safety, it is not easy to foresee. That depends partly on the political changes which may take place in Japan as the result of the defeat which all these speculations assume. There and elsewhere in this region Communism may take root and thrive. The other difficult factor to estimate is technical: is air power now so far superior to naval power, at least in narrow waters and within a fighter's range from its base on shore, that India and China could hope for a fair measure of security, if they possessed a good air force but lacked the means to build a great fleet? As the reader will perceive, in this effort to foresee the future framework within which India will have to shape her own destinies, I am trying to anticipate what is probable rather than what is desirable. It will be a hard world, seared by long familiarity with cruelty and suffering. Its climate will not favour idealism. We do not yet know how completely restrictive monopoly capitalism will dominate it, or for how long. This time it will not even talk about disarmament, save that it will disarm the aggressor of yesterday. To steer an independent course in such a world will demand from Indian statesmen unusual and sagacious courage, and their success will depend mainly on their ability to solve social and economic problems of desperate difficulty within their internal structure. In spite of the dangers, I think that India will at an early moment after the peace choose complete independence, and I hope she will ally herself with a victorious China. It is to be foreseen that any government we are likely to have at Westminster will try to block her road by using the princes. But that device cannot be used for ever.

In a rational and kindly world independence would not be incompatible with mutual aid. At the end of this war, in all the belligerent countries, millions of workers, who had learned to face the enemy's bombers with stout hearts, will stare with terror at the cold forges and clean chimneys of the mills which had employed them through the years of war. The apparatus which made the tools of destruction can with no ruinous cost or delay be adapted to make the tools of peace. The governments which have had in their hands the spending of half the nation's income dare not suddenly desist. They will have to organise and finance the rebuilding and restoration of all that has been destroyed between Severn and Volga. Need they stop there? In the East and above all in India, which has been our ward through two centuries, the hope of the future depends on the rapidity with which her backward and impoverished population can make the transition in field and workshop from an outmoded to a modern organisation of her superabundant labour force. Much is needed which only she can effect, but much also is required which we could supply. She needs tools of every kind, both agricultural and industrial. She needs the machines that would enable her to make her first internal-combustion engines, the equipment that would give her ample hydro-electric power, pumps that would spare her peasants the fantastic labour they spend in irrigating her fields—but the catalogue might be endless. In war, were it to Africa or Asia, we sent all the tools our armies demanded without counting the cost. To lift these Asiatic peoples and above all the

Indians who were our subjects to a level of life more worthy of humanity, would it be amiss to send out the tools that would do it on easy terms of credit, and at cost price? For my part I would dare to propose a free gift of machinery equal in value to a week's cost of the war, or let us say £100,000,000. If it is proper to send out a machine-gun for which we shall never be repaid, would it be amiss to give an irrigation pump? It would cost us only the difference between the wages of the British workers who made it and the dole they would otherwise receive in idleness and discontent. The higher level of productivity and comfort it brought to India would soon be reflected in a rising volume of normal trade between her shores and ours. The terms on which this might be done could be worked out between Whitehall and Delhi in such a way as to arouse no suspicion of any infringement of India's independence. It would be at once a sane and remunerative stroke of economic policy and an imaginative act of statesmanship. If India decides to quit us, then let us give her a dowry worthy of our pride.

If the reader still doubts whether it would be expedient to further the prosperity of an independent India by a splendid gift conceived on a grand scale, may I ask him a question? On a rough estimate, how many hundreds of thousands of millions would it be worth to us during a generation, in goodwill and in a lower level of armament, if across the Atlantic, in Russia and in Asia men ceased to use the two words "British imperialism"? We could, if we dared to act greatly, so treat India that men would be ashamed to utter them.

V. Why India Is Poor

THE old-world legend of India's fabled wealth which dazzled poets and beckoned conquerors has shrunk, long ago, into an antiquarian puzzle. Happy periods and favoured regions there may have been in which it did not wildly distort reality. Today there confronts us an abyss of poverty so deep that we struggle in vain to plumb it. Everyone is familiar with the figures through which statisticians have sought to measure it. Lord Curzon, in 1901, during his viceregal reign, published an official reckoning which estimated the average income per head of the Indian population as £2, or Rs. 30, per annum. Since his day many statisticians have made their estimates, but comparison is difficult, since their methods vary widely, while the exchange value of the rupee and the purchasing power of sterling have also varied. Lord Curzon's startling figure has been more than doubled in the interval. The most accurate and elaborate of these enquiries, that of Professor V. K. R. V. Rao,* yielded for the year 1931-2 an average income of Rs. 62 or £4 13s. It is doubtful, however, whether the real income of the poorer Indian villagers, the mass of the population, has risen in this proportion, if at all. For the previous year, Mr. Colin Clark † estimated the average income of the inhabitants of this island at about £94.

This should mean, in round figures, that for every shilling in an Indian's purse, an Englishman has a pound. But such comparisons convey a seriously exaggerated impression. The English climate exacts a much heavier expenditure on clothing and houseroom, and there is the same disparity in the costs

* *The National Income of India.*

† *National Income and Outlay*, pp. 14 and 88-90. This is the estimated net national income for 1930 divided by the estimated population of the U.K.

of the typical diets required to maintain the body in health. None the less, the traveller has only to look about him to realise that these starved and stunted bodies, these empty and dilapidated hovels, these threadbare rags, these neglected rural roads, these missing hospitals and schools, do mean, in terms of health, comfort and efficiency, that the Indian income is a pitiable fraction of our own.

In this chapter I shall attempt an analysis, which can be only a sketch, of this startling Indian poverty. What are its causes? How far is it due to Indian institutions? How far is the policy of India's British rulers to blame? After this study of the production of wealth we must attempt, though the data are inadequate, some consideration of its distribution. What share in causing this poverty do the exactions of the usurer and the landlord play? How much of it must we ascribe to taxation and the "drain" of wealth to the Metropolis?

THE PRODUCTION OF WEALTH

IN embarking on this difficult exploration, it seems proper to begin with the human factor. What are the forces of labour available for the production of wealth? The census can show how the gigantic potential labour forces of this population, which in 1941 numbered 389 million persons in all India, is distributed among the various occupations. Roughly 70 per cent are engaged in agriculture and only 4.3 per cent in industry.* The traveller notes immediately the relatively small contribution which women make. They have hardly yet begun, as

---

* The proportion engaged in agriculture rose from 61 per cent in 1891 to 73 per cent in 1921. In 1931 it fell to 65.6, but this was due solely to a new method of classification. (See Anstey, p. 6.) The proportion of industrial workers to the total population fell from 5.5 per cent in 1911, to 4.9 in 1921 and 4.3 in 1931. Industry in this connection means chiefly small-scale concerns which use no mechanical power. In 1931 the daily average employed in factories under the Act was only 1,751,137.

clerks and typists, to enter commerce and the public service, and it was only in the few fashionable *swadeshi* shops, started to foster the sale of native goods, that I ever saw an Indian woman serving behind the counter. In the cotton industry women's labour plays a much smaller part than in Europe. Women, so far as my own observation went, take little part, save as helpers, in the traditional handicrafts. Gandhi's propaganda has, however, induced vast numbers of them, both in the villages and among the middle class in the towns, to take up spinning. In the North, where *purdah* prevailed until recently, for it is now breaking down, the women of the higher castes, which include the cultivators, were sometimes confined so strictly to the house that they dared not carry a meal to their husbands while they were working in the fields. On the other hand, women of the lower castes work habitually in the fields, as they do also in plantations, and in some districts the caste-line is not strictly drawn. In the towns they labour, usually as porters, at the roughest tasks, in the docks, in building operations, and until the other day in the coal-mines. A European may admire the grace of their carriage as they poise heavy burdens on their heads, but he is revolted at this misuse of their slender bodies. Without attempting any statistical estimate, it is evident that women play a much smaller part in the production and distribution of wealth than they do in the West, and far too often, when they are employed outside the home, it is upon unsuitable tasks. Custom curses the higher strata of Indian womanhood with too much shelter, while it fails to protect the lowly. A lavish use is made, on the other hand, of child labour. If this adds something to the productive forces of India it is at the cost of its efficiency, intelligence and health in after-life. Finally, we must deduct from the working forces of the people a large intellectual proletariat, which fails, after a literary education, to find permanent work. Here the blame lies partly with mis-education and the system which Macaulay helped to introduce, partly with the traditions of the higher castes.

That this enormous labour force does not, in physical

strength, endurance or efficiency, approach any Western race is a fact of which all European residents are aware. It is repeated in daily conversation, in tones that vary from contempt and impatience to sympathy and pity. The low standard of life has had its inevitable effect. I need not be at pains to quote the many authorities, ranging from Gandhi to certain high British officials, who have said that half the population of India never eats enough to satisfy hunger. There are fine men among the peasants, giant Sikhs, athletic Mahrattas, though even among these races the women are often puny. But the coolies of the towns and the villagers of the poorer districts are an undersized race, pitiably slight of build, with poorly-developed muscles—mere fractions of men. Nature has developed a miniature race which can sustain a shadowy life for a short span on a minimum of proteids and vitamins. The average Indian expectation of life is 23.5 years: the same figure for the British population is 54 years. Worse still, the physical life of most of these workers, the villagers no less than the townsmen, is all the time subnormal. They never know what health or vigour means. The All-India Conference of Medical Research Workers, which met in 1926, recorded in a formal resolution its belief that the annual deaths from preventable disease amount to 5 or 6 millions; that the loss of efficiency from preventable malnutrition and disease is not less than 20 per cent; and, finally, that while today 50 per cent of the infants reach wage-earning age, the proportion might easily be raised to 80 or 90—and these, it is declared, are under-statements. Of the preventable diseases the most deadly are malaria and the anæmia caused by the hook-worm, a parasite engendered by insanitary habits. Malaria accounts annually for about a million deaths, disables permanently another two millions and causes about 50 million cases of sickness, which ought to be (but seldom are) treated in hospital.*

* Linlithgow, p. 490. There are in British India 6,700 hospitals, which means one hospital for 163 square miles, or for 45,000 people. Quinine is a Government monopoly, yielding an annual profit of £40,000. Produced at 9s. per lb., it is sold at 27s.

The average child in a malarious district suffers from an enlargement of the spleen in infancy, and never knows full vitality. With money and organisation both these diseases could be stamped out. There is no justification for the fatalism which blames climate for the high mortality and heavy sickness rates of the Indian population. When I first read that the Indian death-rate fluctuated from 62 in 1918 to 24 per 1,000 in 1922 (the lowest recent figure), while the English mortality rate stood in 1927 at 12.3, I did not know what to think. When I learned that the death-rate in Benares Cantonment stood at 12.3 (the home figure), while that of the native town was 46.1, I had no further doubt. The cantonment and the town have the same climate, but in the cantonment a well-nourished population lives in roomy houses, amid gardens, in wide streets, while in the city a congested and poorly-fed population inhabits narrow gullies of streets and defies within these fastnesses of darkness every rule of health and sanitation. Yet the white population is never at its ease in this climate, to which Indians have adapted themselves through several millennia. I ceased to feel surprise, when I had seen the slums of Calcutta and Bombay, that their infantile death-rates stood at 317 and 419 in 1924, while that of London was 70: the marvel is that any infants survive the foulness of the hot and stagnant air, the parasites, the din, the stench and the opium with which nine working mothers in ten attempt to still their wailing. After the neglect of sanitation, we must include among the causes which enfeeble the mothers and bring puny babes into the world the custom of early marriage and premature child-bearing. Malnutrition begins with the weaning of the child and lasts through life. India, with its excessive population of useless cattle, produces a wholly inadequate supply of milk, and what can be bought is usually dirty and diluted. It is safe to say that a worker's child rarely tastes milk (unless one reckons buttermilk) either in the village or the town, save under a few of the more progressive municipalities which have begun to organise a supply. The usual diet of rice and other grains lacks fat, protein and the protective vitamins and contains an excess of starch. The villagers rarely taste fruit, save in the mango season, nor do they grow salads. Wheat is a luxury raised for export: the staple rice, especially if it is "polished," is a deplorable food. This monotonous and ill-balanced diet, in which salt is often the only relish, is for a great proportion of the working population deficient also in quantity: they cannot earn enough for health and vigour. It is doubtful, indeed, whether India raises more than a bare sufficiency of food for its population. The production of grains and pulses (and nothing else comes into the reckoning for this vegetarian population) would yield a daily ration of 1.2 lbs. per head of the population, after allowing for exports, which amount, even in a good year, only to 4 per cent. This may be measured against the scale of the Bombay jails, which allow 1.7 lbs. to a prisoner on hard labour, while the standard allowance in times of famine for diggers on relief works is 1.29 lbs.* Since the daily output of food is an average which rich and poor must divide, it is probable that slightly too little is raised to provide a sufficiency for the poorer workers.

What this under-nourished labour force loses in efficiency through psychological causes, which determined leadership could alter, cannot be estimated in figures. The percentage of literates in the adult male population has slowly risen in British India to 18.3 per cent, but among women the figure is only 1.9 per cent, and in the whole population 9 per cent. The children of the workers rarely spend more than a year or two at school and quickly forget what little they have learned. It has been reckoned that before provincial self-government came into force, two-thirds of India's 700,000 villages had no school at all. The quality of the education is often deplorable. Malaria affects the children even of the middle class, and Sir Ronald Ross has drawn a mordant picture of a class of children, all with enlarged spleens, struggling to learn by rote a table of the Plantagenet kings. Living still in a primitive

* Anstey, p. 442.

world of superstition and fable, unable to read the clock, to decipher the simplest written calculation, or to read a leaflet, these workers are bewildered amid the mechanism of a factory, cannot grasp the foundations of rational agriculture, and fall an easy prey to the trickery of usurers, foremen and landlords. With their low physical vitality they are strangers to ambition and lack the self-reliance and individualism of Western workers. The big communal family of Indian society stands behind them: it will always succour a man when he is down, and with it he must divide his gains. The economic motive as our competitive individualistic Western society knows it, stirs him but feebly. Caste holds him in a tight framework of rules, prohibitions and customs. Religion, through the doctrine of reincarnation, plays its usual part in promoting other-worldliness and repressing discontent. When my average life of one score years and three has run its brief course on the lowly rung which I occupy on the ladder of births, my soul, when it quits this despised body, whose very shadow defiles, may rise, if I have observed every rule of ceremonial duty, to inhabit the frame of a Brahman or a prince. So Lazarus scrambles, passive if not contented, under the table for fallen grains of rice.

That the efforts of this labour force are not employed to the best advantage in the production of wealth everyone knows, and many agencies are at work, though as yet on a small scale, to improve the methods of cultivation—for 88 per cent of India's workers are engaged in agriculture. In any attempt to estimate the incredible waste of labour, we must begin by recognising that there is a long period of the year, varying considerably in different regions, during which no work can be done upon the land. A low official estimate reckons this interval of absolute idleness as two to four months,* and there is, of course, much under-employment at other times. It would be safe to say that this labour force is unemployed through one-third of every year. When we recollect

* Linlithgow, p. 566.

the 20 per cent of inefficiency through preventable malnutrition and disease, and the slight use and misuse of woman's labour, it is obvious that the first and simplest explanation of Indian poverty is that not half of India is effectively at work.

Can we reach any measure of the waste of labour due to primitive methods of cultivation? I reckoned with the peasants in some villages near Agra the time required to cultivate an acre under wheat. From the first ploughing to the final threshing, including the laborious watering, forty days of one man's work were consumed. Professor C. S. Orwin has reckoned that on an English farm, using horses, the comparable time is 40 horse-hours, and at most 42 man-hours.* But the wheat raised by 40 days' labour must compete in the world's market and sell at the same price as the wheat raised by 40 hours' labour. It seems to follow that the Indian worker can expect, as his daily remuneration, only an eighth or a twelfth part of what the English worker enjoys.

Let us suppose that a dictator, working on some Indian equivalent of the Five Year Plan, were to reorganise these villages with Russian ruthlessness for the scientific production of food and raw materials. The same output could be attained by a fraction of the present rural population, and the immense majority would be left wholly unemployed. That is, however, to underestimate the present waste. Even without machinery, science or large-scale organization, the village at present has twice the population it requires to cultivate the fields by the traditional methods. A family can be supported in India upon five to seven acres of irrigated, or twenty to twenty-five acres of "dry," land. If holdings were actually rearranged on this basis, more than half the present rural population would be displaced.†

Given the present level of economic development, India is manifestly over-populated: her villages are congested by undernourished multitudes who cannot find full-time work in the fields. It is possible in some cases to trace from local records

* *Times*, March 9, 1942.
† Anstey, p. 40.

the progress of this congestion. Dr. Mann (*Land and Labour in a Deccan Village,* Vol. I) found that in the village which he studied holdings had averaged 40 acres in 1771: by 1915 they had dropped to an average of 7 acres. Seven acres may in the Deccan provide a bare living, but in Bengal holdings average 3.1 acres, and in the United Provinces only 2.5 acres. This sub-division has come about through the breaking up of holdings at each generation among the heirs. Hindu law, though based on primogeniture in most parts of India, else-where requires an equal division of inherited property among all the children. Hindu custom, however, in the past, kept the land as the farm of the undivided communal family; and near Poona I found such families still cultivating their common estate collectively under the direction of the eldest brother. It is only too probable that English judges, interpreting this Hindu law, gave it an individualist twist and promoted sub-division. Worse still, since soils differ in quality, the custom grew up (as in the old Russian village) of assigning to each heir samples of each type of land, and these might be scattered in minute fragments over a wide area. Sometimes the individual plot may run, a few yards wide, for the length of over a mile; or again, the plots are mere garden beds, five or six yards square.*

With this evil of fragmentation an energetic administration could cope, and indeed in the Punjab, by far the best-governed province, the semi-official co-operative movement, using persuasion alone, has had an encouraging success in consolidating holdings; but compulsion is necessary.

The easier remedies for this tragic over-population are rarely available. Most of the soil of India is fully cultivated; indeed, the cultivated area has trenched unduly on the pastures. There may be scope for some further internal migration to the plantations of Assam. From emigration, given the racial prejudice against Indians, little is to be hoped, save that British Guiana might take another two millions. More

* Linlithgow, p. 134.

can be done by the extension of irrigation. The canalisation of the Punjab rivers, and the establishment, on what recently were deserts of barren sand, of colonies which show a level of wealth and enterprise far above the general average, make the brightest chapter in the record of the Indian Empire. The same transformation is taking place in Sind, since the Sukkur barrage was completed. Over the whole country some 50 million acres are irrigated, or about 20 per cent of the cropped area. Of this about half is watered by canals, some of them ancient, and the remainder by tanks and wells. The methods used are often primitive, for from the older canals which lie below the level of the fields a couple of peasants must lift the water by hand, dipping and swinging a skin bucket. It is commonly said that there is not scope for many more schemes on any ambitious scale, but since the Government's irrigation works yield an average profit of 7-8 per cent, it is clear that the margin of economic expansion has not yet been approached. The chief need of today is the introduction of a cheap oil-driven pump to work the wells, or, better still, of an electric pump; but without a great development of co-operation this is impossible on any considerable scale.

Even without any outlay of capital, however, the villager could be taught to increase the output of his fields several times over. The yield of wheat per acre is half the English average; that of cotton half the American figure; and that of sugar one-third of what is usual in Cuba. The employment of selected seeds of improved varieties would do much, but as yet these are used only over about 4 per cent of the area sown. The substitution of long-staple cotton of the Egyptian type for the poor short-staple Indian variety is proceeding, but very slowly. Ridge-cultivation increases the yield of certain crops by 55-60 per cent, and shallow hoeing some 25 per cent. A great part of the cultivated area (about 21 per cent) is annually wasted under fallow: if leguminous fodder crops were grown upon it, not only could the cattle be adequately fed, but the soil would be improved.

After noting these easy paths to progress, we soon reach

others, which are barred by deep-rooted prohibitions of religion
or custom. Of manure of any kind too little use is made,
and this was always so. The soil seems, however, to have
reached the limit of impoverishment long centuries back: it
does not deteriorate further. Farmyard manure is available only
in very small quantities, for the peasants use the cattle-dung
as fuel. Coal is far beyond their means. Wood and charcoal
are available only round the forests; but something might be
done by planting for this purpose and by cheaper transport.*
It seemed to me that the customs and law regulating tenancy
discouraged planting, even on waste land, by the tenants. The
easiest remedy, however, would be to induce the peasants, as
Gandhi is doing, to use composts of night soil for manure, as
the Chinese do. Here, however, the Hindu dread of ceremonial
defilement stands in the way.

The obstacle of religious belief is still more serious when
we turn from cultivation to the rearing of cattle. The sanctity
of the cow forbids any rational management of the herds.
India has a vast and excessive cattle population, for she maintains 67 cattle for every 100 acres sown, while Holland has
only 38 and Egypt 25. Yet the Hindus eat no beef, and drink a
negligible quantity of milk. Vast numbers of starved and
aged beasts, of poor stocks and diminutive stature, pick up a
living as best they may, when the common pasture land will
yield no more, from the stubble, the weeds or the fallows, or
by raiding the crops. In spite of her sanctity, the cow is not
valued, and often leads a miserable existence. More care is
bestowed on the female buffalo, valued for her milk, and upon
the oxen used for ploughing and draught. Aged beasts must
not be slaughtered, though life is a burden, yet unwanted buffalo bull-calves are allowed to starve to death. It is not love
or care for the beasts, but a tabu on the act of taking life
that underlies the Hindu doctrine of *ahimsa*. India will
greatly increase her wealth, and with it the happiness of her
animals, when she can bring herself to slaughter useless beasts,

* Linlithgow, p. 263.

and conserve the available food for those that remain. If better bulls for breeding were readily obtainable, an annual yield of 8,000 lbs. of milk could be obtained, given adequate fodder, where today the cows furnish virtually no milk. Early cutting and storage of the jungle grass would yield ample food in some regions. Egyptian clover (*berseem*) could be grown on the wastes and the fallow land. Much, also, might be done to popularise the silo.* The scope for progress seems unlimited, but little can be achieved until a frontal attack is made on custom. The unchecked ravages of monkeys and other wild animals, especially rats, must be mentioned in this connection.†

We might, on these lines, give rein to our imagination through a long vista of day-dreams. It is evident that the theoretical possibilities exist for an immense increase of India's income from agriculture and the rearing of cattle. If we choose to suppose that this inert, ignorant, half-starved peasantry could be galvanised into zeal for economic progress, and organised for a concerted effort, it could, within a brief span of years, abolish the poverty that renders Indian life subnormal, raise for much more than the present population a sufficiency of nourishing and varied food (which need not include meat), and dispose in addition of an increased surplus for export. But it is no less evident that if the labour force in the fields were intelligently organised, there would be work on the land only for a fraction of the village population. At an early stage in the process of reorganisation half of it would be found to be superfluous. The problem of over-population turns out to be a problem of wasted labour. One must have seen women squatting on the ground and cutting the grain listlessly with a tiny sickle; one must have watched the men spending fifteen days to water an acre of wheat, by laboriously raising water from a well with the aid of a pair of leisurely oxen, to realise what this waste of labour means.

What alternative employment is available? Our assump-

* See generally Linlithgow, chap. vii.

† Anstey, p. 54. Cheese is also forbidden, since it involves the use of rennet: perhaps research could discover a synthetic substitute.

tion that progress has begun in the fields, carries with it the further consequence that the cultivators have now some little surplus income, after the needs of bare subsistence have been satisfied. There will be a growing demand for clothing, furniture, better housing, and even for cheap luxuries. Start with the improvement of agriculture and it is possible (but not otherwise) to reckon on a great expansion of industry, and of rural enterprises which at present are neglected by the peasantry. The rearing of poultry is neglected, partly because the Hindu respect for life extends even to an unfertilized egg. The present generation, however, is growing much less strict, and in Bengal even Brahmans will eat not only eggs, but fish. Much might be done to expand the fisheries, and to build up a fruit-canning industry. Much might be done with sericulture, but again religion forbids, though Hindus will wear silk without scruple. There should be promise also, in other trades subsidiary to agriculture such as the making of implements * and ropes. The trade in *lac*, for which the gramophone has created a great demand, might be much better organised. In the long run, however, India must depend on the staple industries: she must clothe herself, and provide her masses with houses in which they may lead a healthy and self-respecting existence. In satisfying these new needs, it should be possible to find employment for the superfluous population of the villages. Indian thinkers and politicians who rely mainly upon a policy of high protection to foster their national industry are ignoring the fundamentals of the problem. Tariffs may be a proper means to use, but they can at best divert to the native mills the demand lately satisfied by Japan and Lancashire, and they may impoverish the peasantry further, if they raise prices by the whole amount of a high duty.† They cannot

---

* Linlithgow, pp. 567-9.

† A system of quotas might be more satisfactory than tariffs, if it were so used as to control the price of staple goods, *e.g.*, the cheaper cotton cloths, subject to a regulated competition by imported wares. By raising or lowering the quantity of imports the price of the native article could be kept at a proper level.

create an expanded demand in the main internal market. That is the village. The first step must be to assist the cultivator to produce more, and to produce it with less labour. When two men can raise twice as much wheat as four grow today, the third may weave the clothes they will demand, and the fourth set to work to build them a sanitary house. That, put in the language of childlike simplicity, is the only conceivable solution for this relative over-population. Fewer men must draw more wealth from the soil—so much more that their surplus will support those cultivators whose labour in the fields has become superfluous, and reward them while they cater for the expanded needs of those still active on the soil.

Two schools of thought will struggle violently when India is free to plan her own industrial development. Gandhi's school will strive to restore village handicrafts. The Bombay millowners and the Indian capitalist class generally will press for the encouragement of machine industry. As an immediate expedient for the relief of impoverished villagers, who can find nothing better to do through months of inevitable unemployment, the revival of the spinning-wheel can be justified. It is, however, a most primitive tool, and Congress invited inventors to design better machinery for carding and spinning, which can be worked by hand. With official encouragement an improved handloom has been popularized in some districts, which raises output by 40 per cent. The attraction of the little *charka* is, however, its simplicity and cheapness. If more elaborate and costly implements are suggested for the craftsman, he must be provided with credit to purchase them, and it is no less necessary to enlist him in a co-operative organisation which will market his products and deliver him from the exploitation of the middleman. I talked to a village weaver, who usually wove for his neighbours the yarn they had spun, making a small charge for his labour; but the demand was erratic, and he was often without work. The attempts to organise the weavers co-operatively have so far had little success; perhaps because they are all enslaved to usurers. But if co-operation can be made a success, need it stop short at individual production? At present weaving is confined to the hereditary weavers' castes, and each village tends to have its one weaver and its one potter. The caste line will have to be broken, if industrial work is to be provided for the superfluous cultivators. Could we then move on to co-operative workshops as the Chinese are doing? In that case, why not call in electric power?

It is easy to sympathise with some of the grounds that underlie Gandhi's hatred of machine industry. If it necessarily meant that the peasant, uprooted from his village, where at least he has sun, clean air, and the pageant of Nature round him, must live in a filthy and congested slum within a great city, and work under a petty tyrant of a foreman, a wise people would sacrifice much of the wealth of nations to escape it. It need not mean this. A relatively comfortable and healthy worker's dwelling (though with outside sanitation) can be built in India for £26;* town planning could break up these slums, and forbid their growth in the future. There remains the worker's attachment to his village, and his reluctance to lose himself for ever in a vast alien city, where men speak an unknown tongue and honour strange gods. Electricity, by dispersing industry and cheapening transport (for in the Bombay Presidency electrification has transformed the railways) may go some way towards meeting these objections, and may in the future provide industrial work at home, in co-operative workshops and even in factories, for the villagers without compelling them to expatriate themselves.

There has been in recent years a considerable development of hydro-electric power in India, especially in the Punjab and in the region of Bombay, for the benefit of its large-scale industries. The capital cost of constructing dams is, however,

* Whitley, p. 291.

heavy, and current expensive.* It is probable that the private monopolies are exploiting the public, but India's poverty restricts the demand. With an increased load, the charge could be much reduced. As yet, however, even the best of the few good model dwelling schemes for workmen stop short at the provision of electric light. We turn in a circle. If India were richer, she could provide cheap electric power and develop her industries: until she develops them, she will remain over-populated and poor.

A vicious circle of this kind is broken, as a rule, by calling up or calling in new capital or unemployed reserves. India has these reserves in abundance, and need not depend on imported capital for her future development. Everyone has heard of her fabulous hoards of gold and jewels: she has been called the sink of the world's precious metals, and estimates which look fantastic, but may in fact be sober, have been compiled in the attempt to measure this sterile wealth. The one fact that is certainly known is that India annually imports, as part payment for her exports, gold to an annual value which has varied greatly but averaged in the last five years before the present war £19,400,000. This gold does not serve as a basis for credit, and little of it finds its way to the banks; indeed, the banking system is yet in its infancy. It lies in safes and chests: it is deposited in temples: it adorns the persons of the women: it is even buried. This process has been going on through time immemorial, and the total accumulated stock (even if we refuse to believe the statisticians who have tried to guess at its amount) would suffice for an immense capital development. Every Rs. 100 of this gold if it went into a bank would presumably serve, according to the usual rules, as a basis for another Rs. 900 of bankers' credit. This will doubt-

* The cheapest rate for power in India is 0·5 anna (Tata Hydro-electric Power Supply), which compares with 0·1 anna in Norway. But this is exceptionally low. Elsewhere it may range from 2 to 3 annas per unit. (*Second Supplement to Electric Undertakings in India* 1931-2, and Anstey, p. 33.)

less happen, very slowly and gradually, as Indian society modernises its outlook and its habits. Could the process be accelerated? A foreign government cannot touch the keys of emotion which might release it, nor can it be mobilised by the usual commercial appeal. In so far as it is in the hands of Muslims, they think it wrong to lay it out to interest. It is possible, however, that patriotism might conjure a part of it out of the ground, and if once a habit were formed, the rest of it would gradually follow. Women brought their ornaments to Gandhi, freely giving them for the purpose of liberating India from foreign rule. Would they do as much if an Indian administration, with some magnetic personality at its head, and a powerful party organisation behind it, were to appeal for this hoarded gold to swell a guaranteed development loan? A really dynamic party could achieve this miracle. This money, however, is in the villages: it cannot be reached by prospectuses and newspaper articles: missionaries must go out and fetch it, aided by the appeal of cartoons and films to the eyes and wireless propaganda to the ears. The capital, in short, can be raised if the Indian village can be magnetised into a belief in planned development and scientific progress. That is an abstract way of summing up its belief in a large number of very simple propositions: that the village should sow selected seeds, breed from pedigree bulls, plant certain grains in ridges, sow clover on the fallows, consolidate its holdings and overcome its shrinking from the use of night soil. A loudspeaker under the central banyan-tree in every village, amusing and teaching the people by turns each evening, might in a few years transform their whole mental outlook. A foreign bureaucratic machine could not execute, or even conceive such a task. It implies a deliberate war upon traditions, which no alien rulers dare risk. Only a powerful and popular Indian party, controlling the resources of the public administration, yet touching the common people intimately in their daily lives, could essay such a task with success. When it begins to interest the Indian masses, and to fire them with a constructive national ambition, such a government will be able to extract this hoarded wealth, which it will employ to finance land banks, irrigation and electricity schemes, housing plans, the sinking of wells, the supply of pumps and the organisation of rural industries. This gold might also be used, after the war, to buy machinery from America or Europe, if gold still retains its traditional function in international trade.

RESPONSIBILITIES

ON the basis of a study so slight as this of the production of wealth in India, it may be rash to apportion the responsibility for the astonishing waste of labour which explains the general poverty. But some rough, summary opinions about India's economic history since British rule began, we cannot refrain from forming. The first reflection, when one has seen it at work, is that its efficiency is unduly concentrated upon the elementary tasks of government—police, justice, and the maintenance of order. The constructive tasks of economic development and popular education it neglected entirely through many generations: when it did attempt them, it did so on a small scale, tentatively and with stinted funds. This unlucky balance of efficiency in one direction, with neglect in the other, goes far to explain why the development of industry failed to keep pace with the growth of population. One of the "natural" checks on population (to use Malthusian language) was entirely abolished. Save on the fringes of the North-West Frontier, war ceased to slay over the vast area of the Peninsula, where before it had raged incessantly. The other checks were undoubtedly lessened. Famine, by the end of the last century, had been so far disciplined by the improvement of communications and the gradual development of an official technique of relief, that it no longer causes the former mortality: under the Moguls it literally depopulated wide regions. Again, while painfully little has been done to raise the general health of the population, some success has been achieved in fighting plague and cholera, though an epidemic of influenza (in 1918-19) swept off some 13 millions. These benefits of British rule have done their work. India enjoys peace with semi-starvation, and her population has been doubled in 150 years.* When I travelled in this crowded land, the reproach of the Hebrew prophet rang in my ears: "Thou hast multiplied the people and not increased the joy."

The same ambiguity hangs over other gains. The Western conquerors built railways and trunk roads. The balance of benefit, social, political and economic, is overwhelming: yet this penetration of the villages involved the gradual decay of the traditional crafts. Over the roads poured a flood of cheap machine-made goods, and today the motor-bus is completing their ruin, for it carries their customers for a trifle to the nearest market-town. Slowly at first, but at last with remorseless swiftness, the village craftsmen have had to abandon their trades, and have been flung back upon the land for a living. Even in the later part of the period, the census reveals this process, for between 1891 and 1921 the percentage of the population occupied in "pasture and agriculture" rose from 61 to 72. The ugliest chapter in the records of our early Empire is that which relates the deliberate destruction by prohibitive duties of the thriving export trade of India in fine textile goods.

Our forefathers, when they imposed a duty of 78 per cent, the rate prevailing in 1813, on Indian muslins imported into England, knew perfectly well what they were doing. They

* Over most of the period the Indian rate of increase was low. Between 1870 and 1910 it was only 18·9 per cent, as against 58 per cent in England and Wales and 59 per cent in Germany. But between 1921 and 1931 it rose to 10.6 per cent in a decade, a higher figure than any in western Europe, though less than those of the U.S.A. and U.S.S.R. None the less, in this decade agricultural production rose by 16 per cent and industrial production by 51 per cent. On this showing, overpopulation does not account for Indian poverty. The case would, however, be grave, if infantile mortality were checked and the span of life lengthened, without a great increase in production. (See *India Today* by R. Palme Dutt, pp. 60-73.)

were reversing the current of trade in Lancashire's favour. The home market of the Indian weavers was soon flooded with English machine-made cotton cloth, which paid only a trifling revenue duty of 3½ per cent. The export of British muslins to India expanded tenfold between 1824 and 1837. The result was the ruin of the Indian textile towns. The population of Dacca, to take as an example one only of these thriving centres, as Sir Charles Trevelyan testified in 1840, fell from 150,000 to 30,000: "the jungle and malaria are fast encroaching upon the town." A few years earlier, in his report for 1834-5, the Governor-General, Lord William Cavendish-Bentinck, a good and humane man, said that "the misery hardly finds a parallel in the history of commerce. The bones of the cotton-weaver are bleaching the plains of India." * The ruin went on, in spite of such protests, with pitiless logic. What happened first to the weaver was soon to overtake the potter and the smith. Is man too wicked an animal to be trusted with powerful machines? The steam engine, as the early Victorians used it, was deadly as the bombing-plane today

Our economic doctrines shifted according to circumstances with our interests. In the early period we used every known device of fiscal policy to destroy Indian manufactures and foster our own imports. Thereafter, when our own earlier adoption of power-machinery had given our goods an overwhelming advantage, we went over to free trade and imposed it on India also. The result was that an abnormally long interval of several generations stretched between the destruction of India's traditional home-industries and the belated effort on a small scale to create a native machine-industry. It may be said that this was an inevitable consequence of the industrial revolution. Not at all. In England the hand-weaver was ruined. But his pauper children were taken from the workhouse as soon as they could toddle and placed in the "dark

* It was Marx who first saw the full significance of this report (*Capital*, Vol I, ch. xv, § 5). I am indebted to Mr. Palme Dutt's *India Today*, Chap. V, p. 99, for this quotation.

Satanic mills." That did not happen in India. It is often said that she is suffering today from arrested development: she lags a century behind the rest of the civilised world in her entry into the machine age. This is a true but incomplete statement of the facts: the delay was imposed by the policy of her conquerors. The consequences in their bearing on population were, and still are, ruinous. Under native rule, her handicraft industries and exports would have survived much longer: power-driven machinery would have been introduced by native capitalists much earlier, and would have progressed more rapidly under the protection of a tariff. The craftsmen would not have been driven to seek their livelihood from the soil, and the average income might have risen to something like the Japanese level." *

To trace all the consequences of this major wrong our fathers did to India would fill a volume. One paradoxical result was that when modern industries did at last establish themselves in India, they had no sufficient motive to achieve efficiency. The destruction of native handicrafts and the consequent overcrowding of the soil rendered labour so cheap that any capitalist who installed out-of-date machinery might hope for the profits of exploitation. Worse still, only a minimum of machinery was installed: it was even cheaper to use human beings than beasts of burden. In the Bengal coal-field, until

* Dr. Buchanan, who spent several years in Japan before he studied India, is worth quoting on this point. After explaining (p. 471) how as a result of British policy Indian "craftsmen who had formerly been paid in food were left with neither occupation nor income," he draws a moral from Japan. "A governing group which understood its people and really cared for their welfare should make an effort to teach them better ways of earning a living. This the Government of Japan tried to do, and as a result the Japanese are about two generations in advance of India. While Indian craftsmen were literally starving, unemployed Japanese of the same group were learning to operate modern machinery. Often this was set up by the Government itself for demonstration to both capitalists and labourers; and as soon as possible the home market was preserved to the home producers. There have been anomalies in the Japanese protective system, but it has 'worked'."

the other day, coal was carried hundreds of yards up steep grades on women's heads. Capstans worked by women were in some of these pits the chief source of power as recently as 1927. It was not worth while to lay rails for the trucks in these mines, except in the main galleries: the coal was carried half-a-mile on women's heads. In many mines no ponies were used and as late as 1929 not a single mechanical conveyor existed in these pits, which none the less earned fabulous profits.* Of all the reasons why India is poor today, the commercial policy followed by Great Britain, as its owner and ruler, throughout the last century and during the first twenty years of the present century is beyond question the chief. The consequences, social, psychological and even physiological, are so deep-seated, that one and even two generations of enlightened administration may be required, before they can be undone. In this peninsula, under our rule, the value of human life sank to the lowest imaginable level.

Partly in obedience to British interests, partly under the influence of doctrinaire principles, the Government of India adhered, throughout the nineteenth century, to *laissez faire* in its extremest form.† *Laissez faire* is the principle that expressed in the domain of theory the perfect indifference with which the propertied class in the first half of the nineteenth century contemplated the condition of the masses. The Government did nothing to foster Indian industries, and would have denied that it was any part of its duty to concern itself with such matters. Military considerations would alone have compelled it to favour the building of railways: in addition they served

* See Buchanan (p. 261) who was an eye-witness. The recent prohibition of women's labour underground has led to a great improvement. Electric power is now coming widely into use in these mines.

† Professor Buchanan, a decidedly friendly observer, also comments on the attachment of the bureaucracy to *laissez faire* (op. cit. p. 459). So does Sir George Schuster (*India and Democracy*, p. 317), who writes: "Though there has been much advance recently, the Victorian traditions of *laissez faire* tended to survive longer in India than elsewhere."

as an outlet for British capital, which was protected from any element of risk by a guarantee of its interest. The inland waterways were neglected—as they were at home. There is one mile of metalled roads for every seven miles in France. On the other hand, much was done for irrigation, especially in the Punjab, for the benefit of its "martial races"—a duty which the better of India's oriental rulers had also fulfilled within their capacity. The good record in this matter is balanced, however, as Sir William Willcocks, perhaps the foremost hydraulic engineer of his day, has shown, by grave mistakes in Bengal, where railway embankments were allowed to cut across drainage canals, while other ancient canals were mistaken for rivers, with the result that they silted up under neglect. If deserts have been gloriously reclaimed in the Punjab, whole regions in Bengal have lost their fertility, and have become malarious swamps. There is no difficulty in understanding the stern adherence to free trade dogma, which forbade India to foster her infant industries by a tariff: the immutable principles of economic science favoured Lancashire. When at length duties on imports were imposed for revenue purposes, a counter-balancing excise was levied on Indian cotton manufacturers.

Under Lord Curzon, in some respects, with all his notorious foibles, an enlightened Viceroy, we note the beginning of an attempt to foster minor Indian industries, especially by research. Lord Morley, the last of the consistent Victorian Liberals, sharply intervened to check this departure from *laissez faire,* and the opinion of the English business community, not in other respects conspicuously liberal in its outlook, supported him. The test case was raised by the Madras Government, which created a Department of Industries in 1906, and named Mr. Alfred Chatterton "Director of Industrial and Technical Inquiries." He established an experimental aluminum industry, a chrome tannery, some handloom weaving factories, and started research upon well-boring and the adaptation of oil-engines to irrigation. Lord Morley suppressed the Department and would sanction nothing beyond technical education, whereupon Mr. Chatterton took service with the Indian State of Mysore. With the last war this obstructive Liberalism vanished, and the Indian Government for several years followed an active policy on the lines inaugurated in Madras. A reaction set in, however, under the financial stringency which prevailed from 1924 onwards. This decade, however, saw the adoption of protection. From 1921 onwards it became the accepted policy for India; the excise on cotton was abolished, and the Indian industry has since enjoyed a tariff advantage on piece goods which rose in 1934 to 25 per cent against British cloth. Against Japan the duty rose to 50 per cent. The Tata firm was helped by a 33⅓ per cent duty and for a time by bounties also, to create an Indian steel industry. The Empire surrendered in the economic field to Indian nationalism somewhat earlier than in politics. The accepted principle is now fiscal autonomy for India. A system of preferences for British goods was, however, imposed after the Ottawa Conference. The results have been all that Lancashire feared; its export of piece-goods to India had fallen by 1939 to a tenth of what it had been a quarter of a century earlier. In general, British goods which formed 63 per cent of India's imports in 1914 amounted to only 30 per cent in 1938: in value the drop was from £61 to £34 millions. It is possible that the British Government may have hoped to detach the Indian capitalist class from the nationalist movement. This has happened only in a minor degree.

It is harder to understand the long delay in adopting a policy of constructive aid for agriculture, for no British interest here stood in the way. On the contrary, every advance in farming and every addition to the farmer's buying power would have promoted British trade and eased the task of government. Nothing was done, even in the way of research, until 1903, and then only when Lord Curzon accepted a gift of £30,000 from Mr. Henry Phipps of Chicago to establish an experimental station at Pusa. It has done much admirable scientific work, and the same may be said of some of the provincial stations which have followed it, notably in the Punjab. But the new seeds and the new knowledge, in spite of the care taken to adapt all the results to the conditions of the small peasant cultivator, reach him very slowly. The problem of teaching the peasant cannot be solved officially, from above. The co-operative societies, which should have been the chief means for aiding the villager to make improvements and to market his produce to advantage, make little progress. It was only after 1912 that the law permitted their formation. Virtually nothing has been done to help the peasants with their marketing, and they remain the prey of rapacious middlemen, who are often usurers also. The attempts made to cope with the usurer by restrictive legislation have all admittedly failed.* The best way to defeat him is to furnish cheaper credit. This the co-operative banks are doing, especially in the Punjab, with a measure of success. They date from 1904, and have now, all over British India, 5,329,110 members, which seems a large number until one realises that it includes only 8 per cent of the cultivators. The Government everywhere took the initiative in forming these credit societies, with the result that the members rarely have much understanding of co-operative principles: the Punjabi peasants with whom I talked invariably spoke of the Co-operative Credit Society as "the Government bank." Since they must accumulate capital by their profits, they charge high rates of interest, which range from 6 to 15 per cent. Useful though they are, these banks do not seem, even in the Punjab, to drive the usurer out of the field, and the load of debt continues to grow. Even in the Punjab, which is in this, as in other respects, a model far in advance of the rest of British India, the expenditure of the Government on agriculture is still pitiably low, when compared with that of Western countries, where farming interests a much smaller proportion of the population. As Sir Malcolm Darling pointed out, a decade ago, the Punjab spent in promoting agriculture Rs. 79 per 1,000 of the popu-

* Linlithgow, p. 436.

lation, against an expenditure of Rs. 960 in Great Britain, Rs. 945 in Germany, and Rs. 1,020 in the United States.*

This negative record, qualified though it is in our own day by a belated but niggardly amendment, must figure as a central fact in any verdict on the results of British rule. Through a century the English conquerors took upon their own shoulders the responsibility for governing this population. They dwelt amid its poverty, its ignorance, its physical misery and its helplessness, and never dreamed of using the immense resources of the efficient machinery of government which they had created to teach it, to heal it, to organise it out of its backwardness and inertia. They aggravated the pressure on the soil by hurrying the destruction of handicraft, and postponing the growth of industry. By suppressing, until our own day, all political initiative among the governed, they lamed its will and checked the working of its powers of adaptation; they violently changed its economic environment, yet they held in check the forces in Indian society which would have reacted to the new conditions and remodelled its structure.

While the argument of this chapter points to British commercial policy and to *laissez faire* as the central facts that account for Indian poverty, this sketch has also thrown into relief the factors inherent in the social structure of India and in Hindu belief which militate against economic progress. It is part of the curse of subjection that Indians, when once they have set their minds towards freedom, ascribe every ill from which they suffer to the foreigners among them, and either ignore the effect of their own institutions, or even idealise them, because these things, at least, are their own. But the more one realises that this heritage of obsolete thinking is a fatal obstacle to economic well-being, social justice and physical health, the more passionately does one long to see the end of the daily conquest of India. To remove these obstacles, to transform the mind which the masses inherit, to fight the native forces which maintain superstition, the Indian nation

* *The Punjab Peasant in Prosperity and Debt*, p. 715.

must first be self-governing and free. No radical movement for the overthrow of these customs and beliefs could gather momentum under the present system of government. India suffers from arrested development not merely because her equipment of machinery, measured in horse-power, is far behind that of any Western country. That is an external detail, easily remedied: machines can be bought. The arrest of development which matters, is that Indian society, as a whole, has passed through no experience comparable to the rationalistic and realistic movements which between the seventeenth and nineteenth centuries lifted Europe out of the Middle Ages. Such movements could take no root, because so soon as India was ripe for any collective thinking, she inevitably turned nationalist. Nationalism criticises the foreigner: it does not turn inward to analyse the inheritance of the past.

THE DISTRIBUTION OF WEALTH

THE MEAGRE wealth which India produces in her congested villages by ill-organised toil is ill distributed. In that respect her case is not peculiar. What is singular in her misfortune is that the parasitic classes which her labour must support for the most part turn their incomes to no economic use. It is impossible to make for the accumulations of the village usurer and the *zemindar* (land-owner) the plausible defence which capitalist economics can muster for the *entrepreneur*, the banker and the more progressive type of landlord in the West. The usurer levies a merciless tribute, but when he has grown rich by charging anything from $37\frac{1}{2}$–75 per cent for loans of a trifling amount, which breed at compound interest, he rarely turns the capital which he has amassed to any productive use. Cases occur in which a *bania* (the word means "trader" as well as "usurer") will start a flour-mill or a cotton ginnery, but they are rare. Nor can it be said that the rural usurer often performs an economically useful service by lend-

ing money. The peasant borrows because misfortune has over-
taken him—his plough-oxen or his milch-buffalo have died—
or because he must celebrate a marriage. Marriages are, as
we are often told, a common cause of debt. But the peasant
is sometimes driven to the usurer because he must pay his
land tax or his rent before his crop is ripe. He borrows on
the security of the standing grain and so begins a series of
ruinous transactions in which the *bania* doubles the parts of
usurer and dealer. In short, the debts of the village are for the
most part unproductive. If a man has intelligence to improve
his land, he will go to the co-operative bank for a loan, and
not to the usurer.

Apart from its direct effect in lessening the cultivator's income, this institution of usury is the root of many social mis-
chiefs. It saps any fund of energy and ambition that malaria
and semi-starvation may have left in the peasant's nervous
system. Why toil unduly when everything beyond a dish of
porridge seasoned with salt must go to the moneylender? The
land is slowly passing in the poorer districts into the ownership of the usurers: the former owner continues to till it as a
tenant, but without interest or hope. Again, this institution is
one of the chief causes of communal strife: Islam forbids
usury, and it is accordingly Hindus who draw from Muslim
peasants and labourers their curses with their pence. Pathans,
however, have no scruples and press their victims ruthlessly.
Finally, the usurer, holding entire villages in his grip, commands enormous social and political power, which he wields
invariably for reactionary ends. Of course he uses it to thwart
co-operation: but he will even resist the use by indebted
weavers of improved looms, which might render these wretches
independent. He has in his pay lawyers who fight his cases for
him, and prostitute their brains to serve his interests in elected
assemblies. The capitalist party in India is small: the industrial capitalists may be reckoned in tens of thousands.* But
politics are dominated by parties based on property, which is

* There were in 1939 only 10,466 industrial concerns large enough to
come under the Factory Acts.

apt to mean in India the interest of the usurer, the middleman and the *zemindar*, with their legal spokesmen. The tax returns reveal the importance of this great section of the propertied class. Even in the Punjab (where co-operative banking trenches considerably on its field of action) one in four of the payers of income tax is a usurer. What is the part which they draw from India's income may be guessed approximately. Estimates have been rising steeply. Agricultural debt was estimated in 1921 by Sir Malcolm Darling at £400 millions. In 1931 the Central Banking Enquiry Committee Report put it at £675 millions. In 1937 the first Report of the Agricultural Credit Department of the Reserve Bank of India estimated it at the startling figure of £1,350 millions (Rs. 1,800 crores). This is twice the annual income from agriculture, as Professor Rao estimated it for 1931-2.* The price-level had in the meanwhile risen, but this figure will, none the less, serve as a rough measure of the peasants' burden of debt and of the severity of the agrarian crisis. Land, both in Bengal and in the United Provinces, was going out of cultivation. In the provinces where peasant-ownership prevailed, the moneylender was foreclosing with increasing frequency. He then became a landlord of the worst type, while the peasant sank into the position of a debt-slave working without hope for a bare subsistence. Even in the period of relative agricultural prosperity this process had been going on, for the census of 1931 shows an increase in the number of non-cultivating landlords, a heavy fall in the number of cultivators (owners and tenants) and a big increase (from 21.7 to 33.5 millions) in the number of landless agricultural labourers. It is to be feared that the figures for the next decade will show an even more rapid growth of this village proletariat. We know too little of the real history of the Indian village, but there is reason to think that the fact with which this chapter started—a considerable rise in money income during the present century—may be misleading. This startling table compiled by a competent Indian economist

* *The National Income of British India*, p. 187.

(R. Mukerjee: *Land Problems of India*, p. 222) tells its own story:—

Year	1842	1852	1862	1872	1911	1922
Day Wage (annas) of Field Labourer without food......	1	1½	2	3	4	4 to 6
Seers of rice sold for one rupee	40	30	27	23	15	5

While the money wage was quadrupled, the cost of the main article in the worker's diet rose eight times: in other words, the labourer's real wage was halved in eighty years. Something of the kind happened in the wickedest period of English history, the uglier years under the Tudor dynasty when the Church was looted, and the common fields turned into sheepruns, while Henry VIII debased the currency. These figures (like the comparable data in Thorold Rogers *) apply in their full horror only to the landless labourer, who had to buy his rice. The peasant who retained his own land and lived largely on the produce did not suffer in the same way. But such peasants are growing fewer. Our last word on this subject of debt may be relatively cheerful. In most if not all the Congress provinces legislation has been passed cancelling a proportion of the arrears, scaling down the principal and fixing 6 to 9 per cent as the legally enforcible maximum rates of interest. How far this restriction is in fact observed I do not know.

The dealers and middlemen who handle the villager's produce are numerous, and some harvests, on the road from the village to the port, must run the gauntlet of a long chain of them. Attempts at co-operative marketing have failed, notably in the case of jute, where the dealers (an exceptional case) are Europeans. The local village dealer is usually the usurer, who may also keep a shop. The profits of dealing are high and the most rascally cheating common. Denunciations of these "thugs" (a word which sober economists will use) are com-

* *Six Centuries of Work and Wages*, pp. 342-3 and 427.

mon, even in official documents; but I know of no attempts to estimate the proportion of the income of the village which they annually drain off.

Finally, among the parasites who live upon the labour of the village, we must set in the place of honour the landlord, or *zemindar*. He is occasionally a prince whose family has lost its soverign rights: more often (as in Bengal) his family, though wealthy, reckons its distinction only by four or five generations: oftener still he is a parvenu who has bought out a degenerate old family: finally, he may be a usurer who has foreclosed, and appropriated a debtor's fields. The system of land tenure, as its exists today, was a British creation. The East India Company found tax-farmers everywhere established, who collected the land revenues of the Mogul, for which service they retained a commission. Whether ignorantly, or from policy, it chose, throughout northern India, to regard these functionaries as landlords, and it conferred upon them what India law and usage had never allowed them—the ownership of the soil. This arrangement doubtless seemed natural to younger sons who brought with them to India the outlook of an English squire's family: it was also an act of policy, for the foreign conqueror bought the loyalty of this new squirearchy by authorising it to exploit the peasants. The creation of landlords was continued: it mars the good work of the Punjab irrigation colonies and has reappeared round the Sukkur barrage in Sind. The worst form of this system is to be found in Bengal, where Lord Cornwallis made a "permanent settlement" on the basis of the values of 1793. The revenue due from the *zemindar* can never be increased, but he may rack-rent his tenants by raising their rents every twelve years, a privilege of which he has mercilessly availed himself. Under these permanent settlements an average of about a quarter of the rent goes to the Government as land-revenue: three-fourths remain to the *zemindar*. In other parts of the North, notably the United Provinces, assessments are made every thirty years and the *zemindar* retains 55 per cent as "rent," paying the remainder as tax. The variable assessment is the more reasonable system, but it, too, works harshly in a period of falling prices.* Finally, throughout the South, in the province of Bombay as well as Madras, over an area which is approximately half the peninsula, the peasant-cultivator is virtually the owner and pays land-revenue, which some consider a tax and others rent, direct to the state, without the intervention of a *zemindar*. In these regions the only landlords are usurers or "kulaks" (to use the Russian word) who have turned debtors into tenants. In these *ryotwari* (*i.e.* peasant-owner) provinces also, the British imposed their own ideas of landed property, though with less disastrous results than in the *zemindari* provinces. There can be little doubt that the prevalent native system was some form of collective ownership, which admitted of several variations and may have been slowly decaying. Occasionally there was tillage in common: more often a periodic redistribution of the land took place: never was the peasant regarded as an owner who could dispose at his pleasure of his land, even when he enjoyed the full usufruct for life. With the enforced individualism of the British system the weaker peasants went to the wall, since they could now mortgage their land. In vain had the officials of the Company who were familiar with the villages protested against this revolutionary change: the Directors in London knew better.†

The evolution, due to British policy, of the tax-farmer, the "publican" of Roman times, into a landlord, will be the worst of our legacies to the villages of northern India, for it will survive our direct responsibility for their government. In function and outlook this landlord remains a tax-farmer. He draws

---

* Lord Ripon proposed that assessments should vary only as prices vary, but the Home Government vetoed this reform. Clearly, land charges ought to vary according to an annual price index.

† The reader is asked to excuse this dogmatic statement on a hotly controverted subject. I feel no doubt that (broadly) Sir Henry Maine was right, and the school of B. H. Baden-Powell, despite his minute knowledge, demonstrably mistaken.

a tribute and he does nothing else. He has laid out no capital on his "estate": he does not attempt to manage it scientifically: nor is he usually by his example an influence for agricultural progress.* He is often a harsh overlord: he exacts, over and above the money rent, sundry services in kind and, like the usurer, he often stoops to petty trickery. Since he has the power to exact a price from the tenant for his permission to make improvements, he acts as a formidable obstacle to economic progress. He wields great political power and disposes of the votes of his richer tenants—the poor have none. This oppression the early British rulers of India introduced, and to this day the landlord is the object of peculiar official solicitude. All "agricultural incomes" in India are exempt from income-tax. This mercy was not devised from any concern for the tenant, whose income, save in a few exceptional cases, is far below the limit of exemption. It spares the great incomes of the landlords, which sometimes run into princely figures. The great landowners are, moreover, separately represented, as a special interest, like the European merchants, in legislative bodies.

To what proportion of the peasant's income this tribute to the landlord amounts it would be interesting to know. It comes to three times the land revenue in Bengal and to a little more than the land revenue in the United Provinces. In the Punjab, as we shall see, it may amount to three times the value of the peasant's net income from his land.† Some part of that revenue —much too small a part, it is true—is spent on purposes which benefit the peasant: from the landlord's tribute not an anna comes back to him in service. Our analysis of the distribution of Indian wealth has brought to light several indigenous para-sites who contrive to eat up a part of the produce of the peasant's toil several times greater than that which the Government appropriates. But native though they may be, it is

* If the reader suspects my Socialist bias he may consult the Marquis of Linlithgow's Report, p. 425, or such an orthodox economist as Dr. Anstey, who calls the zemindars (p. 99) "mere parasites who batten on the products of the cultivators."

† See p. 246.

the strong arm of the British Raj that upholds them in the exercise of their—rights.

"THE DRAIN"

NATIONALIST criticism, inevitably and naturally, has been concentrated not on the social aspects of the mal-distribution of wealth in India, which have their parallels in other lands, but on the peculiarity of India's case. The peasant pays a tribute, which in part explains his dire poverty, to landlord and usurer: but they are Indians: what they grab unearned remains within the country. But does not the Indian nation, as a unit, also pay what may fairly be called a tribute to the power which conquered and controls her—not, indeed, to its Exchequer but to its owning class?

The fact is there: the payments go out. They are withdrawn from India; they do not continue to circulate there, paying Indians for goods and services as the tributes of the landlord and usurer do. That cannot be gainsaid. What can be urged on the other side is that these charges are payments to England or to Englishmen for services rendered. To that Indians counter with the reply that the services are overpaid and that they are performed without India's invitation and against her will. There arises, when we have heard both sides, the further question whether this "drain" of India's wealth plays a major part in explaining her poverty.

The classical controversy over the "drain" turned within narrow limits, for it concerned the so-called Home Charges; the payments, that is to say, which the Indian Government annually makes in London. The major charges are for the management of the external debt, with the interest on the capital cost of railways and irrigation works: after these come smaller charges for part of the expenses of the India Office in London, army pensions, allowances paid to British officials and soldiers absent on furlough, stores purchased in London and some minor items. The total sum, at the turn of the century, was about £17 millions and has since ranged from £30 to £35 millions. The earlier figure was approximately that of the land revenue, which measured it for Indian eyes.*

The answer, in so far as the productive debt is concerned, is easy. The railways and irrigation works have been of great service to India: the necessary capital could not have been raised in India, or if raised there, must have paid a greatly higher interest rate. I think, however, that an Indian Government would have known how to raise this money. A democracy would have done it by a patriotic appeal; a despot would have tortured a few rich men to encourage the rest. To the criticism over pensions and furlough allowances, there is the general reply that over the greater part of the period of British rule Indians lacked the training to perform the services which Englishmen rendered. To this it may be answered that the Indianisation of the services ought to have begun much earlier and proceeded much faster.

The Indian attack is morally successful when it points to the debt incurred to compensate the East India Company for the loss of its privileges after the Mutiny. The Home Government, which resumed them for itself, was certainly the party to this transaction which ought to have paid. India was a passive and indifferent object in this transfer of power. Again, Indians have an easy case to argue when they point to the many wars, some unnecessary, some iniquitous and some with no imaginable relation to any Indian interest, for which in part they have had to pay. India has paid in this way for her own reconquest after the Mutiny: an indemnity, as it were, for her defeat. The Opium Wars opened China above all to British trade. Hong Kong was not annexed to India. What Indian aspired to the conquest of Burma? Who now would defend the First Afghan War? If a part of the Indian army could be spared for Napier's expedition to Abyssinia, then manifestly it was, for purely Indian purposes, to that extent too large.

* See *India in the Victorian Age*, by Romesh Dutt, p. xiv.

And so, from one item to another we may go on.* It is often answered that in fact these charges no longer figure in the account; the debts have been wiped out. That is no answer: year after year they did reduce the surplus available for India's own development.

In morals, the Indian advocates are entitled on these counts to a verdict—if this be a moral world. An empire took India by force, and used her for its purposes. If, however, we are dealing with the economic problem of Indian poverty the case is not so simple. Foolish and unjust wars and mean reckonings there have been. Would India have escaped such wars, if Clive had never been born? The Indian argument assumes that the Peninsula, without the British, would have been a paradise of peace in which armaments and taxation to finance bloodshed would have been unknown. It might have weltered to this day in internecine war: but if some strong native power had unified it—the Mahrattas, for example—would it have escaped the military burdens which Japan must bear? She must pay for a navy: India escapes that charge. The broad economic defence for all these military charges, and also for the police, is that they are details in an immensely valuable contribution British rule brought a new security, internal and (save on the North-West fringe) external peace, immunity from brigandage, civil war and invasion. That is an economic gain which means something in income for every Indian and something, in the opportunity to accumulate wealth, for the whole nation. On the economic plane the answer may well be successful: freed from these British military charges it is possible that India would have been not richer but poorer. What stings is the sense that

* The Great War does not figure among these Home Charges. India, in so far as she had at this time a will which she could freely express, made two "gifts" amounting to about £150 millions to the Empire. These great sums were raised in India by rupee loans: the interest is not "drained" away. Oddly enough, India did catch the war fever, and even Gandhi, in spite of his pacifism, made a recruiting tour in Gujarat. The "gifts" may at the time have been made willingly, influenced by an inflated expectation of favours to come.

even this security was imposed: the laurels with the pensions went overseas.

There arises out of this somewhat sterile controversy over the past the urgent question whether the whole machine of government, civil and military, is more costly than India can bear; or to put it in another way, whether India is gravely overtaxed? Gandhi, with his instinct for simplifying knotty problems, has summed up the popular attitude in the twin demands that the cost of the army and the civil service should be cut by half, and the land revenue by as much, while the salt tax should be abolished. The land revenue has no longer its old importance in the Indian budget: between 1883 and 1923 it fell from 53 to 20 per cent of the total revenue from taxes. It is, however, as important as ever in its social effects. The poor of the villages are taxed only on their land and their salt, for they do not consume imported goods subject to customs: if they pay on cotton piece goods they need not do so, for as Gandhi would say, they can wear home-spun: if they pay also on toddy, again, as he would say, they ought not to drink it.* The land tax is involved in a muddle of insincere controversy. Is it tax or rent? If one answers "tax," then why should the cultivators of the South escape rent? If one answers "rent," then why should the North be bled by the *zemindars* also? Again, is it of much use to reduce this "tax," if the *zemindar* continues to levy his heavier tribute? The hated salt tax will, of course, go so soon as India controls her budget. It is difficult to ascertain the real burden of the land tax upon income, for it varies immensely from province to province and with the date of the assessment and the level of prices. But Sir Malcolm Darling's estimate may be quoted that in the Punjab it absorbed 20 per cent of the net income from the land.† Sir George Schuster, a former Finance Member, accepts as accurate the estimate of 8s. (Rs. 5⅓) as the burden of tax-

* Since 1937 prohibition has prevailed in the Congress provinces.
† *The Punjab Peasant in Prosperity and Debt*, pp. 10, 248.

ation per head.* This looks like a very low figure, until we recollect that the *per capita* income of the rural population may be about Rs. 51 (Professor Rao's estimate) or measure it against the even lower figure of Rs. 42 for the agricultural population, adopted in the Majority Report of the Central Banking Enquiry Committee (p. 39). To this burden of taxation must be added in northern India the rent and everywhere the interest on debt, if we are to form any idea of the total tribute levied on this average *per capita* income of the peasants. The plain fact is that in the poorer villages any tax whatever is intolerable and unjustifiable—if the land revenue be a tax. If it is rent, then the *zemindar* must be swept away, and if that cannot be done without some compensation over a brief term of years, then England—if this were a moral world —rather than India should pay it, for she invented this parasite. From a due development of income tax it would be possible, even without a reduction of expenditure, to satisfy Gandhi, by freeing the poorest of the poor entirely from taxation. No civilised state will tax an income too low to provide a bare subsistence, and that is the case of the majority of these peasants. The proportion prevailing in Indian budgets between direct and indirect taxation is grossly unfair to the poorer strata of the population. Income tax has in recent years yielded only round about 10 to 12 per cent of the total revenue.† At home in a normal year of peace even Conservative chancellors used to aim at a rough parity between direct and indirect taxation—indeed between 1924 and 1936 direct taxation ranged from 53 to 60 per cent. The level of income tax in India has been rising in recent years, but it is still, when compared with British or American rates, so ludicrously low as to be nearly negligible. The conclusion may well be that the total burden of taxation in India is not too high, but that its incidence, since it falls too heavily on the workers, is among the factors in the distribution of Indian wealth which explains the general poverty.

* *India and Democracy*, p. 271.
† Anstey, p. 388.

On the subject of expenditure it is enough to quote the official reckoning, which shows that 26 per cent, taking the provincial and central expenditure together, goes to the military services, 6 per cent to education and 1 per cent to public health.* Of this military expenditure a part is evidently due to the fear of another Mutiny. The native army is still officered largely by Englishmen and is held in check by a high proportion of British troops (one in three). A British soldier costs four times what an Indian soldier costs, and a British officer as much as twenty-four Indian soldiers. On such counts as these Indians have a heavy case against British military policy. But the lesson which this war has taught us is that the defences of India were in every sense—military, economic and political—perilously weak. Ill adapted to India's needs, and in respect of its racial composition uneconomical this army may have been, but it was also too small: an adequate and fully mechanised, yet wholly Indian army, would, doubtless, cost more. It is a grave mistake to suppose that the Indian Government is extravagant. On the contrary it is excessively economical. It manages the debt according to the severest canons of sound finance. Its instincts are invariably for deflation. It increases taxation when compelled to do so with reluctance: it cuts down expenditure in times of stress, even on essential productive services, with an approach to enthusiasm. But given political realities, it dared not cut down military charges, for it dared not go much further in arming India, or (what comes to the same thing) in withdrawing the British garrison. For the same reason it dared not cut down the cost (9 per cent) of police, jails and justice, the first line of defence in coping with disaffection.

* I have given these percentages as they stood, on the eve of the reforms, in the official year book, *India in 1928-29* (p. 223). They seem to me, however, seriously misleading. Among expenditure in this reckoning is included that of departments which produce a net revenue, railways, irrigation, forests and land revenue. If these items are excluded, then the military expenditure amounts to 33 per cent, and that on the two social services (education and health) together to 9 per cent.

The costs of the general administration are swollen by the salaries of British civil servants. Able men may expect some compensation if they expatriate themselves, to live often in lonely and unhealthy stations. But their salaries are out of all proportion to the standards of the Indian educated classes. The Viceroy is paid considerably more than the President of the United States and the members of his Council much more than British or American cabinet ministers. Other official salaries, to which allowances must be added, are on the same extravagant scale. Europeans in India, it seems to me, live at a needlessly high level of expense: the reason is less the climate than their sense of the prestige of their white skins. Governors and other high personages are expected to maintain a pompous establishment which offends the better strata of Indian opinion, though possibly the pace was originally set by the luxury of Indian potentates. A Viceroy who had dared to live, if not precisely as an ascetic, yet with the thought of India's poverty ever present with him, would have won India's respect as pomp will never win it. But apart from the privileged position which civil servants of British origin may occupy, the fact seems to be that in India every type of professional service is too highly rewarded in comparison with the incomes derived from agriculture and industry.* Government in India is costly not merely because civil servants, Indians as well as Englishmen, are highly paid, but also because the legal profession levies an enormous tribute on the productive part of the population. That is the case in all capitalist countries, but hardly on the scale that prevails in India. These, then, are the reasons —distrust and a false sense of the conqueror's prestige—why, year after year, the Finance Member faces an inelastic revenue, mortgaged in advance to the indispensable costs of a perennial conquest. Even so, a bolder way of thinking, a more imaginative sense of what even a modest expenditure can effect to promote industry, foster agriculture, and lay the foundations of intelligence and health, could have solved this problem in part. The rulers of India seem never to have realised

* See Professor Rao: *The National Income of British India*, p. 187.

that if they could double the income of the country, the present and, indeed, a much higher expenditure could be cheerfully borne. If the little that Lord Curzon was able to do in this direction had begun a generation earlier, if we had gradually raised the expenditure on industrial and agricultural research and organisation, on housing, health and education, till the present miserable percentages were doubled and quadrupled, we might have found that a prosperous and contented India could have been trusted to handle even artillery without British regiments to watch her.

The controversy over the "drain" is commonly argued on narrow political lines. The Home Charges (justifiable as in part they are) form, however, a small portion of the annual tribute to which India must submit. A people living in the Middle Ages has been penetrated by the commerce, industry and capital of a nation formed by the industrial revolution. It erected its factories, laid out its plantations, sunk coal pits and built railways and ports on the basis of a labour supply which is still exceedingly cheap, even when allowance is made for its physical weakness and inefficiency. In the cotton-mills of Bombay Presidency it has been reckoned that 34 Indians do the work of 12 Lancashire hands for 60 per cent of their wage-bill.* In turning this opportunity to advantage, European capitalists had behind them a friendly government which, until our own day, rather retarded than promoted the emergence of this backward people from its economically primitive phase, and only recently, and still inadequately, began to protect its workers from the grosser forms of exploitation. In addition to manufacture (in which Indian competition is even now formidable only in the cotton trade), the British forces of penetration included modern banking and sea-transport. The profits of this

* By the delegates of the International Textile Unions who visited India in 1926-27. See *Das Werktätige Indien* by Schrader and Furtwängler, p. 266. But other authorities rate Indian efficiency much higher. The management of the Tata Steel Works rates one Indian worker at two-thirds of a European.

exploitation under favourable conditions often put a strain on our powers of belief. Coal-mines have been known to pay 160 per cent on a daily wage of 8*d*., nor were such rates attained only in boom years: * the dividends of one of these mines averaged over 80 per cent throughout the period 1901-29. Out of 51 jute-mills, 32 paid as much as 100 per cent in one or more years between 1918 and 1927; 29 never paid less than 20 per cent, and 10 never less than 40 per cent.†

With sufficiently full figures before me I reckon that during the early post-war years, for every £100 which these jute mills paid in profits to their shareholders in Scotland they paid £12 in wages to their Indian workers.‡ India is, indeed, the brightest jewel in the British Crown.

Even these monstrous figures do not tell the whole of the story. Most of these British companies are registered in London, which means that the income tax levied on profits won by exploiting Indian workers go not to the Indian but to the British Exchequer—a form of tribute from which the whole dependent Empire suffers, Africa as well as Asia. To the reader these are merely figures: to my memory they recall the barely human existence to which in stinking and dilapidated hovels those workers were condemned. A civilised government would have contrived to raise their standard of life by taxing such profits. It may be as well to remind the English reader—to Indians the bare mention of such a thing may look like a joke in the worst of taste—that not even in a rudimentary form does any system of social security exist in this profiteer's para-

* Buchanan, p. 266.

† Anstey, quoting *Capital*, p. 282 note.

‡ A similar reckoning will be found in *Das Werktätige Indien*, p. 103 —that profits amount to six or eight times the wages bill—and also in *Exploitation in India*, a valuable little study of conditions in this industry by the Rt. Hon. Thomas Johnston, M.P., and John F. Sime, Secretary of the Dundee Union of Jute and Flax Workers. They put the earnings of the jute-mills on their capital for the decade 1915-24 at 90 per cent and state that "the average annual profit is eight times the wages bill."

dise. But the most cold-blooded economist would condemn this record for reasons of another order. These industrialists, the Indians * as well as the British, were starving their own market, when they rationed the buying-power of their wage-earners in this niggardly way. Mass-production cannot thrive without mass-consumption. But the aspect of this exploitation which concerns us at this stage of our argument is that these industrial profits, transferred to the shareholder at home, were, with the pensions of officers and civilians and the fixed interest on the debt, a big item in the tribute the Empire drew from India.

There is a simple yet accurate way in which we may measure the total tribute India pays, not indeed to the United Kingdom as a political entity, but to a section of its inhabitants. The balance of trade should reveal it. Under British rule until the other day, India's exports have exceeded her imports: the amount of the excess should disclose what she pays as debtor to her Western creditors, together with the profits which foreign industrialists, bankers, merchants and carriers make on her territory for their shareholders and sleeping partners overseas. It will also include the sums earned in India and transmitted to Great Britain as pensions, or for the support of the families of civilians, soldiers, and others resident out of India. A negligible part of it may go to capitalists of other than British nationality, and to Indians living in Great Britain. This total does not include the very considerable sums which

* There is little or nothing to choose between the two, save the fact that Indian profits mainly went into home consumption. The most efficient of the Indian cotton-mills show an even greater prosperity. (See Buchanan, p. 209.) Thus between the years 1916 and 1929 a mill at Sholapur paid during three years dividends of 200 per cent and over, and during seven years of 100 per cent and over: its lowest dividend in this period was 35 per cent. When the slump came (1930-32) it still paid 6 per cent. The record may be held by the Empress Mills at Nagpur, a Tata concern, which boasted (Buchanan, p. 210) that the original shareholders could reckon their actual dividends in 1920 as 488 per cent. That was a boom year, and this was an exceptionally capable concern. There were, of course, less efficient concerns which made no profits at all in bad years.

Englishmen in India enjoy or reinvest, whether as salaries or profits, upon her soil. It represents the profits, fixed interest and pensions, of which the equivalent is physically sent out of India in the form of goods, as a surplus of exports over imports, less the excess of imports of treasure over exports. An exact statistical reckoning is difficult, because the value of the rupee has varied considerably and so has the area included within India's frontiers. Over a century, starting in 1835, when we may consider that the relationship had entered on its modern phase, the annual tribute grew steadily from about £3 millions at the start to £12 millions in the decade beginning 1875. By the turn of the century it was nearing £20 millions. It shot up to its maximum in 1916 at £43 millions, and then rapidly declined. During the first quarter of this century it averaged £23 millions. In 1931 the balance was suddenly reversed and has remained favourable to India down to the present day. These figures mean that even if we disregard the early predatory period altogether, we withdrew from India by the normal processes of trade and administration a sum that cannot well have been less than £1,000 millions in the course of the century that ended in 1930. A considerable part of this great sum, in a period when sterling was worth much more than its value today, must have gone to add to the capital equipment of these islands. It built in England the steel-mills, the electrical plant, the ships and the workers' dwellings which India lacks.*

* It would be desirable to have an exact study of these figures over the whole period of British rule; but this is a task for a professional statistician. I have used the decennial averages for the period 1835-1922 given in the *Statistics of British India*, 1922, p. 129, which are quoted in Buchanan, p. 190. For the later period I used the Statistical Yearbooks of the League of Nations, down to the year 1937-8. In making use of its tables, I have disregarded, as for the purpose of comparison I was obliged to do, the refinements and corrections of its final column, which allows for certain errors and omissions. Some Indian economists have made estimates which seem to me greatly exaggerated. Wealth can be transferred from one country to another only by the physical export of goods, treasure and services. It seems to me for this reason

In what sense is it reasonable to call this great sum a tribute? Much of was payment at a rather excessive rate for honest and valuable services: much of it was the somewhat extravagant reward of enterprise, knowledge and skill which India did not possess. Much of it, as certainly, represented ruthless exploitation. It is not the total profit arising from British trade with India, or the total earnings of Englishmen arising out of the political relationship: these would come to a much higher total. It is, broadly, that part of the gain arising from the actual relationship with India, economic and political, which Englishmen enjoy in England. It is this geographical distinction that marks it off from the usual profits of capitalistic exploitation. If we had settled in India as the Moguls did and buried our fathers' bones in its soil, we might have levied a much more ruthless tribute and yet have done less economic and social harm. Let me illustrate the distinction. Mr. Smith is a sleeping partner in a jute-mill in Dundee: he has also invested in British War Loan and railways. All this is unearned income, derived from the active work of mill-hands and railway servants, and from taxpayers in this country. He spends it, however, for the most part also in this country on goods and services originating here. Much of it returns promptly as wages to the workers of this country, or in some form continues to circulate here. Mr. Brown, on the other hand, has shares in a jute-mill in Calcutta, in Indian railways

---

impossible that the annual "drain" can exceed the balance of trade, so defined.

It will be asked whether invisible items modify these balances of visible imports and exports. The chief of these are shipping and insurance charges. Full allowance has been made for these in the League's statistical tables, where the original data have been adjusted to represent the c.i.f. value of imports and the f.o.b. value of exports. The services include estimates for tourists, emigrants' remittances, etc. This means that the figures in Column Six ("total") represent the true balance of trade—goods, services and gold. Since the earlier returns have not been compiled on this exact model, I cannot claim more for the figures in the text than that they reveal the tendency of the balance of trade.

and the Indian debt. His income also is unearned, and is derived from the active work of Indian mill-hands, railwaymen and taxpayers. But it is spent on goods and services in Kensington or Tunbridge Wells: it ceases to circulate in India, and evokes no further goods or services there. It is a gain that Indians were far from inviting Mr. Brown to make at their expense. There would have been no Scottish jute-mills in Calcutta but for Clive's indispensable preliminary operations. Assuredly it represents a "drain" on India's resources and it swells, when we add it up, to a formidable total.

It is clear, however, when we examine the recent figures of India's trade balance, that a transitional period started in 1931, when it swung in her favour and remained steadily positive. This surprising phenomenon must be interpreted with due caution and I must confess that I lack the knowledge to analyse it with any confidence. It seems with a brief time-lag to coincide with the new era in our economic relationship which started with the adoption by India of a protective tariff. Again, as a result of the recommendations of the Simon Commission a very much more equitable plan, greatly to India's advantage, was adopted in apportioning some of the military charges between the home country and the dependency. The Empire bore the cost of mechanising her army, nor has she been made to pay, as in the past, for its services outside the Peninsula. The policy of buying virtually all the requirements of the army, the railways and other governmental services in Great Britain was gradually modified in India's favour. On the other hand, to circumvent the tariff, a number of British industries which make light consumers' goods, such as candles, matches and soap, have opened factories in India: of these the most important is a branch of Imperial Chemicals. This investment would be reflected in the trade returns by the export of machinery, which was still British property after its arrival. To that extent the figures may be misleading, though only to a limited degree and for a brief period.

During the war India's financial status has undergone a startling transformation, so that she is no longer a debtor country. She exported troops, which do not figure in the balance of trade. The United Kingdom has shouldered a great part of "her" expenditure on defence which it imposed on her. India has been able to "repatriate" the sterling debt on a massive scale, so that by January 1943 it was virtually wiped out. Nor is this all. The Government of India has been able to purchase the few remaining British-owned railways, four in number. There still remains a sterling balance in India's favour which may be used to acquire the title to other British investments in India. In short, the war has had in India the same general effects that it has had throughout the Empire. The supplies of raw materials which the war devoured, in this case jute, pig iron, leather and wheat, have been paid for by mobilising British overseas investments. The economic empire is being liquidated, and India has become, for a moment, a creditor country.

THE FUTURE

OUR ATTEMPT to analyse the causes of India's poverty, brief and superficial though it may have been, has led us to conclusions which justify brighter hopes for the future. The dislocation of her traditional economic structure which resulted from her entry into the machine age, unprotected and subject to foreign rule, caused a misery which will haunt her for decades to come. The waste and the under-employment of her vast labour force will persist. Its consequences, mental and physiological, through under-nourishment and lack of ambition, will yield to no quick remedy. But the record shows that even under direct British rule the decisive change in her status has already begun. Hers can no longer be called a typical colonial economy. She has enjoyed, with some serious qualifications, fiscal autonomy for many years. The trade balance has at last turned in her favour, so that she no longer pays a tribute to the Imperial Metropolis. During the Second World War she has ceased to rank as a debtor country.

All this means that when she achieves her political freedom, her economic destiny will be effectively in her own hands. If she can evolve a creative leadership, it should then be possible for her to deal with the causes of poverty that lie embedded in her own social institutions—her traditional attitude to animal life, the habit of hoarding—with caste and much else. When her leaders are her rulers, they should be able, with a modern technique of education and propaganda, to cope with these psychological impediments to economic progress. That is a task which no foreign bureaucracy could hope to accomplish. The problem of the mal-distribution of wealth confronts us in several forms—the excessive cost of the machinery of government, the enormous exploitation of the wage-earners by industry, the low level and the partial incidence of direct taxation, the tribute levied by the functionless landlord and the usurer, and outside British India the exactions of the princes. These problems have haunted the fringes of Indian political life for a generation, spectres which nationalists tried to dodge, because they threatened the unity of a people still at issue with the foreign conqueror. This class struggle cannot be postponed after India is free. What solutions, gradualist or revolutionary, she will reach, I will not try to guess.

The technical problem of increasing the production of wealth presented itself to us as we went along in two phases : fewer hands must raise richer harvests from the soil; the labour power released by better organisation on the land must be diverted to industry. Of the immense untapped resources the Peninsula possesses the younger generation of Indians is now keenly aware. The utilisation of its hydro-electric energy has only just begun, while its minerals are as yet wastefully and inadequately used. It lacks within its own borders nothing essential for an immense industrial development. The catalogue, in which I have not included cotton, jute and other primary products of agriculture, is impressive :

(1) It has been estimated that India's resources of hydro-electric energy, which may amount to 27 million horse-power, are second only to those of the United States with 35 millions.

But India had by 1932 developed only 3 per cent of her resources, as against 33 per cent in the U.S.A., 72 per cent in Switzerland and 55 per cent in Germany. She has, however, made some progress since the date of these figures. The first pioneering work was done by the private enterprise of the Tata firm in the Bombay Presidency. The remarkable development in the Punjab was due to British official initiative. Mysore was in this as in other matters progressive. Schemes on the model of the New Deal's triumph over rural poverty in the Tennessee Valley might be adapted to India's needs. It supplies cheap fertilisers which the exhausted soil of the Peninsula sorely needs.

(2) India possesses enormous reserves of coal, chiefly in and around western Bengal. Most of it is easily worked, but while some of it is as good as the imported Natal coal, much of it is of a rather poor quality. There is good coking coal, but the supply is limited.

(3) The iron-ore deposits of India exceed in quantity those of Great Britain and Germany. In quality they are among the best in the world, yielding from 60 to 70 per cent of pure iron, and they are very easily worked. The best deposits, moreover, lie conveniently near to the Bengal coal-field. Their development is due to the enterprise of Mr. Tata, the Parsi millionaire. Failing to obtain the Government's consent, his pioneering work was delayed for some twenty years. Eventually Lord Curzon encouraged him, and his firm, now under his sons, has built up at Jamshedpur what is said to be the largest steel and iron plant in the British Empire, employing 50,000 men.

(4) Of manganese India has the largest reserves in the world and her production is second only to Russia's. But the uneconomic and unprofitable plan is followed of exporting the ore to Europe, America and Japan, instead of extracting the manganese on the spot.

(5) With mica India is well supplied. There is much bauxite, some copper in Bihar, some pyrites as yet unworked and abundant salt in Baroda. There is some oil in Assam and the

Punjab, of which little use has been made. But the Geological Survey has been starved and its work is still incomplete.

With these great natural resources the progress of industry in India under British rule has been slow in its tempo and disappointing in its scale. The verdict of the American economist, Professor Buchanan (dated 1934), is worth quoting, because he made his thorough study of Indian economics on the spot after a residence in Japan, which gave him a basis for comparison:

Here was a country with all the crude elements upon which manufacturing depends, yet during more than a century it has imported factory-made goods in large quantities and has developed only a few of the simplest industries for which machinery and organisation had been highly perfected in other countries. With abundant supplies of raw cotton, raw jute, easily mined coal, easily mined and exceptionally high-grade iron ore; with a redundant population often starving because of lack of profitable employment; with a hoard of gold and silver second perhaps to that of no other country in the world and with access through the British Government to a money market which was lending large quantities of capital to the entire world; with an opening under their own flag for British business leaders who were developing both at home and in numerous new countries all sorts of capitalistic industries; with an excellent market within her own borders and near at hand in which others were selling great quantities of manufactures; with all these advantages, India, after a century, was supporting only about two per cent of her population by factory industry. . . . While the proportions are gradually changing, Indian economic life is still characterised by the export of raw materials and the import of manufactures. In spite of her factories and her low standard of living, India is less nearly self-sufficient in manufactured products than she was a century ago.*

* Pp. 450-1. Professor Buchanan formed a very favourable opinion of that "singularly able and high-minded body of men," the British bureaucracy in India, but he thinks that their "aristocratic background" led them to "despise business." India needed "practical rulers" who

Able and fair-minded though Mrs. Anstey and Professor Buchanan are, given their capitalistic viewpoint, the adequate economic history of our rule in India has still to be written. My Socialist scheme of values disqualifies me, nor have I the intimate knowledge which should underlie even a brief sketch and a summary judgment, but there are some questions and perhaps some opinions even a diffident outsider may risk. To me the record seems to be poor in the creative daring which orthodox economists advance, often with good reason, as the justification of capitalistic enterprise, at least in its early phases. Where in this story is the inventive pioneer, who perceives a public need, stakes his all to satisfy it, and draws a possibly excessive reward for good service? It was the Government rather than any capitalistic *entrepreneur* which took the initiative in providing the most impressive of the services we have rendered—the trunk roads, the railways, the irrigation works and the Punjab hydro-electric scheme. It is true that the railways were constructed and run by private companies for many years before they were nationalised. But the initiative came from above, largely for strategic reasons. So far from taking a risk, the capitalist had an ample guarantee from the state. The chief industry in which British capital has been engaged, jute, can hardly be classed as risky, since India has a world monopoly of this material. One family does, indeed, stand out as a type of the wonder-working *entrepreneur* who

would "adapt their industrial technique to the use of her people. For this particular task a less effective group could scarcely have been found." He refuses to decide how far their adherence to *laissez faire* and free trade was due to a "desire to favour British industry and commerce" and how far it sprang from a disinterested academic belief; but he has no doubt that British policy did gravely retard India's industrial development. It was dictated, as Lord Curzon pointed out, by Manchester, and "has been the most damaging feature of British rule." Charitable though Professor Buchanan is throughout in judging motives, he makes it clear that British currency policy in India has in effect injured Indian traders. He criticises also the habit of buying all government stores, including railway material, until very recently in England, and the failure to develop banking.

figures in the classical textbooks, the Tatas, father and sons. After making fabulous wealth in the safe routine of cotton manufacture, they did pioneer on a great scale, first with hydro-electricity round Bombay and then with steel at Jamshedpur. Nor is that all, for they have interested themselves in aluminum also, to mention only one of their many prospects. But they are native Parsis. Only too often—though not always—when we look at the record of British concerns in India which dealt with indigo, tea, and coal, they were manifestly demoralised by the cheapness of Indian labour.

Why, one asks, are the Tatas unique—or nearly so? Where were the *entrepreneurs* of the same calibre, whether Indians or Englishmen, who should have been doing what they did, and much more of the same kind, fifty or sixty years earlier? That a clever Indian could grow rich with fatal ease as a lawyer is part of the answer. That certain functions and trades had been appropriated by the British business community as theirs by custom, if not by right—this also is important. Shipping, banking by the modern Western technique, insurance, foreign trade —these came to India with the Company and remained stubbornly British. Again, this mighty Government spent so large a proportion of the Indian national income on railways, the army, public buildings, telegraphs and the like, that without the assurance of its patronage it would have been risky even for Englishmen to start industries in India to make such things as steel rails, girders, cables or locomotives. Until recent years, as an unquestioned part of the Imperial routine, if a hideous railway bridge was required to span the Ganges at Benares the material was fetched from England. That was one of the most valuable perquisites of empire. The virtual monopoly of shipping was another. The typical fact in our relationship with India is that British ships carry Indian pig-iron and manganese ore to England and then back again to India as finished steel and machinery.

The *laissez-faire* principles of the bureaucracy would never have allowed it to sit down and plan the development of Indian industries, as the Russians and it may be the American New

Dealers would have done. But to conclude from this that private enterprise, whether Indian, British or foreign, had a clear field to make the most of the resources of the Peninsula would be to fall into a serious error. A veto this Government had in the early days, and a negative plan of sorts must have persisted as part of the continuous tradition of the bureaucracy. The Company had up to 1813 a monopoly of all forms of trade, but it could and did permit others to embark under licence in private ventures such as coal-mining. This tradition of control has persisted down to our own times. Englishmen are often puzzled, and even irritated, when Indians assail the Government because this or the other industry is lacking in India. There are many wealthy Indians: why do not they club together and start it? The answer is that an informal system of negative control, wholly alien to British traditions, prevails and always has prevailed in India. Without the goodwill and the active support of the Government, neither a heavy industry nor an engineering industry could be started. Behind the Government the white business community entrenched in the banks, the railways, and the managing agencies thinks and acts with an astonishing racial unanimity. In war-time the formal consent of the Government is, of course, required. This war has made us aware how primitive Indian industry still is. Imported aeroplane parts can be assembled. The chassis of a lorry can be constructed. But in all India there is no plant capable of making an internal-combustion engine for any purpose whatever. It is absurd to suggest that this nation of exquisite craftsmen cannot learn how to do it, or even that the managerial ability shown at Jamshedpur would fail here. The responsibility lies with the Government and it does not disclaim it. The House of Commons was told (October 9, 1941) that it would not be "a practical proposition" to start such an industry during this war. In the following year Indian indignation was hot enough to secure the promise of a commission to study this question. The veto, however, has not yet been lifted. It may be that some charitable explanation could be suggested for such an act of policy as this, but I cannot supply it. To me it seems that from the days of the monopolist Company onwards, the rulers of India have been fighting a slow rearguard action, to keep India as long as possible a source of raw materials, a market for British manufacturers and a field for British investment. In our own day so much has been conceded, that India is now a protectionist country, and a creditor rather than a debtor. But even today her rulers cling, while they can, to the last keys of power. Much as they kept the artillery in white hands after the Mutiny, so now they will not surrender the sole right to make the engine which is the motor of modern life. With majestic impartiality they protect all the minorities, princes and untouchables, Muslims and the British makers of internal-combustion engines.

For these reasons India is poor. We gave her, indeed, the blessing of unity and internal order: we built railways, and famine ceased to slay. But over this peace brooded the incubus of our control, which distorted and retarded her economic development. When she surmounts the immense obstacles which still keep her politically subject, this incubus, lighter by far than once it was, will be lifted from her shoulders. Some time will pass before she will learn to stand erect and use her atrophied muscles. If with courage as well as wisdom her leaders have the sagacity to plan with the aid of science, there is no reason why India should remain for ever poor.

VI. Looking Forward

THIS BOOK is nearing its end, and I will now try to sum up the conclusions to which it points. There is much in it that many readers will have found unwelcome, eccentric, unacceptable. But whatever their intrinsic value may be, some few opinions stand out for me, about aspects of Indian life and British rule, which I shall try to restate briefly, since they are commonly overlooked. They formed themselves in my mind partly from things seen, partly from a process of reflection that covers half a lifetime.

(1) The fact which for me overshadows every other is the immeasurable, the inhuman poverty of the Indian masses. To grasp it, to analyse its causes, to discover the beginnings of a remedy—that is the Indian problem. If politics rather than economics have filled the greater part of this book, the reason is that the solution of this complicated evil is and for long has been hopelessly beyond the competence of India's British rulers.

Our day in India is over. We have no creative part to play. India's poverty has its psychological aspect, which we can only complicate. Her social institutions, which our presence tends to stereotype, play some part among its causes. It involves a latent class struggle which Indians must themselves bring to a decision. No foreign rulers could do in the way of planning and popular education what must be done, least of all a foreign bureaucracy. But, to be blunt, the major cause of this poverty has been the impact of our way of life on the unshielded, passive body of Indian society, from the Conquest to the present day. The true cause of Indian poverty is not over-population. India is over-populated only in the sense that her colossal labor forces are but half-employed and that their effort is wastefully organised. The excessive concentration on agriculture dates from the deliberate destruction of Indian handicraft industry in the early days of the Company. The ill-effects were prolonged by the policy, not yet wholly discarded, which sought to use India solely as a source of raw materials, a market for our manufactured goods and a field for our capital investment. From this policy, from the charges of our costly military and administrative apparatus and from the inordinate profits of the few industries we established, there resulted an annual drain on India's resources, in effect a tribute, which was apparent until the other day in India's adverse balance of trade. This checked the formation of Indian capital. Our educational system failed to give Indians what they chiefly lacked, a training in the natural sciences and technology. No less unfortunate in retarding their industrial development was the attachment of the bureaucracy to *laissez faire* and until recently to free trade. The incubus of our policy on India's progress outweighs the great gifts we brought—peace, order, the end of famine, and our distinguished engineering work in the fields of transport and irrigation. To the average illiterate villager, who rarely sees a white man and has never caught even a distant glimpse of the intellectual treasures of Western civilisation, our rule means chiefly the predatory landlord we imposed and our native police, as brutal as it is corrupt.

But in sight of this unparalleled poverty, India possesses great natural resources, which a capable and dynamic government that knew how to harness Indian patriotism to an intelligent plan could develop, while it organised to some purpose the labour of the peasants on the land.

(2) The Indian masses, rural as well as urban, while they endure this degrading and enfeebling poverty must face the spectacle of great and conspicuous wealth in the hands of the few, while they endure the harsh exploitation of an owning class which relies on a conscienceless police force. This, as any social chemist would recognise, is a highly explosive mixture. There are here the makings of social revolution. A resolute government which made the necessary changes promptly by peaceful means might perhaps secure its fruits without a period

of bloody civil war. In northern India the first step is to sweep away the functionless landlords with a minimum of compensation—enough to prevent these men from becoming in their turn a fascist counter-revolutionary force. The ideal solution of peasant poverty may be in many regions the adoption of mechanised and socialised farming on something like the Russian plan. This, however, is not yet possible, save on an experimental scale, for lack firstly of education and secondly of the ability to manufacture machinery. For many years, therefore, Indians will have to rely on less drastic solutions, most of them familiar and easily applied.

But even for a reformist programme, in addition to the elimination of the landlords, three or four other measures are indispensable, which propertied interests will resist. Enough has been said about usury to give the reader some idea of the curse it is. But it fulfils a function. It is the primitive, traditional way of financing India's chief productive activity, agriculture. Perhaps it can be fought by restricting the rate of interest and cancelling arrears. But the only way to kill it is to create a socially satisfactory way of financing farming. In the long run the only satisfactory solution is for the state (in this case the province) to take over the land and act as a benevolent and scientific landlord, who will as soon as possible organise big communal, mechanised farms, and will in the meantime supply the peasants with the capital needed for improvement.

Short of this radical solution, much might be done by developing co-operation for marketing and purchase as well as credit, by a land bank and by a development fund. Other indispensable measures include the adoption of drastic direct taxation, especially on unearned incomes. Another is the canalisation of investment into socially useful enterprises, in accordance with a long-range plan of development. A third is some technique of price-control, perhaps by variable quotas of imported goods, to check the ill-effects of protection on the impoverished consumer. A policy of this kind presupposes a well-organised democracy, which means not merely the right of

poor men to vote, but their organisation in peasant leagues
and trade unions which can work effectively without having to
dread the coercion of an omnipotent police force. The adoption of an occupational franchise should be considered. In short,
there can be no hopeful attack on Indian poverty without some
shift in the balance of class power. The Indian social structure,
it should be noted, is doubly unstable. The impoverished
peasantry, with the relatively few industrial workers, are po-
tentially a revolutionary force. Secondly, the embittered and
unemployed youth of the middle class might be turned in a
fascist direction. Subhas Bose was doing this and so are the
Muslim Khaksars, organised as they are on the Nazi model.

(3) The nationalist struggle against the imperial power has
postponed and repressed this latent class struggle. None the
less, it casts its shadow before it and influences both Congress
and the Muslim League today. This is the clue to some aspects
of current politics in India which admit on the surface of a
simpler interpretation. Gandhi is well aware of this class
cleavage and manages, on the whole, to suppress it. That is
why he will not countenance any form of agitation, such as a
refusal to pay the land-tax, which would antagonise the landlords. To maintain the internal unity of Indian society as long
as possible, in order to mobilise it as a single whole against
the imperial adversary, seems to him an axiom of strategy.
But in attempting to forecast the future we should not assume
that Congress, after the liberation of India, will manage for
long to preserve its present unity and discipline. Either it will
dodge any fundamental solution of the agrarian question, in
which case it will forfeit the support of the peasants, or else
it will boldly eliminate the landlords, in which case it will be
split from top to bottom—for Gandhi, with the wealthy industrialists, will defend landed property.

(4) This class issue cuts across the Muslim-Hindu feud and
goes some way to explain the increasing tension. The Muslim
League is a great power, but it reflects the fears and interests
chiefly of the propertied element and primarily of the landed
gentry. It tries by an appeal to religious separatism to post-

pone the class issue and prevent the fraternisation and co-operation of Muslim and Hindu tenants and landless labourers. Though it is obliged, like every Indian party, to demand "independence," it is in fact fairly well content to lean on the protection of the British Raj: but if this tactic can no longer succeed, it will insist on Pakistan. Cut off from Hindu radicalism, it believes that within a Muslim state it could maintain its ascendancy as the ruling class. The popular forces among the Muslims have a potential and in some regions an actual majority, but they are poor and ill-organised and have no leader of Mr. Jinnah's calibre. None the less, while this feud is at the moment a very grave evil which admits of no easy cure, it is not rooted in unchangeable instincts or in inherited character, as is commonly supposed. Economic causes give it most of its contemporary force. It has been fostered in the last generation chiefly by the official classification of Indians for all political purposes according to religious labels. This has had effects which may be difficult to obliterate quickly. Yet on nearly every contemporary issue, Indians divide themselves naturally not on religious lines, but according to functional and class interests. In short, however potent as a disturbing force this feud may be today, it is factitious and was swollen to its present dimensions by our political arrangements.

(5) In any attempt to solve the Indian problem we must proceed on the assumption that Indians distrust us and dislike us. There are exceptions to this rule, but such men are not typical; their motives are often interested and their advice may mislead us. Dangerous counsellors also are those liberal and well-meaning Englishmen who, because they themselves like Indians, shut their eyes both to the behaviour of their cruder fellow-countrymen and to the emotional reactions of a subject nation to this conduct. Our promises and professions are not believed: we have no credit. We must either pay cash down or find a surety. How far this distrust is justified I have discussed, indirectly perhaps, by a close scrutiny of our recent attempts at a solution. Throughout Sir Samuel Hoare's Act of 1935, to take only the most glaring instance, a certain effect—

dividing to rule—was provided for by highly appropriate means in clause after clause, but more especially by the allocation of votes to the princes and the Muslims. If anyone chooses to argue that Sir Samuel did not intend that these means should be used for this end, I am not disposed to carry the discussion further. He may, for all I know, lack the habit of self-analysis. The historian will have to say what Indians said: This act was an essay in the imperial art of division, which failed because it admitted of only one, the obvious, interpretation. So many of our offers and policies have been open to this criticism that we must expect mistrust, even when we are sincere.

(6) The Cripps offer was not, as even our Liberal press maintained, a satisfactory attempt, either in the procedure adopted, or in its contents. No preliminary soundings had been taken: the offer itself was rigid and subject to modification only in minor details. It failed because not Congress only but Indians generally saw in it no intention to surrender the reality of power today. It was not the communal feud that wrecked it, and though this doubtless would have caused difficulties at a later stage, these had not arisen during the discussions with C████ ██s.

(7) The religious feud occupies so much of our attention that we are apt to forget that the intricate problem of the princes is at least equally important. Congress raised it during the Delhi negotiations in a form which readily won sympathy from progressive Englishmen. It is indefensible that the autocratic princes should nominate the representatives of their states in the future constituent assembly, while the provinces elect theirs. An Indian union cannot be formed by a medley of autocracies and democracies, nor would this hybrid be long-lived, if it could be begotten.

So much most of us grasped. But an even graver issue is involved. It is highly unlikely that the princes, so long as they remain autocrats, will ever enter any Indian union that includes the more radical provinces within a democratic framework. But if they stay out, Indian independence is impossible.

The geographical pattern is too intricate: the states cut across all the lines of communication. The paramount power could use them to maintain its garrisons at its choice all over the Peninsula. Under such conditions a lame and limping Dominion could, perhaps, come into being, but it could never take the next step of declaring its independence by seceding from the Empire. Again, if the princes should come in, as autocrats, it will be on terms which for the mass of Indians, including their own subjects, would be intolerable and unacceptable. In other words, five hundred princelings still, under the Cripps formula, enjoy a veto over the will of all the millions of this nation. This *impasse* might continue indefinitely, or until it resulted in civil war or revolution.

The gravity of this business lies in the fact that the princes are not principals or free agents. They are the protected puppets of the paramount power. If they obstruct or push their bargaining to the limits of blackmail, few Indians will waste much breath in cursing them. In these manœuvres Indians will see only the hidden hand of the imperial power. Not a single indiscreet word would be uttered, meanwhile, in public, either at Delhi or Westminster. The game could be played entirely behind the scenes, and by officials whose names fe   know. The average Englishman, even the average Member of Parliament, would look on bewildered and somewhat distressed. "These princes," he would say, "seem rather unreasonable, but after all they ought to know their own business. Besides, they stuck to us in the hour of danger. So we must leave it at that."

At the risk of offending the reader grossly, I will state my conclusion bluntly. As yet we have made no offer of eventual independence to India. The Cripps mission carried no such offer. So long as we stand behind the princes, protecting autocratic rights which depend on our armed power, India's independence is a meaningless word. It is to be presumed that the shrewder men in Delhi and Whitehall understand and understood this all the time. This may be imperial statecraft, but is it honesty? I believe that independence is what Indians want and mean to get. Dominion status is not what they desire. But so much is certain: we cannot keep them contented with this less attractive condition by manipulating the princes against them. We shall deserve both their anger and their contempt if we try.

WHAT CAN BE DONE?

LET US now turn to the future. I think it unlikely that any fresh attempt to reach a settlement will be made by the British Government, until the war is over. Certainly none will be made until Lord Linlithgow's prolonged viceregal reign ends in October, 1943. I assume with even greater confidence that no attempt by Indians can succeed, or will be encouraged, so long as Gandhi is in prison and Congress remains in revolt. The realists of Whitehall and New Delhi may reckon that when the war is won, or as good as won, our prestige and authority will have been recovered; while available military sources will be unlimited and our dependence on American goodwill will no longer hamper us. In short, we may then be able to deal with the Indians as empires are wont to deal with subject peoples, though it is understood that the offer of Dominion status stands, as also do our peculiar relations with the Muslim League and the princes. By postponing a decision, any liquidation of the Empire, to use Mr. Churchill's phrase, can be averted.

These realists may have vision, a gift of which they have given little proof in the past. For my part I can cast a less flattering horoscope. It is possible that India has escaped the danger of invasion. That is for her and for us a stroke of undeserved good fortune. But it has its political disadvantages. It means that there will be no rally of patriotic sentiment to our side. In that case, the longer we delay a settlement, the more will Indian opinion, over an ever-widening surface, harden against us. That is happening already. Of late both the Hindu Mahasabha and the Muslim League have threatened, though in vague terms, to resort to direct action. They will not do it: wealthy conservatives do not court imprisonment. None the less, their threats do mean something important. They mean that these rivals perceive that the revolt of Congress has added to its popularity. India today is no place for conservatives and it may be an even less congenial sphere of activity for such groups on the day after tomorrow.

Why do I assume this? Not from any partisan pessimism, but because economic distress is driving average men and women to anger and desperation. Food prices have been allowed to soar, uncontrolled, until in January 1943, thanks to reckless exports, to the loss of imported supplies, to profiteering and to hoarding, due as much to fear as to greed, they had risen to levels which in some provinces meant a shortage verging on famine, and this was true also of some other necessities of daily life. The bureaucracy, absorbed in crushing Congress, a policeman's job which it understands, had ignored for six months the onset of this disaster. It then took, belatedly, some of the steps for which the crisis called; but without training, or experience, how competently will it perform this novel and difficult task? Much the same thing, though on a far smaller scale, happened round about the end of the last war. The result was that the model province, the pattern of loyalty, the Punjab, was on the verge of open rebellion and a Sikh crowd had to be mown down at Amritsar. History rarely repeats itself: it is apt to do something worse.

In their other reckonings the realists may be equally astray. Is it certain, for example, that our own troops will patiently remain in India to repress rebellion and shoot starving crowds after the war is won? And again, will our own economic plight permit us to disregard American displeasure? To sum up, the realists may be mistaken in postponing an Indian settlement, until the war is won. The best moment was at its outbreak. A reconciliation could have been reached had a more perceptive messenger carried a better offer at the nadir of our fortunes in the spring of 1942. The next chance will come when the new Viceroy succeeds Lord Linlithgow.

Though no sign of a change is visible in the Government's attitude to India and none can be predicted, let us assume that the improbable will happen. What, then, are the conditions under which it might succeed?

The main condition, if we did but realise it, has been fulfilled. The Empire is being liquidated. No boast of Mr. Churchill's at a Mansion House banquet will suffice to keep it intact. This unusual man has some of the elements of greatness—an indomitable will, the fighting temperament, a single-track mind that runs straight to its goal, an enviable ability to ignore the opinions of men beyond his own chosen circle, an unshakeable faith in his own star, firm roots in tradition, an ability to express much that average Englishmen feel in words that reveal the consummate artist. A blinkered vision is combined with the genius for action. But however high we may rate Mr. Churchill—and it is easy for those who respect courage and artistry to rate him too high—no man's will can turn back the shadow on the dial of history. We have already traced the end of our old economic relationship with India. India has ceased to be a tributary and a debtor dependency. Our empire over her in the economic sense is ended. It can never be resumed—by us. If ever in the future India slips back into the position of a dependent and a debtor, the creditor and economic overlord will be America. By what ties, then, if not by economic bondage, could we still hold India? Our civil servants, our merchants, our soldiers are no longer indispensable to her. Any affection she might have felt we never chose to cherish. We could now hold India only by military power. Possibly for a time we may try. As certainly in the long run we shall fail. Indians are too many and Englishmen too few. The onlookers, also, are as numerous as they are critical—the Americans, Chinese and Russians. Finally, this nation is now too civilised to persevere for long in a task so repugnant to our better nature.

The next condition of success is difficult and perhaps impossible. It is that Mr. Churchill should forget his Mansion House speech—his boast that we will hold our own, his vow that he will not be instrumental in breaking up the Empire, and his threat to carry the issue to a general election. Happily he did not mention India by name. He will not change his mind: he is capable only of a possessive attitude towards our Asiatic dependencies. The best to hope for is that under the pressure of realities he may consent to stand aside in silence and allow others to settle this matter. Which others? I do not see them on either of the Front Benches. I will add, since we are surveying persons, that when we really intend to settle this business, we shall look for a new team. The old team has incurred the distrust of Indians. Whether they deserved it is immaterial. Mr. Amery's abilities have not enabled him to win her confidence. It would be wise at the same time to wind up the India Office and transfer its necessary departmental business to the Dominions Office or the Foreign Office. The new Viceroy should have a new staff to serve him at Delhi. The grey eminences who knew how to rule by dividing are unsuited to this enterprise. There are men in the Indian Civil Service, including some recently retired, who could do this work.

A new point of departure has to be found. The argument from India's imminent danger will no longer serve: that moment of acute alarm is past. Victory, when autumn comes, should be in sight. The emphasis may now be laid, more appropriately than in March 1942, on the future. But the dividing line between the right and the wrong approach to India's future is sharp and clear. The wrong approach is to think of India as our possession on which we propose to confer certain rights. The right approach is to welcome her as an independent nation to the family we are organising. That should be done not by us alone, but by the United Nations, and especially by those which have a footing in the East—America, Russia, China, the Dutch and ourselves. In plain words, we should associate these powers with ourselves in seeking an Indian settlement.

There are several ways in which this might be done. A good beginning might be to negotiate and publish a Pacific Charter as a companion to the Atlantic Charter. It should recognise

that the coming international era in the East must be based
on a new order of equality, social, economic and political. It
should go on to make this promise specifically to each of the
Asiatic peoples in the joint names of the Western peoples. To
China, after recalling our renunciation of "the unequal
treaties," it should promise the restoration of all her lost territories, including by name Hong Kong and Formosa. To the
Filipinos it should renew, in the name of all, the American
pledge of independence. To India it should assure, again in
the name of all, "independence, which she shall enjoy at her
free choice either within the British Commonwealth of Nations
or outside it." I need not fill in the clauses dealing with Burma,
Malaya, the Dutch Islands and Persia, save to say that Burma
and Ceylon cannot be offered less than we offer to India. A
general clause might follow, welcoming any regional grouping
for common purposes which the Asiatic states may see fit to
make within the world-wide organisation. Finally, on the economic side, the Charter might say that in the general effort to
banish want and fear, the Western powers will make it their
constant endeavour by every suitable means to raise the level
of life of the primary producers up to that of the industrial
peoples.

The reader may object that we have had enough of words,
and indeed such a charter would be worthless, unless it were
specific. Its value, as I have sketched it, would lie in its efficacy
as a means of removing India's distrust. She doubts our promises. But in this document we should bring forward America,
China and Russia as our sureties. This we could do without
humiliation, since the Americans and the Dutch would also
call us in to underwrite their pledges. If it were boldly conceived and phrased, such a charter should make in India the
atmosphere in which renewed negotiations could succeed.

Should we go further and call in an American or Chinese
mediator? I will express no decided opinion on this point.
Obviously all the signatories of the charter would have the
right to be informed and consulted over the steps taken to im-
plement it. At some stage mediation might be useful. But

Indian affairs are intricate, and any foreign mediator, however quick-witted, would have to spend some time in preliminary studies. If the American State Department were to choose the mediator, my own enthusiasm for this suggestion would promptly wither.

All the old difficulties would still confront us—the formation of an *interim* government, the Hindu-Muslim tangle and the princes. The first step in solving all these difficulties is that the persons chiefly concerned should grasp at once the fact that we mean to succeed. If they think we are playing at politics, they also will play.

The *interim* government will have two main tasks to fulfil—to wind up the war as far as India's share in it goes and to preside over the framing and adoption of the constitution. The first task should be far less arduous and responsible than that which was anticipated for any team which might have accepted the Cripps offer. India may still be a crucial base for operations against the Japanese, but may not herself be in serious danger. The industrial effort may be more important than the raising of new armies. This easier situation should facilitate the transfer of real power to an Indian administration. We need not traverse the old ground once again. I will assume that it is agreed that the new national government must be "by convention" a cabinet, and that this time the Indian defence member will not be limited in the way first proposed.

No settlement can even begin unless Congress comes into it. The new Viceroy must start his reign with an amnesty. Congress in its turn must call off civil disobedience, which it cannot do till its leaders are released. Self-government must be promptly resumed in the provinces. The national ministry must be formed with the support and participation both of Congress and the Muslim League, but they should not monopolise it. The independent Muslim parties should also be represented.

This presupposes an agreement over Pakistan, which looks difficult. Each side must surrender something. My suggestion is that we offer to meet the views of Congress in the matter of the princes. That we ought to do in any case. Assured of this victory in the struggle for Indian unity, Congress might then go some way to meet the Muslims. It has already said that no province ought to be coerced into joining the Indian union.

A preliminary agreement might be drafted assuring to any province which demands separate self-determination either by (*a*) a bare majority vote of its newly-elected legislative council or (*b*) a three-fourths vote of the members chosen by the most numerous of its communal electorates, the right to have its case decided by an arbitral court which may at its discretion provide for a plebiscite, and make any division of its territory or rectification of its frontiers that may be required to meet the views of minorities.

This is the utmost that reasonable Muslims could fairly claim. We may have to gamble on the chance that this success would satisfy them and that in fact no province will demand separation.

But this is asking much, perhaps too much, from the Hindus. To meet their wholly proper ideal of unity, I would propose that the paramount power should publicly remind the princes that autocracy is an outmoded institution at variance with all the purposes for which the United Nations fought. It should then advise them to prepare for the creation of an Indian union by enfranchising their subjects and conceding civil rights and responsible government on terms not less liberal than those prevailing in the British provinces. Finally, the statement should turn from advice to warning: no prince who disregards these suggestions need expect the support of the paramount power, if disorder should result from his obstinacy.

That would settle the princely problem in twenty-four hours. Incidentally it would remove the last doubt of our sincerity in the mind of the most sceptical Indian. I do not mean to convey the absurdly optimistic idea that the difficulties in the way of a settlement would then vanish. The constitution would still have to be framed. It may not yet be possible to turn the flank of the communal issue, by adopting an occupational franchise. The Muslims may cling to their separate communal electorates. They may even demand parity with the Hindus as their price for consenting to federal unity in any form. Failing that, they may insist on Pakistan. Mr. Churchill's is not the only unusual personality that renders a settlement difficult by its defiant individualism. Gandhi, who is a less flexible conservative than Mr. Churchill, can be fitted with difficulty into any pattern of unity, and the same thing, for other reasons, may be said of Mr. Jinnah. History with all its wrongs and discords and oppressions has personified itself in these three men. I do not pretend to see the way clear to the end: it is much if we can guess how to begin.*

Here is the order in which these tentative suggestions might be carried out:

(1) In a Pacific Charter a joint offer of independence is made to India by all the United Nations interested in Asia.

(2) Indian business is transferred from the India Office to the Dominions Office.

(3) The new Viceroy opens his reign with a political amnesty and states that he hopes to be able to transform his Council into a national government.

(4) Congress simultaneously calls off its revolt.

(5) The Viceroy advises the princes to prepare for entry into an Indian union by conceding full civil and political rights to their subjects.

* A wholly different procedure would be preferable, if it were possible. The problem is to create an Indian federal union. The natural way would be to start with the units, the provinces, and let their governments do the work of negotiating the basis of a settlement. It might be far easier for the premiers of the chief provinces to reach an agreement than for Congress or the Muslim League to do so. But unluckily six of the provinces are without a government of their own. This can be remedied. But a far graver difficulty is that Congress and the League are both highly centralised and disciplined parties, which exact obedience from their members who serve as ministers in the provinces. It follows that no free negotiation between their premiers is possible. Could Congress and the League be induced to renounce this formidable control, at least for an experimental period?

(6) Coalition ministries resume self-government in the six Congress provinces.

(7) Possibly with the help of a mediator, Congress and the Muslim League negotiate an agreement over Pakistan, conceding the right of provinces to separate self-determination, under an arbitral tribunal acceptable to both.

(8) The Viceroy then calls on the best available man, who should probably be a Muslim, to form from Congress, the League and other leading groups a national government, whose chief tasks would be (*a*) to conduct the war-effort and (*b*) to prepare a draft constitution for the Indian union.

(9) As soon as active hostilities are ended in the Indian zone, new elections are held in the provinces and states. The process of self-determination then follows on the lines of the Cripps offer and the Pakistan agreement.

(10) The relations of the single Indian union (or of Hindustan and Pakistan) with the British Commonwealth are then, after negotiation, fixed by treaty. At once, or after an agreed interval, the decision is taken by the Indian Dominion (or Dominions) whether it (or they) will remain within or secede from the British Commonwealth.

There are, to sum up, three active forces in this struggle over India's independence. First, there are the Indians, divided on religious lines traversed by confused class lines. Secondly, there is Mr. Churchill with his deeply entrenched Die hards, omnipotent in England by reason of his personal ascendancy. Thirdly, there is America, critical of British imperialism for mixed reasons. Lastly, there is a passive force which can be brought to bear only in a moment of acute crisis —the opinion of the usually enlightened minority which knows too little about India to form a confident judgment, and the Labour Party absorbed in other things.

In one way or another, but probably not in the way I have ventured to suggest, Dominion status will be offered again. As before, it may seem unacceptable (*a*) because the Muslims will insist on parity or Pakistan and (*b*) because the paramount power will make the customary play with the princes.

My personal view is that the loss of Pakistan, though regrettable, would not be mortal, if Bengal and the Sikh territory were retained. A *modus vivendi* between Pakistan and Hindustan might be reached on the model of the old Austro-Hungarian dual monarchy. Also I doubt whether the separation would last for much more than a generation. The Canadian provinces did not all federate at the start. Muslims can be won for socialism rather more easily than Hindus, and after a decade or two the Muslim League and the landlords may lose their hold over some of the provinces included in Pakistan. Reunion would then be possible.

But, as we have seen, Hindustan could not live or achieve independence if the princes' states remain in the hands of the paramount power. This the Die-hards perfectly understand. Hitherto they have been able to play this card in their imperial game with perfect impunity. If democratic opinion, here and in America, were sufficiently well-informed to follow this manoeuvre, it would feel considerable indignation. It will have no leisure to grasp it amid the headlong rush of events as the war draws to a close. A simpler issue, somewhat later, may awaken the interest of the Labour Party in India. It cannot justify to the working masses of this island the retention of a conscript army so far from home. That may be necessary, if we fail to make peace with the Indian people. A settlement is attainable so soon as we make up our minds to two things. We must hand over the reality of power to an Indian national government now, and clear the road to independence by withdrawing our support of the princes.

Does it matter? Will anything really be won for humanity when India does gain her independence? A blot will be cleared from the consciences of a very few of us: a load will fall from all our shoulders. But is that all? I have attempted in this book no estimate of Indian character or capacity. At one end of the scale is an apathy and inefficiency among the half-starved masses without a parallel on this earth. At the other end, I can recall three or four Indians I have had the honour to know worthy of the first places among the shining examples of goodness and intelligence I have met in my journey through life. But I have also encountered among them some peculiarly ruthless thugs and many conscienceless exploiters. What I have come to expect and usually find is a rather high level of gentleness, courtesy, sensibility and quickness in intuitive perception. Gentleness, indeed, is their salient vice. When they are good, there is a glow of warmth in their goodness. Like all men reared in an unfree society, they find it difficult to behave easily and without tension in the presence of wealth and power. Some are too deferential and others too defiant. We cannot know what they are, until they are free. Something will happen under every dark skin when Indians rule again in Delhi. How much, in a new sense of dignity and a consciousness of liberated power, that will mean to the younger generation, it is difficult for us, who have always been our own masters, to measure. The stigma of racial inferiority will be erased, the paralysis of a nation's will-power ended. India will no longer feel that her destiny is in the hands of strangers: nor in tones alternately of listlessness and exasperation will she be able for all that is amiss to blame this alien power, as far beyond her control as the monsoon. In one startling instance already we have seen in our lifetime what the removal of the stamp of inferiority can achieve to raise the mental stature of human beings. A repressed class in Russia has become the daring architect of a splendid future. That vast country also had its medley of races, its Babel of languages, its illiterate peasants, its backward aborigines. It dared to proclaim the equality of all who work and fused them into a united nation that will defend the common heritage. It too had obstructive traditions to combat and a poverty almost as desperate as India's. It has become in a quarter of a century a mighty industrial power and could have attained comfort, had it not been compelled to make guns instead of butter. Looking around them, when the last British Viceroy quits his palace, Indians will see opportunities where there were closed doors, difficulties to be overcome where once impossibilities confronted them, a country to be re-created and shaped by their own effort and thought, which was a conqueror's possession. It may be that they exaggerate their command over the future. By faith men grow to greatness.

Appendix: Things Seen*

I. Why India Followed Gandhi

FROM my memories of a stay in India during 1930, a scene stands out that staged Gandhi's movement for an English onlooker in its bewildering passivity. It happened in a little country town not far from Agra. Ferozabad is a busy commercial centre. Mechanical lorries make their way through the crowded bazaar between the camels and the bullock carts. The little place lives by making glass bangles for the peasant women. Through a twelve-hour day, squatting in the infernal heat before a clay oven, without a pause for meals, men deftly convert by a turn of the wrist molten glass into bracelets, each served by a little boy who may start his brief life of labour at six years of age. Among these workers I saw no grey heads.

This stirring little town is ardently nationalist, as all commercial India is. In its main street I met a singular procession. Ten adherents of the Indian Congress party were being led to prison for the offence of picketing shops in order to enforce the boycott of British goods. On their wrists they wore steel handcuffs, and they walked within a moving fence of ropes. Behind them, in orderly files, marched a crowd of sympathisers. Some of them carried sticks: all were angry and excited. In chorus they shouted the slogans of the Congress movement, and broke into snatches of song. They numbered a full hundred or more. What force restrained them? I could count only four Indian policemen. In any Western country, that crowd, knowing that the nearest troops were thirty miles away, and sure of the support of every man in the town, would have rescued its friends.

This scene reproduced the Indian sub-continent in little. Everywhere its millions, no longer passive and acquiescent, bent, none the

* The following chapters, reprinted with a few additions from *Rebel India*, record things seen in 1930.

less, before a force which could not have withstood their united assault. The significance of this monumental restraint is obscured by the usual description of Gandhi's followers as "extremists." The word is doubly misleading, for it suggests a minority holding the most radical views. Uncompromising the Congress may be, but to the "left" of it there are groups of young men ready for terrorist action and guerrilla warfare, which wait only for the acknowledged failure of its non-violent tactics. A minority it certainly is not. In all the vast area north of Bombay it has the active support and allegiance of the mass of the Hindu population, in the villages no less than the towns. Its few critics are inaudible in the crowd. The Muslim minority stands aloof as an organised body, but even its more conservative leaders will admit that it neither opposes Congress nor supports the Government. Its younger educated generation is wholly with Congress. A police inspector in Bombay estimated this section as a third of the whole Muslim population; six Muslim barristers with whom I talked put the proportion at a half. The South is relatively apathetic, less easily regimented, less willing to face the test of imprisonment, less devoted to the person of the Mahatma, but it too shares the aspirations of the more active North. At an election, if the Congress deigned to take part, it would sweep the Peninsula.

Throughout this year of agitation, Congress contrived to pervade the entire life of India. It was impossible to forget it. Cars in the street carried its colours. The children sang its songs. It dictated the course of trade. Bombay, I soon perceived, had two governments. To the British Government, with all its apparatus of legality and power, there still were loyal the European population, the Indian sepoys who wore its uniform, and the elder generation of the Muslim minority. The rest of Bombay had transferred its allegiance to one of His Majesty's too numerous prisoners. In Mahatma Gandhi's name Congress ruled this city. Its lightest nod was obeyed. It could fill the streets, when it pleased, and as often as it pleased, with tens of thousands of men and women, who shouted its watchwords. It could with a word close the shutters of every shop in the bazaar. When it proclaimed a *hartal* (a day of mourning), which it did all but every week, by way of protest against some act of the other government, silence descended upon the streets, and even the factories closed their doors. Only with its printed permit on a scrap of coloured paper, dare a driver urge his bullocks and his bales past its uniformed sentries, who kept watch, day and night, in every lane and alley of the business quarter. They had their guardrooms. Their inspectors entered every warehouse

and shop, and watched every cotton-press. They would even confiscate
forbidden goods which a merchant had tried to smuggle past their
patrols. Every day began with its public ritual. The city prayed and
sang. At dawn and even before it, from every street there issued a
little procession of white-robed figures. All wore the home-spun cos-
tume of *kadi*, which is the symbol of India's resolve to provide for
her own needs. The men had on their heads the white Gandhi cap.
A few had Indian drums or triangles; all sang. This movement could
talk English to the educated few: it had its vernacular press for those
who could read only their mother-tongue; but the unlettered mass
knew by heart its numberless rhymed songs and ballads, which extolled
its leader, called for a boycott of British goods, and proclaimed its
vow to win liberty or die. These little bands numbered ten or twelve
persons, sometimes men, sometimes children, sometimes women. They
set the keynote of each day's life. You could not escape them; you
could not forget them. Every man had heard them before he entered
office or shop, nor did they muffle their challenge as their songs followed the car of a British official.*

* This description of Bombay applies to the earlier period of the struggle.
At the end of October 1930, more stringent ordinances came into force. The
Congress was declared an illegal organisation: all its buildings and other
property were liable to confiscation: meetings were unlawful merely because
it summoned them: and all its directing committees and officials were liable
to arrest. These decrees in a certain extent drove Congress underground: it
no longer dominated the streets as undoubtedly as before, but the change
was less marked than one might have expected. Its bulletins were still
printed or manifolded on secret machines and distributed in the streets. A
few volunteers, circulating through the town, could still by word of mouth
collect a great crowd for a meeting, which would be duly dispersed. The
severity of the repression varied with the temperament of the local officials.
In the United Provinces it was relatively gentle. I saw the tricolour flag
still flying in November over the late Motilal Nehru's house in Allahabad,
which served as the national headquarters of Congress, and to and from
this centre the local leaders and couriers from the provinces came and went
undisturbed. Here and there, mildness and good-temper disarmed the local
agitation. I heard of one magistrate, very popular with the people, who
successfully treated the defiance of the salt monopoly as a joke. The local
Congress leader made salt openly, in front of his bungalow. He came out:
bought some of the contraband salt: laughed at its bad quality: chaffed
the bystanders, and went quietly back to his house. The crowd melted
away, and no second attempt was made to defy this genial bureaucrat. On
the other hand, any exceptional severity, especially if physical brutality
accompanied it, usually raised the temper of the local movement and roused
it to fresh daring and further sacrifices. This was not so, however, in the

As the day wore on, even in the European streets I noticed that in ones and twos Indian women were seating themselves on chairs at the doors of certain shops. They all wore the graceful Indian dress, but their *sari* (the long scarf) was of orange, a colour that has in this land its heroic associations. Few entered these shops. You might catch a glimpse of the owner reading or playing chess. But if anyone attempted to enter, the lady joined her hands in supplication: she pleaded, she reasoned, and if all else failed, she would throw herself across the threshold and dare him to walk over her body. These women have been known to fling themselves in front of a car, and lie upon the ground before its wheels, until its owner yielded and took back into the shop the forbidden goods he had bought. But these were the exceptional shops which had refused to give the pledge to sell no foreign cloth and no British goods. Most of the Indian shops gave this undertaking, and where pickets were posted, it rarely happened that an Indian purchaser tried to defy them. The picketers went in their hundreds to prison, but always there were more to take their place. It was in this readiness to suffer that the moral power of this movement resided. When thousands will go gladly to prison, tens of thousands will give money, and hundreds of thousands will obey. It reminded me, in its temper and outlook, of the militant suffrage movement in England, save that it avoided even the minor acts of violence in which these forerunners indulged. A disarmed people had instinctively adopted these tactics. It courted suffering; it faced it, as women will, with a noble, if passive, courage. Women were the natural exponents of its gospel. Out of the seclusion of centuries they stepped at the call of patriotism, and nothing in this astonishing movement was so surprising as their joyful devotion. If they have not yet won *Swaraj* for India, they have completed the emancipation of their own sex. Even in the conservative North, I heard the ripping of curtains and veils.

Like the Suffragists, Congress had an instinct for colour and display. The struggle was not all suffering: this movement could be gay. Its volunteers marched in its processions in military formation. With the Indian tricolour flag, the orange scarves of the women's contingents and the white home-spun of the men, they made a bright pageant, in the dazzling light. After the procession would come the mass-demonstration, which in Bombay would often gather, in the

South. Severity does seem to have checked it in the Andhra district of Madras, where at first it was vigorous.

park by the seashore, as many as twenty thousand people. More sober and orderly meetings I never saw. No Western gathering was ever so silent and passive as these Indian crowds. Few stood: they squatted upon the ground, the women in one wing, the men in another, and so, motionless and silent, in regular files, they listened to speeches and songs, Rabindranath Tagore's national anthem, or the older *Bande Mataram*. The speeches were certainly what lawyers call "seditious," but they were never incitements to disorder: invariably they preached non-violence. Sedition comes near to orthodoxy when a hundred million of one's fellows agree with every word. While the speakers talked, the more devoted members of the audience, men as well as women, would take out the little hand-spindle, the *takli*, and twist it placidly and indefatigably as they listened. In official circles the dispersal by *lathi* charges of such a gathering was described as "maintaining order." *

* I did not myself see any of these *lathi* charges: the practise varied greatly, and while I was in Bombay, these demonstrations were tolerated. I questioned many European eye-witnesses, however, including police inspectors, and saw many photographs. I believe that with one or two possible exceptions, the meetings should have been tolerated: the mistake lay with the higher authorities who prohibited them. Latterly all Congress meetings were forbidden, and as regularly dispersed. If they had been tolerated, there would have been no disorder, and sooner or later the audiences would have grown bored. As it was, especially in Dombay, the policy of rough dispersal moved the whole city to anger. To face the *lathi* charges became a point of honour, and in a spirit of martyrdom volunteers went out in hundreds to be beaten. They gave a display of disciplined, passive courage: we (as all India thought) of brutality. Again and again, I heard descriptions by Europeans of the beating of slight and passive youths by sturdy constables which made one feel physically sick. They did not exaggerate. I have a photograph which shows the "volunteers" squatting motionless on the ground in their files, while from behind, the police (in this case Englishmen) rain blows upon their heads with the *lathi*—a heavy staff, which can inflict disabling bruises and wounds.

That the police, even under English officers, often meant to inflict physical punishment for disaffection I could not doubt. In Calcutta some students, witnessing from a balcony of the University the brutal beating of participants in a peaceful procession, shouted "Cowards!" Two hours later the police returned, rushed into the University under an English officer, invaded the classrooms, and beat the students indiscriminately as they sat at their desks, till the walls were splattered with blood. The University made a protest, some faint expression of official regret followed, but no punishment. I heard details of this affair from professors whose repute in the European scientific world stands high. An Indian Judge of

224

To understand why this nation, at last so nearly united, remained non-violent, we must discard all our Western heritage. Non-violence is more than a religious tenet; it is a racial instinct. What Gandhi has done is to reaffirm it, against the drift of Western example and teaching. India believed in it, while our forefathers were still barbarians. It has formed her conduct. It has even regulated her diet, for it will tolerate no taking of life. For the first time in her recent history India gained in Gandhi a leader who based himself on her silent assumptions, the beliefs that have moulded her body. She had had in her political life commanding figures before his day, but Western thought had shaped their minds. Gandhi, it is true, studied law in London; but did anything remain with him from his Western education, save his command of our language? When India listened to him, she heard herself thinking aloud. He has, indeed, borrowed his nationalism from the West, but he dares to preach that it can triumph by adopting in its struggle the ancient Hindu tactic.

With that word, however, misunderstanding begins. There are millions of Indians for whom non-violence is nothing more than a tactic which they practise because they lack arms and the military tradition against an enemy who has both. Non-violence is, indeed, a tactic from which somewhat contradictory effects are expected. It may embarrass an opponent, as a general strike might do, by making it impossible to conduct the normal course of administration and trade. That is its mechanical aspect, which we of the West grasp readily enough. If none obeys when we command, if no one pays taxes, or buys what we export, empire comes to an end.

But *ahimsa* (non-violence) has also a mystical meaning. It overcomes an enemy by love—an effect hardly likely to follow from the boycott of his trade. Again, by self-restraint, it awakens shame within him for his violence. In the mind of the Mahatma and his immediate followers, *ahimsa* is but part of a moral discipline through which India must pass if she would be free. The deepest conviction of the Indian tradition is that the saint who can control himself may command the universe. Hindu legend loved to tell of the ascetic who won the power, by his austerities, to control the stars in their courses, and

the High Court, whose student son had been beaten, spoke with a vehemence which I wished some member of the Government could have heard. A similar affair occurred at Lahore, where the police, again under an English officer, invaded a college and beat not only students in class but the professor also. These blows were rarely mortal. The victims survive and hate. Many a terrorist has been made by a beating.

bend emperors to his will. The insignificant figure of Gandhi squatting, in contemplation, on the ground with nothing but a loin-cloth to cover him, recalls to the Indian's imagination those stories of the *yogi's* greatness. In his own mind, however, the loin-cloth has another meaning. In this land where naked poverty contrasts with purple wealth, he has ranked himself with the lowest. He will wear no garment and eat no food that might divide him from the outcasts of the village. In this unfamiliar kernel of religion lies the originality of this unique movement, and one, at least, of the secrets of its power.

Men will respond even in the India of today to a religious appeal, undistracted by the hum of our aeroplanes and the clatter of our armoured cars. I heard from a scrupulous man of science this evidence from his own experience. He was among the Santals, a primitive aboriginal tribe of the hills, which from time immemorial has lived by hunting. The legend reached them of this saint who had arisen in the plains below. Over one sentence of his message they pondered deeply, and then with implicit obedience they acted. The saint had said, "Let the creatures of the forest have peace." They burned their bows and arrows and snares and, for the first time in uncounted centuries, took to tilling the soil.

Politics for this singular leader are a mere consequence and by-product of his ethical teaching. From his prison cell, amid the turmoil of the passionate struggle, he issued his weekly sermon. Now it enforced the duty of truth; again it commanded literal and absolute chastity. His disciples tried, at least, to follow this difficult teaching. In a gymnasium in Baroda State, organised by the Congress movement, I saw, decked with fresh flowers, an altar to the god of chastity which the young men had erected beside the parallel bars.

Indians quote the sayings of the Mahatma in a tone of loving reverence, such as only the simplest of believing Christians use when they cite their Master's words. Scarcely a shop in the Hindu quarters of Bombay fails to exhibit his photograph. I have seen it in the wattled hut of an aboriginal tribesman so poor that he owned nothing else, save his tools and his earthen pots. It is sold by peddlers with the gaudy lithographs that portray the adventures of Krishna, and it may be bought, contrary to the law of Islam which forbids portraiture, on the steps of the great mosque at Delhi. By putting this man in prison we made him omnipresent.

This mystical doctrine of self-control, incarnated in the spare person of this all but naked saint, has given to the best among the sixty thousand who have faced the privations of Indian jails, the strength to withstand. One face from among them stands out in my memory: its owner, a lawyer, may have been too fine a spirit to be typical, but his thinking was characteristic of Gandhi's movement. He had been the chief speaker at one of the few meetings (near Meerut) which were dispersed by rifle fire. He had tried to calm an angry crowd, and had stationed a cordon of volunteers round the police station to protect it. He was, none the less, arrested, beaten by the police, and shot by one of them, while under arrest, at close range. The police kicked him as he lay on the ground, and five hours passed before he received first-aid. His right arm had to be amputated, and a day after the operation he was carried from hospital to prison. He told the story without a trace of bitterness, his face lit by a triumphant serenity. "In prison," he went on, "my friends and I were happy and even gay. 'Now we know,' one said to the other, 'that India is free. We have kept the master's sayings. We have faced even the rifle, and refrained from anger.'" As I looked at the face of this man, proud in its gentleness, I ceased to pity the mutilated arm.

When I grasped the psychological meaning of this movement, as Gandhi conceived it, it became easier to understand his uncompromising stiffness in the negotiations of mid-summer, 1930. He was in no hurry to achieve an immediate political end. The immense volume of pain, anxiety, and material loss which the struggle had brought with it counted for little in his mind in the balance against the mental gain. It was, as he saw it, a preparation for freedom. The nation which resists subjection, though it be without violence, achieves liberation in its own soul. It was against the degradation of a servile acquiescence in foreign rule that he rebelled. His methods were designed to make the continuance of British rule impossible, but even more, to train the people of India in self-respect. These methods, accordingly, form a series of steps, each more difficult but also more effective than the last.

THIS ladder of difficulty began, several years ago, with the revival of hand spinning. Nothing, from our Western standpoint, could be more fantastic. To spin had become for Gandhi's devout followers a species of ritual. I came down to breakfast one day to discover my host, a doctor with a Scottish training, squatting at his antiquated hand spindle, bent on completing his obligatory hour's task. In the train a lady will take a folding spindle from a case, assemble it, and calmly set to work. These were the oddities of a most original movement. It is of more consequence that in many a village the peasants, when field work was at a standstill, would turn the spinning-wheel as they squatted in the shade. This revival of a hopelessly uneconomic craft signified, first of all, Gandhi's revolt against our mechanical civilisation—for he is a rebel, reminiscent of Tolstoy rather than of Ruskin, against Western machines no less than the British flag. It was, secondly, a way of freeing India from her tribute to Lancashire.

But chiefly it is a simple device to help the villager in his inconceivable poverty. Save where there is canal irrigation, the Indian climate and the traditional methods of husbandry make it impossible for the peasant to labour in the fields for more than seven or eight months of the year. He may do a little carting, if he has sturdy bullocks. He may work in a mill, if he is in reach of a textile centre. But the great mass is condemned to helpless and compulsory idleness through one-third of the year.

With capital village industries might be created, but it is scarce. A spinning-wheel may be made at home, or bought for a couple of shillings, and the marketing of the yarn calls for no organisation: it need only be taken to the weaver, who in most villages still contrives, half-starved and loaded with debt, to compete with the mills. True, by a day's spinning only one or two pence can be earned. But when a field labourer's day commands, from dawn to dusk, a wage that ranges from fivepence to twopence halfpenny, and no field work is to be had, is a penny to be despised? There is today a demand for hand-woven cloth, for patriotism favours it. Even the Indian official, who must wear European cloth at his desk, will change in the evening into coarse homespun. He helps the Indian village and deals a blow at Lancashire as he does it.

Sedition begins with the next method, the attempt to smash the Government's salt monopoly. It is the kindergarten stage of revolution. The notion that the King-Emperor can be unseated by boiling sea-water in a kettle may seem laughable. Even this mild activity is, however, an attack on the revenue, and it landed thousands of Indians in prison, including Gandhi himself. He knew his public. He staged his salt-making as a quasi-religious pilgrimage. Its pathetic innocence helped this law-abiding people to take the first plunge into disobedience. Here, too, Indians could argue that they were helping the impoverished peasant, and the protectionist motive made itself felt. Why import salt from Liverpool, if salt water can be evaporated by the sun's heat on the shores of Bombay and Bengal? I suspect the play of a traditional association. Salt in the ancient world was a magical substance. If one ate a man's salt one dare not betray him. To eat an overlord's salt was always to incur a debt of loyalty. The salt *gabelle,* on the eve of the French Revolution, roused the same passions. Salt, moreover, is doubly necessary in a hot climate, because the blood rapidly loses its mineral base by sweating. This is a bad tax, as all indirect taxes are, and it greatly enhances the cost of what is often the one relish in the miserable diet of the labourer. To be sure, it works out at no more than $3\frac{1}{2}d$. per head per annum, but even that may mean two days' work for the head of a labouring family.

The attack on the drink monopoly is a subversive method of greater potency. From this monopoly the provincial governments derive in some instances as much as a quarter of their revenue. Custom, save among the more degraded castes, and the teaching of both the great religions of India unite to forbid the use of alcohol. The Congress had Indian morality behind it when it organised a boycott, through peaceful picketing, of the Government's toddy shops. To a great extent it gained its end. In Bombay the usual annual auction of licences collapsed, and they were sold by private treaty for half the usual figure. In many towns the toddy shops were closed; no Indian dare brave the condemnation of his fellows by entering them. In some places the all-powerful caste organisations re-enforced the prohibition of the Congress. The Government was at length driven to permit the sale of spirits anywhere and anyhow, without the usual restrictions—a sure sign of demoralisation. The most interesting aspect of this agitation was the part which women played in it. I have seen these slight figures, accustomed to a life of ease, take their place for eight hours as pickets at the back door of a liquor shop, beside an open drain, amid the unspeakable degradation of the slums.

Reluctantly, since it contradicted his gospel of love, Gandhi consented to the next method—the boycott of foreign goods, and especially of British cloth. It was organised with enthusiasm all over India, and though the motive, as the Mahatma's intimates assured me, may have been rather to help Indian industry than to injure England, I felt the popular resentment, when the passengers in a passing omnibus shouted "Boycott!" as they caught sight of my white skin.

Congress began by exacting pledges from merchants and retailers that they would neither import these forbidden goods, nor sell the stocks which they already had in store. To impose such a veto with general success was an amazing proof of the solidarity of Indian society. The test of the authority of Congress came while I was in Bombay. The merchants who import cotton piece goods had ceased for six months to buy foreign cloth, but they had in stock quantities worth £3½ millions, suited only to the Indian market. They could not be re-exported, and were deteriorating in the warehouses. The merchants met, and in a somewhat apologetic resolution, declared that they would sell these stocks, and thereafter buy no more. The Congress refused to compromise, and as the event showed, it did not over-estimate its strength. Hundreds of its women volunteers marched down to the wholesale market. They would picket every shop and office. Some of them declared that they would go on hunger strike, until the merchants withdrew their resolution. A meeting was held at which some of the leading nationalist orators spoke. And then, even before the pickets had taken up their stations, the struggle was over. The clerks and porters refused to open the warehouse shutters, or to handle one bale of the cloth. Congress had won.

The figures of the other customs service, the British Board of Trade, showed clearly enough the effects of this boycott. By the autumn of 1930 imports of cotton piece goods had dropped to between a third and a fourth of what they were in the months of the previous year. Imported cigarettes had fallen in value to a sixth of the old figure. Sixteen British-owned mills in Bombay had been closed down, and thirty-two thousand textile workers were idle. There were casualties in this bloodless warfare. On the other hand, the Indian-owned mills which had given the pledge were often working double shifts, and were adapting their machinery to spin the finer counts, which hitherto had been imported.

I F India is difficult to understand, it is because her idealism belongs to her own tradition, while the heavier clay of human nature is of one texture the world over. Inextricably they mingled in this movement. Gandhi may have thought out these methods in order to brace the Indian character for freedom, but in fact all of them, save the "dry" campaign, had their roots in economic nationalism. India already enjoys a tariff which gives her industries a moderate degree of protection, even against British imports. But the cry is everywhere for high protection, both to encourage existing and to foster new industries.

In addition to the reasons of self-respect and wounded pride which all Indians have behind their nationalism, the growing industrial group, especially strong in Bombay, found its account in a movement which boycotted foreign goods. These people may be conservatives by temper and interest; yet by generous gifts of money, and sometimes by taking personal risks, they supported an agitation that may end by kindling a revolutionary flame. Some of the wives and daughters of these Bombay millionaires even went to prison.

This demand for protection has mass support, because India suffers from chronic unemployment and grinding poverty among the educated class. To tens of thousands of young men no door opens as they leave school or college, and they are easily induced to believe that if India controlled her own economic life, there would be room for them in her industries or her banks, her railways or her public services—which may be true, though few of them have had a training which could fit them for productive work.

This economic discontent was increased by the action of the Indian Government in raising the exchange value of the rupee from 1s. 4d. to 1s 6d. Like Mr. Churchill's raising of the sterling exchange, it had the effect of favouring the creditor and *rentier* class, while it encouraged imports and penalised exports. In short, it favoured, on the whole, British as against Indian interests.

A long catalogue of economic grievances has ranged Indian capitalists and merchants almost solidly on the side of the Congress, in spite of the indescribable disturbance which its agitation has caused to the whole mechanism of credit and trade. They bowed submissively to its decrees, even when it closed their mills and shops and virtually confiscated their stocks of imported goods, confident that the gains of the future would compensate for the losses of today.

If the action of the Indian Government in establishing a gold standard with the rupee fixed at an unduly high value offended the mercantile class, another phase of its monetary policy struck at the peasants. It de-monetised silver, threw its reserves on the market, and so in some five years helped to bring the value of silver tumbling to a half of what it had been. There were some good reasons for this policy, but it halved the peasant's credit. There are no banks in the Indian village: there are few even in the towns. In this primitive society men hoard their savings. Their wives carry them upon their persons, chiefly as silver ornaments, and on the security of these, the peasant borrows. This drop in the value of silver halved the savings of the village, such as they are, and lowered its barriers against famine.

For background, this movement of economic discontent had the world depression. The catastrophic drop in the prices of agricultural produce explained the wave of revolution which swept over South America. On India it fell with the fury of a tropical tornado. The peasant saw the value of his crops tumbling, from one harvest to another, to one-half or a third. On the Ganges plain, wheat in three years fell from seven, through four, to two rupees per *maund* (82 lbs.). The jute-grower of Bengal had the same experience. The village was ruined. Its savings were halved. Its crops would fetch barely half the wonted price. But its debts, its taxes and its rents stood stolidly at the old figure. Life, it knew not why, had suddenly become impossible. If it paid, it must starve; if it did not pay, it must turn rebel. While it hesitated, the voice it reverenced spoke the word it wished to hear. Gandhi proclaimed the patriotic duty of tax-resistance. In a sense it was an easy duty; the village could not pay. So it was that the world's mysterious dealings with gold and the price level suddenly swung these silent, apathetic villages into politics, ranged them behind Congress as its staunchest supporters, and over wide areas of northern India prepared them for the final phase of the struggle—the refusal to pay taxes. It was never general, for it did not touch the South, or the Punjab. It began in Gujarat (Bombay Presidency) with a refusal to pay land revenue. In Bihar and parts of Bengal the police rate was resisted. In the United Provinces, in the later phases of the struggle, the peasants resisted both rent and tax. While this went on, the head-men and other local officials were summoned to lay down their offices, and in countless villages they responded. In some districts the peasants defied the regulations which conserve the forests. But the struggle in the villages merits a fuller narrative.

The unique personality of Gandhi played a decisive part in firing India for this struggle. Without him she could not have achieved this spectacular unity. He touched, as no leader before him had ever done, her traditional springs of emotion. He gave her effort the solemnity of a high moral endeavour, and appealed to a faith that had its root in racial instinct. But without this material background, the nationalist movement would never have attained these dimensions, would never have roused the villages, nor enlisted the capitalists in its ranks. It was easy to induce shopkeepers to put up their shutters for a *hartal*: they sold little on other days. It was easy to refrain from buying foreign goods: few had the means to buy. Above all, it was satisfactory that patriotism agreed with empty purses in rejecting the tax-gatherer's demands. Finally, among the legion of unemployed young men the movement found it easy to recruit its volunteers. To say this is not to belittle it, or its leader, nor to question its passionate sincerity. It is to recognise the play of economic causes in making history.

II. *The Village Defies the Empire*

FIVE days spent among the villages of Gujarat stand out among the most memorable, and yet the most painful, of my stay in India. Try as I may to think calmly and write quietly about these experiences, they dramatise themselves. The nationalist movement was here at its height, and I realised the extremes of devotion and endurance of which it is capable. The Indian Government was here at its worst, struggling, as it was bound to do, to collect the taxes which the peasants refused, and using or tolerating, in the process, a physical brutality and a contempt for the forms of the law which I should have refused to credit, without the evidence of my senses.

The Indian Police presents to the observer aspects which differ according to the position he occupies. Seen from above, by a member of the ruling race, it is a model of loyalty and reliability, zealous in its dealings with crime and disaffection. Seen from below, with Indian eyes (and during these five days I lived entirely with Indians), it is the ugliest blot on our administrative system. That it is all but universally corrupt, given to taking and extorting bribes, even Englishmen, when they talk frankly, will admit, and this is true of the Indian officers as well as of the men. I saw in a hospital bed one of its victims with the marks of torture still visible after many days. To find its arbitrary brutality credible, it must be viewed in historical perspective.

We trod on the heels of earlier conquerors, and our administration, when it works through Indian agents, is a compromise between the traditions the Moguls left behind them and our own European standards. Vigilance is not easy, for a hedge of native subordinates stands between the British official and the masses, whom an age-long training under many despots had taught to suffer silently. I found in the very correct Oxford *History of India,* by the late Vincent A. Smith, C.I.E., the statement on p. 86 that during his own official career he had found it difficult to prevent the Indian police from using torture to extract evidence, while on p. 540 a passage occurs which seems to imply that beating is, or recently was, a not unusual method in extracting taxes. Confessions of this kind rarely occur in books dealing with Indian politics, but I have met with them from time to time in scientific works. A long and varied official experience lay behind the valuable anthropological study of *The Indian Village Community* published by Mr. B. H. Baden-Powell, C.I.E., in 1896. On p. 346, in a most interesting description of some "joint" villages in the Punjab, in which relics of a primitive agrarian communism still survived in his time, I found the statement that the common funds of the village were used to pay "the revenue," meaning the land-tax, the rates and such common expenses as the entertainment of guests, repairs to village public buildings, "and, I fear, we must add, bribes to officials and cost of supplying free rations to man and beast." The officials in question were, presumably, Indians of subordinate rank: no village is rich enough to bribe a *sahib*, if he were purchasable, as of course he is not. But *sahibs*, including white police officers, do exact "free rations" for man and beast, a charge the peasants deeply resent, though they have to meet it with a show of cheerfulness. Little has changed since 1896. I used to go about in native 'buses, a thing that "is not done," and saw a policeman levying his customary daily bribe on the driver.

The reader may think that these charges of brutality and venality against Indians make a poor case for self-government. On the contrary, they are one of the strongest arguments for it. The Indian police has not yet begun to think of itself as the Indian people's servant. It never will so think of itself, until it has to answer to a truly vigilant Indian minister.* At present it is the servant of an autocracy: its function is to overawe the people into submission. British officials cannot bring about this change of mind, and my own experience taught me that some of them make no attempt to do it. In any event, they are few and busy: the routine of office duty occupies too much of their time: they can never go about incognito, for they can never discard the uniform of their white skins. The peasants with good reason believe that it is useless to complain. A determined man may, at great expense, win a case against a police-officer who has wronged him, by carrying it to the higher courts, which enjoy universal respect. But even then it does not follow that the guilty officer will be punished or dismissed. I had the curiosity to collect the legal records of some cases of this kind. The British official tradition in India is one of personal integrity. But as I looked at it from the angle of the Indian peasant, it had a fault which all but neutralised this

* I have left this passage as I wrote it, before "law and order" had come under Indian ministers in the provinces. Whether in two years the Congress ministries managed to bring about much improvement, I do not know, but think it unlikely. A new training and tradition must first be built up.

virtue. It lives on prestige. This government cannot shake off the age-long tradition of autocracy, that it is above the people. It dare not admit a fault, or rebuke a subordinate for excess of zeal. It exacts loyalty from these Indian officials, and it owes them loyalty in return. It will not dismiss a reliable police-officer, even when a judge has censured him in open court, merely because he has ill-used or tortured peasants. A muzzled watchdog would be useless. That is what any student of human nature would expect, though the grossness of some of these cases startled me.* The British official in India is doubly aloof; first, because in social life he mixes little with unofficial Indians, and secondly because in office hours he is surrounded by Indian subordinates who may have an interest in misleading him. This handicap, always serious, makes good or even tolerable government impossible, so soon as the nationalist resistance attains the proportions of a mass movement. Today the British official moves and works among a hostile people, and his Indian subordinates are subjected

* The worst of these cases known to me happened much later, in 1938, at Rawalpindi, and was in no way political. A man named Kiroo was suspected by the police of a share in a burglary. They tortured him in the presence of several witnesses for six hours. By a ruse he got hold of a knife, stabbed one of his tormentors dead and attempted to commit suicide, but was nursed back to life. Tried for murder in a lower court, he was sentenced to transportation for life. Sir Douglas Young, Chief Justice of the Punjab, acquitted him on appeal, and drew attention to the publicity of the torture. "Many persons witnessed it," including some British soldiers' wives and a sergeant of a Highland Regiment. "The inference," as the Chief Justice put it, "to be drawn is that the police thought they had nothing to conceal, or that torturing such suspects was to them normal procedure." Kiroo was fortunate, because some fearless white witnesses of a rank below the *Sahib* caste saw what was done to him. "In most cases," the judge went on, "wretched suspects subjected to treatment of this illegal and despicable character are helpless and hopeless.... We are satisfied that this method of investigation does exist: it is a disgrace to the police force." An official enquiry followed; and a white inspector and several Indian police officers were suspended. But that was all. The enquiry whitewashed them. That had been my own experience. I had been able to tell the highest authorities that I saw the injuries inflicted by police-torturers in prison on a young man in Bombay, who took part in a Congress demonstration. No redress followed. The favourite method was one much used by Fascist police—a disabling form of cruelty that inflicted protracted pain and left marks visible long afterwards. Hitler and Mussolini were less original in their methods of government than is commonly supposed. (For details of the Kiroo case see *Reynolds News*, February 6, 1938.)

to a rigid social boycott. In these conditions, government becomes a sort of civil war.

The refusal of taxes represents the climax in Gandhi's graduated scale of resistance. It would, if it became general, bring British rule to an early end. But from those who practise it, it requires a readiness to brave material ruin. The Indian Government, when it confiscates the land or attaches the movable property of a tax-resister, has no nice scruples. It appropriates, many times over, the amount due, and a man who refuses his land-tax must be prepared to lose his all. In Gujarat, land worth from 700 to 1,000 rupees per *bigha* (1¾ acres) was offered for sale at one or two rupees, and it happened that two new motor pumps used for irrigation, each worth Rs. 5,000, were sold at Rs. 16 and Rs. 65 to cover taxes of these amounts. That thousands of peasants in Gujarat were willing to face these risks is an amazing proof of their determination.

G UJARAT, for several reasons, was chosen as the pioneer of this formidable but costly method of passive resistance. It stands out, with parts of the Punjab and Bengal, as the most prosperous region of rural India. Most of the peasants own their fields, and, though they are a singularly gentle race, they have something of the self-reliance and stubbornness of the typical yeoman. There is less illiteracy than elsewhere. Many of these villagers have seen the world, for on the coast, they include some castes of hereditary sailors, and others go in large numbers to South Africa, and send home large sums (I heard of £150 in one year) to their families. The land is fertile, and will grow, under irrigation, good cotton, tobacco and sugar, as well as cereals. Though the holdings range only from ten to twenty acres, I was startled by the evidences of prosperity.

Instead of the usual mud-huts, here are villages of brick houses, often of two storeys, with their door-posts elaborately carved, while the outer walls are decorated with naïve and amusing paintings. Ancient and modern subjects mingle in the most natural way. One house will display the adventures of Krishna: its neighbour will show a railway train. Their cattle are the pride of these farmers, and I had to go to Gujarat to realise what a stately and beautiful animal the Indian bullock can be. But this prosperity is rapidly becoming a memory, for here, too, the catastrophic fall in prices has brought hardship, and an acute sense of grievance.

These villages had been for years under the influence of Gandhi and his disciples. In several of them I saw the permanent centres (most of them closed and confiscated) which he had established—here a school for untouchable boys (still open), there a sort of monastery-school created to help a backward, aboriginal tribe, and again a technical school which taught spinning and weaving. Two years earlier the Bardoli district went through the first Indian experiment in tax-resistance, not from political motives, but as a protest against an excessive assessment: it stood its ground stoutly and won. The assessment was reduced.

Finally, Gandhi, everywhere hero and saint, is in this region the intimate neighbour and teacher of the villagers. He has often toured through it, preaching to vast, mesmerised crowds, and here he chose to be arrested on his march to the sea. He is devotedly loved, and so, too, is his lieutenant, Vallabhai Patel. I asked a group of forty or fifty villagers why they faced these risks and hardships. The women, as usual, answered first, and voiced this feeling of personal loyalty. "We'll pay no taxes," they said, "till Mahamaji and Vallabhai tell us to pay." Then the men, slowly collecting their thoughts, voiced their economic grievance: "We won't pay because the tax is unjust," and they went on to explain that at present prices they make, as owner-cultivators, less than a day-labourer's wage. Finally, they added: "We're doing it to win *Swaraj*."

WHAT they were doing almost passes belief. Many villages were totally abandoned. I could see through the windows that every stick of property had been removed. In the silent street nothing moved till a monkey skipped from a roof across the lane of blinding sunlight. Here and there I met a peasant who had returned for the day to plough his fields, or a priest who guarded his temple. For the rest, the people had moved across the frontier of British India into the territory of independent Baroda. There, close to the boundary, they camped in shelters of matting and palm leaves, the ground cumbered with their chests and their beds, their churns and the great clay-coated baskets that hold their grain. In the hot autumn days life was just tolerable for hardy villagers in these conditions, but the rains would test their determination.

How many people there were in these camps, of which I saw three, I could only guess, perhaps three, perhaps five thousand. Even in Baroda, however, these refugees were not always safe. Their camps had more than once been invaded, and the Gaekwar's territory violated by armed British-Indian police, under an Indian official, who beat with their *lathis*, not only their own people but the Gaekwar's subjects also.

The answer to this movement was ruthless, and the English official who directed it strained the forms of law to breaking point. Land-tax is payable in two instalments, after the chief harvests, usually in January and May, but the date (since harvests may be late) can be varied. Of this merciful provision of the Code the Commissioner took advantage to anticipate the date of the instalment which became payable in January 1931. He issued his demand notes in October 1930, and already in October the police, in the effort to collect the following year's tax, began to beat peasants who had duly paid their two instalments for the current year. The date, as the Commissioner told me, was anticipated because it was known that the peasants intended to resist, and it was important to realise the tax before they could sell or remove their crops. He added that a man would not be harassed whose sole reason for non-payment was genuine poverty. In short, it was a method of taking the offensive against villages which had not yet broken the law or challenged the Government: they were known to be disaffected, and the remedy of intimidation was applied.

To find purchasers for the confiscated land and buffaloes was not easy. This population was amazingly solid. There are few Muslims in Gujarat, and the Hindus are knit together by a close caste organisation. In the Kaira district most of the peasant-owners are Patidars. This caste, after two members had given way under a merciless beating, and paid their tax three months before it was normally due, held a meeting, and fined them heavily for their weakness: it then announced that anyone who yielded in future would be fined Rs. 101 (about £7 15s.). The penalty for a refusal to pay that fine would be the dread fate of an out-caste.

In such a society no self-respecting Hindu will buy confiscated land. But in this Kaira district there are low-caste aboriginals, known as Barias, whom the Indian Census classes as a "criminal tribe." They are landless labourers: they habitually carry murderous bill-hooks, and after a recent outbreak of brigandage are required to report themselves twice a day to the village policeman. Perhaps these troublesome but unfortunate people would buy, if the price were low enough? I am bound to report the Commissioner's motive, as he stated it to me: he wished to use the occasion to raise these poor people in the social scale. Motives one cannot judge, but effects may be predicted. Should this strategy succeed, it would drive a wedge into this solid Hindu society, and by dividing, ease the task of the ruler. He might get the revenue at the cost of an unending village feud.

A STRATEGY such as this may be devised by cold English brains: it deteriorates when hot Indian hands carry it out. The responsible Indian official, the sub-collector (Mamlatdar) of the Borsod Taluka, a University graduate and a person of unusual energy, interpreted it in his own way. He carried the class war into the villages. He went round them, collected the Barias and made them a speech varying but little, which five of these Barias from different villages repeated to me. He told them that now was the time for vengeance, that the Patidars had oppressed them in the past, but that if any of them owed a debt to a Patidar he had only to come into court and declare himself bankrupt: "I will be there and see you through. If he demands his debt, beat him, cut him in pieces. Beat any man who wears a white (Gandhi) cap." There followed an invitation to buy their confiscated land for one or two rupees an acre. One witness quoted his advice to burn their houses, and another cited a police sub-inspector to the same effect. I am told (though it occurred after my visit) that some houses were in fact burned.

This strategy was reinforced with punitive expeditions by the police to the disaffected villages, often with this official at their head. These police are partly an armed emergency force carrying rifles; the men have no numbers on their uniforms, as I discovered when one of them, without a shadow of right, tried to bar my way along the high road with his fixed bayonet. It is difficult to identify a man who misbehaves.

The usual procedure, on entering a village, was to round up the few men who might have remained in it, or had returned to do a day's labour in the fields. These were beaten indiscriminately, often in the official's presence, and sometimes he used his own stick to further the work of justice. Some serious injuries were inflicted. I saw a man with a dangling, broken arm, and another with his thumb-joint cut to the bone. A woman had a badly bruised and swollen face. I heard of other more serious cases which had gone to a distant hospital.

As I went about from village to village, covering, however, only part of the area, forty-five peasants gave me their personal stories of recent beating, and in all but two of these cases I saw their injuries. A few had bruises all over their bodies, some from *lathis* and some from the butt ends of rifles. Sometimes the motive of the beating was to extract the tax on the spot, and occasionally this method succeeded. But often the victim was not himself a tax-payer. In Bardoli a certain police officer specialised in compelling any chance man he could catch to pay the tax of someone else who was out of reach. The victim would be dismissed with a kick or a blow, and told to collect the money from his neighbour.

Often the motive was simply to terrorise. In two cases a man was beaten till he took off his Gandhi cap. In one village, where the police tore down the national flags from the trees and the houses, it may have been this display of the Congress standard which led them to beat eight persons. In one case, a man who had an ugly bruise on his body from a rifle butt, and twelve bruises on his body from the *lathi*, was told to salute the police seven times. He saluted and they stopped beating.

THE reader thinks, perhaps, that I was misled by subtle Indians. Well, the Commissioner was good enough to accompany me to one village: he, too, saw the wounds and bruises, and his cross-questioning did not shake the peasants. He expressed doubts only in one case out of nine—that of a girl whom modesty forbade to show her injuries. Moreover, I met two of these Indian officials, and witnessed their bullying manners. One of them in my presence ordered a most wanton and needless *lathi* charge against an unoffending crowd of curious spectators which fled at the first command; but still the *lathi* blows fell. At their invitation I gave my evidence both personally and in writing, with names and dates, both to the local officials and to the highest authority at New Delhi. No action was taken on it.

Up to a point I could trust my own eyes. I saw, for example, at the Borsod Jail, eighteen political prisoners, as yet unconvicted, who had to spend their days and nights in a cage, with a front of iron bars like a den in the Zoo, which measured about thirty feet square.* It

---

* This was a country "lock-up" for unconvicted prisoners. The men and women sentenced for participation in the Congress movement were so numerous—there were at this date approximately 60,000 convictions—that they had to be accommodated largely in improvised prisons. They were classified in three classes, A, B, C, according to the magistrate's impression of their social standing. This division, odious in itself, was carried out with singular caprice. Three of Gandhi's sons were sent to prison, each (as one of them told me) in a different class. The theory of the higher authorities, as the late Inspector of Prisons in Bengal explained it to me, was that those sentenced to Class C were of the coolie class, and that the conditions provided for them were those to which this class is accustomed in India. In fact, very few, if any of them, were of this class. I visited the prison at Dum-Dum, near Calcutta, formerly an arsenal. The situation is malarious, and the prison was infested with mosquitoes. The officers in charge (Indians) seemed to me exceptionally reasonable men, who would listen to complaints,

was the warder who told me that they are let out only once a day, for three-quarters of an hour, to wash and visit the latrine. One of them, without books or work, had spent six weeks in this cage, and this the warder could not deny. When another prisoner told me that he himself and two others had been beaten in jail in the Mamlatdar's presence, perhaps I should have rebuked him for traducing one of His Majesty's officials, but in that House of Mercy I was dumb.

---

and do all in their power to remedy grievances. Under harsh officers life in this overcrowded prison would have been literally unendurable. The prisoners fortunately had each other's society: there was no solitary confinement. Even so, the conditions of Class C were shocking. The prisoners were all, or nearly all, of the educated class, and most of them spoke English. The majority were of the clerk class, but there were lawyers and doctors among them. The whole place was dirty, shockingly ill-ventilated, and overrun with parasites. The diet was coarse, monotonous and insufficient. No soap was provided, nor oil (which Indians habitually use), nor could such things be obtained from outside. Many prisoners in consequence contracted skin disease. For Class C there were no mosquito nets, though these were provided for Classes A and B. As a result a large proportion of the prisoners had malaria. The hospital was so overcrowded that there were barely six inches between the beds.

III. How the Village Lives

WE fly to India in these days by aeroplane, but the indispensable vehicle in which to approach a village is the time-machine of Mr. Wells' romance, and its engines must be reversed some thirty centuries. In the shade of a wall a potter, squatting on the ground, spins his wheel by hand and deftly turns elegant shapes of clay that were fashionable in the Bronze Age. Inside a doorway, marked with the print of stencilled hands to avert pestilence and ill-luck, a woman, squatting, turns her spindle. In an open space other figures are crushing sugar-cane in a hand-mill. Against its creaking one hears at a little distance the rhythmical twang of the bow used to card the fleecy cotton. A humble little shrine, which contains a shapeless stone painted with red ochre, fails somehow to persuade me of God's goodness.

The village cultivates much as our forefathers did when Stonehenge was erected. The fields are often mere garden plots of half an acre or less: one could not use a machine in them if one possessed it. Much of the land is wasted in raised boundary ridges. The plough has hardly changed since the mysterious people of the Indus Valley built up a civilisation contemporary with that of Ur of the Chaldees. It is a dwarf instrument of wood, with an iron point; the ploughman guides it with his right hand, and at seed time his left hand may trickle the grain into a drill of bamboo. The peasant threshes by treading out the grain with bullocks, and winnows by tossing it in the air.

Irrigation is usual, but only a few favoured regions have a canal system. If a farmer is prosperous, and the water is not too far below the soil level, he may construct a Persian well. In the villages to which I now invite the reader, we had to be content with a much more primitive device. A pair of bullocks ran down an inclined plane, dragging by a rope, over a grooved wheel, a skin of water from the depths of the well; when it reached the top, the driver laboriously poured its contents into the channels. At harvest-time India knows nothing of the scythe: the people squat on the ground and cut the grain with a tiny sickle. I was curious to discover how much labour these childlike operations involved, and reckoned it out with a group of peasants. For wheat ten ploughings were necessary, and even then the soil was only scratched four inches deep; on the other hand, it must be recorded that a weed is rarely seen in an Indian field. To raise an acre of wheat fifteen days are spent in giving it three waterings. It will take eight men and women from dawn to dusk to reap it.

All told, we reckoned that it cost the labour of one man for forty days to raise an acre of wheat. I should have distrusted this incredible calculation, had I not afterwards found the same total in an official publication. I began with this figure to probe the secret of India's poverty. She must waste her man-power by spending forty days to attain a result which a modern farmer would achieve in as many hours. That is the first reflection, but the thought which follows it is still more disconcerting. These peasants would gain nothing, save leisure, if they could be presented with modern machines. Their holdings range from five to ten acres, and they have nothing else to occupy their time if they should learn to economise it. Trudging through these fields, the baffling problem of India's wasted labour power stared me in the face, and I met it again in the huddled huts of the village.

On the way through the fields to the first of these villages—its obscure name is Kishanpur, and it lies in the great plain between Jumna and Ganges, about thirty miles from the once royal Mogul city of Agra and the graces of the Taj Mahal—I met one of the landlords of the district. Though his clothes were rather shabby, he carried himself with distinction, as became a man of power. We fell into talk, and I asked him whether the *zemindars* in this part of the United Provinces were still the descendants of the old feudal gentry who used to hold the land under the Mogul Emperors, on a military tenure, pledged to lead so many horse and foot into the field when their sovereign summoned them. No, he told me—most of those old families were extinct; he and most of his fellows had bought the land from embarrassed grandees. They held it under an arrangement which prevails over a great part of northern and central India: they draw a rent from the peasants, and must pay 45 per cent of it to the government as land tax.

My eye fell on a pair of white bullocks, as we talked, trotting down the inclined plane of a well. Who dug these wells? The peasants themselves dug them before the memory of the oldest inhabitant, and they also (as I learned in answer to a further question) had erected their huts. What, then, did the *zemindar* contribute to the resources of the village? What outlay of capital did his rent represent? I asked him, bluntly, whether, in return for this tribute, he performed any social or economic service whatever. "No," he replied, with a frankness that disarmed: "we're just filling our bellies as everyone else does. We bought our rights and owe no obligation to the peasants."

Round the drinking-well of the village I counted five heaps of refuse and dung. In the narrow lanes between the mud walls, there was garbage and stagnant filth. The huts were the usual boxes of mud, without windows or chimneys; on their flat roofs the people sleep in summer. The open space round which the hamlet clustered was dominated by a shady tree. Under it I took my seat on the bamboo bed which the headman had carried out for my use. In a few minutes the whole male population was squatting round me and answering my questions.

Three direct inquiries sufficed to outline the condition of this village: the rest was detail. Everyone was in debt; no one could read: not one of the children attended school. I realised, as the villagers helped me to fill in this sketch, that the entire economic life of the village is based on a pervasive system of debt, from which a man never escapes. To a heritage of debt every baby is born; loaded with debt the emaciated corpse is carried to the funeral pyre. The usual rate of interest is 37½ per cent. The *bania* (money-lender) makes full use of compound interest, and these debts multiply like the bacilli in the dung-heaps. When a milch buffalo dies, the peasant obtains another from the money-lender, on the understanding that all the butter (*ghee*) goes to this universal provider, who is also the universal consumer; only the sour buttermilk remains in the village.

The crops, raised with so much painful labour, found their way to the *bania*'s capacious granary. He took the harvest in payment for past debts, and then lent it back to the village as a new debt. In these two transactions it was never valued at the same price: grain is worth more when a *bania* gives than when he receives. The wheat, I should add, never came back when once it had left the threshing-floor, for this village ate wheaten bread only at weddings. Millet and *gram* (the grain used for horses in India) are its daily diet, and it eats little else. The children, who never taste milk after they are weaned, were shadows nourished on debts. Most of them had some disease of the eyes or the skin. Many had the swollen belly that indicates a spleen enlarged by malaria, and the limbs of most of them looked like dark sticks fitted into joints.

The mention of weddings set me inquiring what the village spent on these festivities. It would borrow £14 to celebrate them, doubtless a shocking extravagance for people whose daily income was round about threepence. But weddings were infrequent: the village is becoming too poor to marry, and the one item of good news that I carried away from this talk was that its population is declining. Four stalwart young men stood up and assured me that though they were eager to marry, their families could not afford to help them, although, according to the sentiment of old-world India, it is the worst of social sins to delay the duty of continuation of one's race. Marriages are always within the caste, but outside the village; and of late the scarcity of women has introduced the custom (to put it brutally) of buying wives. "Our religion," as a priest said to me in a neighbouring village, "is no more, for we have been forced by poverty to sell our daughters."

At this point I noticed a ripple of laughter spreading through the ranks, and I asked what had amused them. "We're laughing," they said, "because we never before met a *sahib* who asked such questions as these." (*Sahib* is the title of respect which Indians give to English-men.) "The Collector *Sahib* [that is, the district magistrate and ad-ministrative official] never asks us what we eat." "Oh!" said I, "and what sort of questions does he ask you?" "He asks us about crime in the village, and whether there have been any robberies lately." That struck me as the shrewdest criticism, unconscious though it was, I heard from Indians of this capable but unsympathetic bureaucracy.

Another man was standing up, to attract my attention. He tore off the long length of cotton cloth which Indians drape around their persons: the dark frame beneath it was gaunt. "Look, *sahib*, this is the only shred of clothing I possess. I have no change." It was tattered and threadbare. I asked him what he earned. He had no land, but worked as a labourer on the railway, a State concern, at a wage of sixpence for a day of ten hours, without a break for meals. I gathered that his neighbours envied this owner of one shirt, who kept himself, a wife, and two children on sixpence a day. A man made less, they assured me, when he had land, for he had rent to pay. The rent would soon be due, and they did not know what they would do when the *zemindar* demanded it.

But it was time to walk back to the village of my friend and host— a Brahman, and a man of exceptional ability, who after some years spent at the University and in teaching, had returned to live as a peasant in his native village; indeed, it was already dark. He asked if anyone could lend us a lantern to light us over the fields. There was not one in Kishanpur.

As my stay among these villages went on, I was to learn much more of how they lived. I witnessed the dumb misery of a father, as fever struck his child down, far from any doctor. I surprised a usurer bullying a weaver at work under the shade of a great tree. The weaver had stretched his web on stakes. Bending over it, he was brushing the coarse threads, with his wife and his small boy to aid him. An angry voice, scolding and bullying, broke the peace. The sullen weaver did not answer: he had heard it all before. "What is amiss?" I asked, and discovered that the shifty, cross-eyed little man who owned the voice was the *bania* (moneylender). He told me, without shame, that he was collecting interest at 75 per cent. I asked him whether he had many bad debts, since his rate was so high. No: he said, before the present slump, a bad debt was almost unknown. The weaver, it seems, owed Rs. 300 (over £23) to various usurers. He could weave six yards of coarse cloth in a day, using the yarn which his neighbours spun, and he made 4*d.* by his labour, an income, if he worked 300 days, of £5 a year.

I began to revise my first impression of village life. The mud walls do not confine it. The drama of its existence turns on its relations with the outer world. To it come the *bania* for interest, and the *zemindar* for rent, and behind them both looms the overshadowing bulk of Government, with its courts and its police. The usurer knew that its strong arm sustained him in his right.

The economics of village life seemed to invite an exploitation. This matter of rents took my breath away. There were two classes of tenants in these villages. Some had ancient "occupancy" rights, and paid relatively low rents of Rs. 5-10 the acre (13 rupees, roughly, go to the pound). The majority were so-called life-tenants, and their land-hunger, as they competed for soil to till, had forced their rents up to figures ranging from Rs. 10 to as much, in a few cases, as Rs. 30.*

On an acre an Indian villager, who uses no manure, but waters well, raises six to eight *maunds* of wheat (the *maund* being 82 lbs.), though I heard in the Punjab of a capable farmer who achieved twelve. With eight *maunds* at the price quoted at Delhi in the daily paper, a peasant would make 16 rupees, with a trifle extra for the straw, but the usurer, who is also the local dealer, would give less. Prices this year are half of last year's figures, but rents do not drop with prices.

* These figures were above the average, which in the United Provinces seems to be Rs. 4-6 for occupancy, and Rs. 10-15 for life-tenants. But *zemindars,* sometimes by private arrangements with the tenants, exact higher rents than the registers record.

The reader can do the sum in subtraction which will show how much remains for the cultivator after he has paid a rent of 30 rupees out of a yield of 16 rupees. Even the favoured few who paid a rent of 10 rupees would have a negligible trifle, when they had set aside seed (say, 3 rupees) and fed their bullocks.

For weeks after this experience, these figures haunted me. Were they credible? Were the peasants deceiving me? I might have distrusted them, had I not found confirmation in a cold official publication. It is an analysis of farm accounts in the Punjab, a much richer and technically more advanced province than the region which I studied. Yet even in the Punjab it appeared from the averages of accounts chosen as typical that, under the tenancy system, the income from the land is divided between landlord and tenant respectively, in the proportion of three to one.* The same publication showed that even in that prosperous province, in a year of relatively high prices, the daily income of a tenant was less than fourpence. Clearly my peasants, though they were not scientific statisticians, were telling the truth about this monstrous system of exploitation.

That the landlord (sharing his unearned rent with the State) levied an intolerable tribute was not, however, the end of the story. He held these tenants in a merciless and arbitrary grip. The law did, indeed, provide that a tenant may not be evicted save for non-payment of rent; rents may be enhanced only once in twenty years, and an appeal lies to the courts. But it is not the practice to give receipts for rent, and the peasants told me that the landlord always contrives that there shall be some trifling arrears.

I felt sceptical, and insisted that they should produce an instance to me. Promptly they brought her—a widow woman. She had paid in three years Rs. 210 as rent, but she owed Rs. 6, and therefore nothing had been entered to her credit in the official register. She had no receipts to show, and she was under notice of eviction. The agent of the *zemindar* who owned this village was squatting in the circle; he could not deny it. I turned to my acquaintance, the *zemindar* of an adjoining estate, for an explanation of his neighbour's conduct. It came with all the frankness that I had learned to expect from him. "When a tiger is hungry," he answered, "it will even eat a cow" (the sacred animal of India). His own lands were mortgaged (he went on); he had some social standards to keep up; he must be loyal to the

* The exact ratio was as 150 to 55. See *Farm Accounts in the Punjab* 1927-28), the Board of Economic Inquiry, Punjab Rural Section, Publication No. 20.

government; money was hard to find, and so "he had to think out oppressions to pay his way."

Even now I had not quite fathomed this astonishing system. It seemed to block all improvements. The landlord himself did nothing to improve his property, and he would allow his tenants to do nothing, lest he should be required to compensate them, if he were minded, by the trick of nominal arrears, to evict them. I had noticed that no one grew fruit trees. They answered my inquiry about this with the statement that the landlord would not grant permission, or would charge heavily for it if he did. I was shocked to find that little if any of the cow-dung was used as manure; it had to serve as fuel. There is a quick-growing Indian tree (the *babul*) which would serve admirably for fuel, and of waste land on which it might have been planted there was enough. But even this improvement the landlord forbade, and such was the general practice. But, indeed, one might go on indefinitely. These landlords, who are not splendid feudal magnates but mere tax farmers, still insist on some of the old feudal servitudes. The tenants may be summoned to bring a yoke of bullocks and plough his home farm, and when he gives a feast, they must contribute milk and fodder.

Half the rent goes to the landlord, the rest to the State. What does it give in return? I tested its contribution in a school which served this group of villages. As yet elementary education is compulsory only in a few exceptionally progressive districts in India, and this was not one of them. The school was a little bungalow of two rooms and a verandah. It was dirty—the rooms cannot have been swept for some days; the walls were bare and stained, and the matting which served as a carpet was in tatters. No pictures decorated the walls. Two maps there were, but so worn and ragged that I could not tell whether they represented India or England—but perhaps it was Utopia.

The one good thing to be said for the school is that among its fifty-nine children, all boys, seventeen came from the lowest castes; and of these some were untouchables, who mixed with the rest. The curriculum was academically aloof from the daily life of the villages. Nothing was taught that had a bearing on Nature or farm life, nor was there any physical training or any attempt at games. Reading, writing, arithmetic, and the geography of that vague land of the tattered maps were taught to four classes by two teachers, at a fee which ranged from a halfpenny to a penny a month. These men had had a year's training, after an entrance examination, in a vernacular college, and they earned Rs. 22 and Rs. 19 a month, salaries which rank far above the Indian average. To measure them, it may be said that in these parts a young policeman begins at a wage of Rs. 17, while an unskilled labourer earns Rs. 8 a month.

As I looked at the bright, well-mannered little boys—one does not spend even a halfpenny on girls—squatting as they painted their letters with white on black boards, I began to wonder what place reading and writing really filled in the life of a society engaged in an unending duel with hunger and drought. I asked the teachers what books they possessed. Apart from schoolbooks, they had one between them, which was, significantly enough, a history of the renaissance of the military power of the Rajputs. I next tried the boys, and inquired in the highest class how many of their families had any books at home. Two out of fourteen had one book apiece, a work of Hindu devotion. One family only subscribed to a weekly vernacular newspaper.

Only five of these boys ever drank milk at home, and in this school were represented only the more prosperous families of the neighbourhood, capable of paying a penny a month for learning. Four boys had no change of clothes. One boy boasted that he had four changes and he, of course, was the usurer's son and heir. The senior teacher invited me to question the class, and with a glance at those intriguing maps, I tried geography. Opinions were equally divided as to whether England or India was the hotter and the larger country.

I left this school wondering what these villages gained by paying to the Indian Government one half of their rents. But I know the correct answer. There is no more war in India. Today epidemics never slay more than twelve millions at one blow. The population has doubled as the result of a century and a half of British rule, and Malthus, if he could return to earth, would find in India all his predictions verified. In spite of appearances, I think he would be mistaken. (See above, p. 164 n.)

WHILE reading these pages the reader, I should guess, has been impatiently framing a question to hurl at me: "Why don't these peasants and workers revolt, if your account of their wretched lives is truthful?" That question, let me answer, reveals a Western mind. It comes from the mental world that belongs to a white skin. To answer it I might have to begin by qualifying some particulars.

Life is not all drabness, even in a poor village. The traditional round of ritual and festival goes on, even when rent and taxes are overdue.

There are carnivals and dances, and even the daily worship of the temple is often a happy ceremony, for in Hindu religion there is no oppressive solemnity. But I suspect that part of the reason why Indians are so astonishingly patient and passive is that most of them are half starved. The average "coolie" lacks the physique which instinctively resists wrong by an impulsive movement of the fists. Over wide areas he has about half the muscular power of a European worker. Rebels do not start life with malarious spleens.

More potent still is the pressure of tradition and social usage. Caste and religion prescribe an inconceivably elaborate code of conduct. Life is hedged round from infancy by a net-work of prohibitions and commandments so intricate that the mind of the average man and woman is trained only to obey. An Indian can become a protestant or a rebel only by an effort of which none but the strongest natures are capable. Every caste has its appropriate ideals of conduct and character, and a man no more tries to step outside his caste than a European tries to transcend his sex.

Courage and initiative belong to the warrior or ruling castes. Others do not ape them or envy them. An Indian will plead guilty to physical cowardice without shame. All this makes, and for untold centuries has made, for a deadly patience under wrong.

This institution of caste, and the habit of mind which it begets, works, however, in two contrary ways. It makes of the individual a unit submissive in mind and body to a degree which startles and shocks the European observer. But when a whole society, a whole village, or a whole nation revolt, they develop a solidarity which Europeans may well envy. The same individual who will submit without a show of anger, and even without feeling anger, to insults and blows will develop a passive but disciplined courage of a high order if the group to which he belongs expects it of him.

Caste is breaking down in the towns. But the sensitiveness to public opinion which caste creates will long survive its decay. The workers in the textile mills of Bombay and Calcutta belong to a hundred castes, mostly of the lower order, and speak several languages. It is nearly impossible to regiment them as permanent, paying members in a trade union. Yet, when a strike is called, they will show a steadiness and endurance, with neither savings nor strike pay to help them, which would do credit to any body of Western workers. Indian society does not breed individuality. It inculcates passivity and obedience. But when once it stirs as a mass, there are few traitors and little audible dissent.

Gandhi's movement has awakened the villages to a sense of their power. They no longer feel isolated. Bengal hears that Gujarat is refusing taxes: why should it lag behind? The novel conception of motion has shot across the changeless horizon. I could see the workings of it even in the minds of those abysmally poor peasants at Kishanpur, in the United Provinces. I should not have asked them any political questions—they seemed too miserable for such abstractions—but suddenly one of them happened to mention *Swaraj*. I saw their faces light up, as if the idea meant hope. I asked them how *Swaraj* would improve their lot. Several answered at once. In a chorus from lean throats came the confident reply, "It will mean that we shall pay next to no rent." They knew what they were talking about, they assured me. Most of them once saw Gandhi, when he passed through a neighbouring district. I recalled his demands for halving the army, official salaries, and land-tax.

As yet these villagers had not conceived the possibility of resistance to rent and taxes. They could not pay: that was all they knew. They would tell the landlord so, when he demanded the rent: perhaps he would postpone it.

EVERYWHERE in India, but especially in these villages, I found myself deploring and ever cursing the gentleness of this race. At the next stage in my journey, round Allahabad, the revolt had actually begun. Stranger still, the Congress Party was leading it. It had long hesitated. Like all nationalist parties, it includes all classes. Landlords and moneylenders and the lawyers who serve them make up part of its membership, though the rank and file of its volunteers belong rather to the impoverished clerk class. It was easy to mobilise the peasants of Gujarat to resist the Land Tax, for they own their fields. Elsewhere, in Bengal, for instance, Congress suggested rather a refusal to pay the police rate.

For over most of the North and Centre the landlord system prevails, and land tax is paid by him out of the rent. Congress did not want to start a class-war among Indians. But round Allahabad the peasants called on it to lead them. They were determined to refuse payments of rents which in fact they could not pay. The Congress Party symbolised for them the idea of mass action and resistance to wrong. It had summoned them to smash the salt monopoly and to picket the liquor shops. Who else should lead them in resisting the intolerable burden of rent? They clamoured for the Congress to organise them. It hesitated for a time, but in the end the ardour of the peasants swept its doubts away.

It did, indeed, invent a subtle strategy which saved it from the reproach of any deliberate attack on the rights of Indian men of property. It advised the peasants to offer to the *zemindar* half his rent, on condition that he would sign a bond promising to pay nothing to the Government. Should he refuse, then the peasant would pay nothing at all. These *zemindars* may be more or less nationalist in sentiment: they have dark skins. But they are not cast in an heroic mould. Needless to say, they signed no seditious bond. The movement went forward as a simple and wholehearted "no rent" campaign. In November organisation had begun; and in Allahabad, while I was there, a press was confiscated for printing leaflets which summoned the tenants to resist. In January a "no rent" demonstration of peasants was dispersed by rifle fire. On that for me the curtain falls.*

It is hard to see into the immediate future, but one prediction formed itself in my mind as I left this land behind me. The nationalist struggle has roused its millions from their apathy, taught them the power of their own solidarity, and drilled them in the tactics of organised, if passive revolt. Congress will not remain a united party, and it has within it men and women whose temperaments will one day place them at the head of a peasant movement. Once India is free from her absorption in the national struggle, the problem of village poverty must focus her attention. I came away from these villages reflecting that in the minds of their peasants the same thoughts were stirring which in 1905, to little purpose, and in 1918 with irresistible impulse mobilised the Russian *muzhiks* to sweep their landlords down the steep road that led to exile.

* This peasant movement in the United Provinces continued after the truce. A letter from my friend and host, Mr. S. R. Sharma, describes some happenings, in May 1931, in a village near those which I have described. The crops of a tenant who could not have paid his rent, even if he had sold his cattle, were declared forfeited. He removed the corn from his threshing-floor, whereupon the *zemindar* lodged a complaint for theft. When a lorry carrying armed police arrived in the village, the defiant tenant escaped, but the police seized many of his neighbours, few of whom were involved in what he had done, bound them, threw them on scorching sand, and kept them there without water for several hours. Some were beaten. The police entered the houses and took property amounting, more or less, to the value of the "stolen" corn. Somewhat later the provincial government carried out a general reduction of rents.

ANOTHER SCHOOL

To leave that dismal picture of the village school in the United Provinces as my only record of education in India would be grossly unfair. Indians, when they are free to experiment and create, can do better than that. I will add, therefore, a brief note on another school, this time in Calcutta. It grew there naturally. It had as its background the Bengali Renaissance which has brought new life to all the arts. It has given a new freedom of expression to music; restored the dance, which had fallen to professionals, as a form of utterance in which the young generation delights; brought new life to the theatre and wider horizons to creative literature. I had the good fortune to have as my hosts in Calcutta Lady Bose and Jagadhis Chandra Bose, the most lovable of men, who remained the poet he was at heart, even in the meticulously accurate experiments which led to his discovery of the sensibility of plants. It was the director of Calcutta's municipal schools, Mr. Chatterji, in his younger days a student of anthropology, who took me to visit this elementary school —the best they had. Without the right to compel attendance, the city had at this time got 60 per cent of its children into its schools.

The building of the school was unpretentious, nor was it large. We saw first the studio in which the boys model clay. Their work was astonishing in its vitality—little statues of animals so living and expressive, so true in form, so suggestive of movement, that one was forced to accept Professor Cisek's theory of the artistic genius of children. We paused in a class where very young boys were beginning to talk English by the direct method: they had not gone far, but the little they knew was perfect in accent, idiom and grammar. The three of us, the Mayor, Mr. Chatterji and myself, then went along the corridor and paused at the open door of a classroom. On the floor the teacher, dressed in homespun, was squatting, making with sand a model of the Himalayas and the river system of Northern India. Every eye in the room was focused on him: every ear was bent to catch each syllable of his explanation. Not one of the children noticed the three strangers at the door. We broke the spell, at the exciting moment when rain was about to descend through an improvised strainer. We talked a little with the teacher, and moved on. I had the curiosity to turn back. Barely a minute had passed, but once more every eye was glued on the teacher, and no one saw me at the door. I know no word of Bengali, yet I dare say that I have never met a better teacher.

If all India could pass through that school, the next generation would solve any problem that is soluble.

IV. The Empire's Slums

How shall the English visitor to India, who speaks none of its
languages, explore the mental life below the brown skins of its
inarticulate workers?

I think that for a moment I did it as I stood beside a water tap in
Ahmedabad. Water in this sweltering climate is more than money,
more even than food. My shirt was wet through after ten minutes'
quick walk in the sun. I survived by taking four cold baths a day,
and in the intervals between them I envied the black buffaloes who
wallowed, submerged to their horns, in every wayside tank.

The tap which helped me to understand served two rows of workers'
tenements. It was the only tap they had. Left and right of me they
stretched, and I counted 153 dwellings, of which 140 were occupied.
In each was a family, with its lodgers, usually of five or six, occasionally of nine, persons. On this tap seven hundred human bodies depended
for the water of life. Here they must drink; here they must refresh
their sweating backs; here they must wash their clothes. I felt the
water with my hand. I could not call it warm; it was hot.

My skin had told me what life is like for the Indian worker. And
then I entered two or three of their dwellings. I paced them; perhaps
ten, perhaps twelve, feet square. They had no window, and in the
semi-darkness never a through breath of air has blown. They had no
chimney, and in some of them I noticed the acrid fumes of the cakes
of cow dung which serve for cooking fuel. The floors were a foot below
the street level, and in heavy rain they must be flooded.

The roofs were of tumble-down tiles, which certainly would not
resist the rains of the monsoon. The two rows stood back to back,
and the narrow lane behind them was littered with garbage and green
with filthy slime. Each family had only one of these rooms, with a
verandah on which there was space for only one person to sleep. But
to sleep in such dens is difficult, while the hot weather lasts. Even in
Bombay the streets are littered every night with men who have sought
refuge in them from their stifling dwellings. They stretch a mat or a
bed in the gutter, or even on the pavement, and there amid the roar
of traffic and the trampling of feet, they endeavour to sleep. These
workers are inefficient. What would you expect? Rarely does sleep

bring rest, and rarely do they eat to satisfy hunger. The women fare still worse. They dare not sleep in the open air, and modesty forbids them to bathe naked, as the men will do, under the public water-tap.

From Bombay to Calcutta I saw many specimens of workers' dwellings. Some few, erected by kindly employers, were creditable: many were worse than the row I have just described.*

THE export of leather is one of India's staple trades, but tanning is work that only untouchables may do. I visited the place, outside Bombay, where hundreds of them work. They are all Tamils, who have left behind them the relative penury of Madras for the opulence which I witnessed. At home they are landless labourers who possess their naked bodies and little else. There their wage is seven rupees a month, equal to half a guinea. In Bombay they earned up to last February some eighteen rupees monthly, which has now risen, thanks to a successful strike, to twenty-five rupees. The strike succeeded, though Bombay was full of unemployed workers, because these men enjoy a monopoly of their degradation. A Hindu, even of a lowly caste, will not touch raw hides.

The tannery stands amid malarious marshes. Inside it, and even outside, heaps of decaying animal refuse poison the air. These dark Tamils work all but naked, for they must stand up to the waist in the vats among the hides, their skins alternately burned and tanned by the lime and the tannic acid. Their hands are coated with human leather as thick as the sole of a shoe. Among them are boys of ten and twelve, and all of them, boys and men alike, work twelve hours a day, three-hundred-and-sixty-five days in the year. Mills have the protection of a most inadequate Factory Act, loosely enforced by an under-staffed corps of inspectors. But to works which use no mechanical power the Act does not apply.

* The Report of the Whitley Commission confirms this picture. In Bombay, it states, 97 per cent of the working classes live in one-roomed tenements, with six to nine persons to a room (p. 270). Of the industrial suburb of Calcutta (Howrah) it writes that the overcrowding is "probably unequalled in any other industrial area of India" (p. 272). Of Ahmedabad it writes: "the areas occupied by the working classes in Ahmedabad present pictures of terrible squalor. Nearly 92 per cent of the houses are one-roomed: they are badly built, insanitary, ill-ventilated and overcrowded, while water supplies are altogether inadequate and latrine accommodation is almost entirely wanting. Resulting evils are physical deterioration, high infant mortality, and a high general death-rate" (p. 277).

In huts and sheds built with their own hands, among the garbage and the skins, these workers cook and sleep all the year round. In one of these tumble-down shelters, which measured about 23 ft. by 18 ft., as many as thirty were housed. Even that was not the worst of these dwellings. Against the wall of one of the tanning-sheds I noticed a lean-to, which I mistook at first for a tool-house. But its door was open, and through it I saw three beds. The floor was of earth, and measured 12 ft. by 7 ft.: it was not quite 3 feet high. In this den three human beings were housed.

The owner of this tannery was an Indian. But the landlord of the greater part of this squalid suburb was an institution known as the Bombay Improvement Trust, an immensely wealthy semi-official cor- poration, run by Englishmen. For the hovels outside the tannery it drew a monthly rent of 5s. These ramshackle structures had tiled roofs and walls of galvanised iron (imagine it in this climate), which the tenants had improved by cutting up kerosene tins. These black holes were 10 feet square, with a small verandah, and each housed from six to eight persons. There were three water-taps for about 400 persons, and six stinking privies at a distance of 200 yards. It was growing dark as I left this place, in imminent danger of slipping on the green slime into an open drain. Among the refuse-heaps the great rats were already hurrying.

In fairness I must go on to describe what the Government in its various incarnations is doing to improve the conditions of these workers. I might describe the gaunt, comfortless tenements official on the outskirts of Bombay, but most of them have found a more appro- priate use as a prison. There is the rudimentary Factory Act. In such matters a truthful account would have to say that what the Govern- ment has done it has done grudgingly, tardily, and with an impressive regard for economy.

In one respect, however, its solicitude for the workers far surpasses that of the most enlightened government of Europe. It knows the temptations to which they stand exposed. Beside that tap of hot water, under the 3-foot shelter, the virus of Bolshevism might flourish with the rats and mosquitoes. It had, indeed, found a lodging in Calcutta and Bombay, and of an evening, round these unsavoury tenements, the mill-workers, during the leisure of the two prolonged strikes of 1928 and 1929, were actually listening to speeches by Communist orators, and translating into Gujarati the slogans of the Soviet. From this moral peril the Government of India has rescued the workers, and here it has not confined itself to half-measures. Indeed, as the candid reader will acknowledge, it has spared neither energy, time nor money.

A T Meerut I found these agitators safe under lock and key. Thirty-one prisoners, three of them Englishmen, are answering a charge of "conspiracy to deprive the King of his sovereignty" over British India.

How they set about it I learned from the Committal Order, a book of 287 pages. They organised the workers into trade unions. They led two strikes. They talked of the class struggle, and created a Workers' and Peasants' Party, which, in its turn, was linked to a select little Communist Party. It is said that some of them corresponded with London, and even, it may be, with Moscow in cipher and invisible ink. No reasonable man who reads the magistrates' summing-up of the evidence against them can doubt that they went further. It is elaborately proved against them that they celebrated May Day, and used such incendiary watchwords as "Workers of all lands, unite." Had they bombs, perhaps? On the contrary, they opposed, as Communists are bound to do, all individual acts of terrorism. Did they incite to rioting? That is not alleged, nor any act which in England might deprive the King of his sovereignty. In India, where one tap serves 150 families, the throne may rest on more fragile foundations.

The Government of India leaves nothing to chance. The trial, accordingly, was held in Meerut, though the "conspiracy" against the King and his water-tap was hatched in Calcutta and Bombay, eight hundred miles away. In these cities trial by jury could have been demanded: in Meerut the cause of right ran no such risk. Justice in India is slow but sure, and, as you shall see, it spares no expense.

The prisoners were arrested in March, 1929: the trial began in June. The case for the prosecution occupied a full two years. The charge carries with it a penalty of transportation for life, and bail, save to one fragile prisoner, was refused.

The defence, one may add, costs nothing. There was once a fund; it is exhausted. There was once a defence committee; it is mostly in prison. To the devotion of Mr. D. P. Sinha the prisoners owe it that they do not face the judge unhelped.

During the midday interval I was allowed to talk with the prisoners. Two of the Indians I had known in London as eager and studious young men, who aspired to work for socialism and trade unionism in India. The purpose of this trial is plainly to stamp as illegal the mere existence of a Communist Party. But these young men are not Communists, and, indeed, only half the prisoners deserve that name. Let me hasten to add that the case against the Communists was as flimsy as that against their Socialist comrades. Some years will have been cut out of their lives, even if they should be acquitted, and that for actions or words which thousands of us repeat every day with impunity amid the more numerous water-taps of Europe. For robbery with violence they could not have received a severer punishment.

I listened to some of the proceedings. An hour passed in verifying the origin of a letter, another in tracing printed reports of a speech. The court has no shorthand reporter, and it is the judge, who is not a trained lawyer, but a member of the Civil Service, who must make the record with his typewriter. A sentence or two of evidence, and then click, click, click, while we all sat idle, public and prisoners, counsel and police.

I began to grasp why justice is slow. The click, click, click of that typewriter has cost thirty young men a year of their lives. Others have less reason to complain of the time they must spend in vindicating the King's sovereignty over India's slums. For each day of this interminable trial the Crown prosecutor earns a thousand and twenty rupees (about £78), together with expenses and sundry allowances. He sat and earned it on this day with silent dignity.

The proceedings were as dull as they were slow, and I confess that I fell asleep. I wakened as the court rose, in some confusion of mind. I could still hear the remorseless ticking of that loyal typewriter, but in my dream it had got mixed with the dripping of that unique tap in the Ahmedabad slum—perhaps a seditious dream. For I left the court trying to reckon out how many water taps might be erected with one thousand and twenty rupees a day, spread over two years. It might have been a cheaper method of assuring King George's sovereignty over India.

A POSTSCRIPT

This chapter was written (as a newspaper article) in hot anger after a first visit to Meerut. In cold blood I find nothing in it to modify. I returned to Meerut a second time, and gave evidence on behalf of my two Indian friends among the accused: the court heard with evident surprise that every socialist party in Europe, including the British Labour Party, with His Majesty's late ministers at its head, habitually does most of the acts, teaches most of the doctrines, and uses most of the phrases which figured in the indictment as clear evidence of sedition.

The thirty-two prisoners included S. A. Dange, the Assistant Secretary of the Indian Trade Union Congress, a former President, a Vice-

President and another Assistant Secretary, with officials of various railwaymen's and textile unions and of Workers' and Peasants' parties in Bombay, Bengal and the United Provinces. To their honour, three Englishmen were among the prisoners, B. F. Bradley, Lester Hutchinson and Philip Spratt. The trial lasted three and a half years. The Judge conceded in his summing up that the accused were not "charged with having done any illegal act in pursuance of the alleged conspiracy." The real charge was "the incitement of antagonism between capital and labour," "the creation of Workers' and Peasants' Parties, Youth Leagues, Unions, etc." and "the encouragement of strikes." These things they certainly did, though I should phrase the first count otherwise: they made the workers aware that capital exploits them. In January 1933, as Hitler's reign began in Berlin, one of the prisoners, Muzaffar Ahmad, was sentenced to transportation for life; five to transportation for twelve years, three to transportation for ten years and so on down to the lightest sentence, three years rigorous imprisonment. These sentences, however, were drastically reduced on appeal.

The arrests were made while a Conservative Government was in office, but the trial began and ran most of its course under a Labour Government. Technically there would have been no difficulty in stopping the proceedings. But a weak minister may have to reckon, in such cases, with the possibility that important persons in India may resign or threaten to resign; much clamour would follow in the press and in Parliament. Save under a Secretary of State who possesses character and can count on the Cabinet and the Party to back him, India is governed rather from Delhi than from London. It rarely happens that the Secretary has first-hand knowledge of India; he sees it through the eyes of the Viceroy, and of the officials round him in the India Office, who have spent their lives there. I do not offer this as an excuse for the failure to stop the Meerut trial; it is, however, the explanation of a scandal which has left an indelible stain upon the record of the Labour Party.

I wish I could report that the coming to power of a Labour Government at Westminster had in any way eased the task of its comrades who are struggling to better the lot of the Indian worker. Nothing in these two years has changed in the spirit and methods of the Indian administration. It rules, as it always did, in the interests of capital. It still uses the tremendous coercive powers of the Indian Penal Code (so drastic that one wonders why emergency ordinances are ever necessary) to check the effort to organise the workers in unions. Does a union send down an organiser, not to foment a strike, but merely to enlist the men in a town which as yet has no organisation? The owner of the local mills (I am reporting an actual case) will call on his friend the magistrate, who promptly issues an order under §144. This at once stops every possible activity on that organiser's part. He may not deliver a speech: he may not even meet the workers in small groups.

Does a powerful oil company fear a strike? Orders are issued which restrain "agitators" from entering its territory. Does a strike, in spite of all, break out in some provincial town? The whole official personnel is mobilised to combat it; even the law courts may close down till this more urgent business is settled. As for the railways, which are state concerns, they work under what is in spirit military discipline, with Royal Engineer officers at their head. Even a strong organisation like the General Workers' Union of the N.W. Railway (Punjab), with over ten thousand paying members, cannot secure recognition.

In short, the Meerut Trial is but an exceptionally gross instance of an official attitude towards labour which is normally and habitually suspicious and hostile.

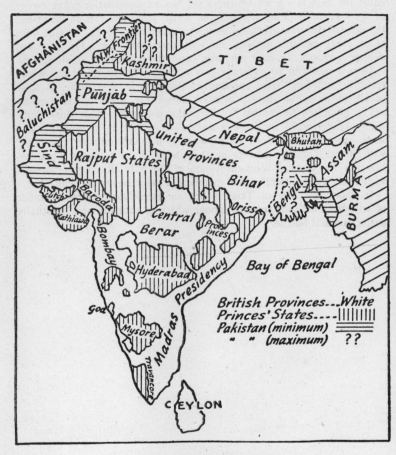

A sketch map of India (political)

INDEX

Index